Reading the Pentateuch

A Historical Introduction

Reading the Pentateuch

A Historical Introduction

John J. McDermott

PAULIST PRESS

NEW YORK / MAHWAH, N.J.

Cover design by Valerie Petro

Book design by Céline M. Allen

Library of Congress Cataloging-in-Publication Data

McDermott, John J., 1960–
    Reading the Pentateuch : a historical introduction / John J. McDermott.
      p. cm.
Includes bibliographical references.
    ISBN 0-8091-4082-9
  1. Bible. O.T. Pentateuch—History of Biblical events. 2. Bible. O.T. Pentateuch—Criticism, interpretation, etc. I. Title.
    BS1225.52 .M33 2002
    222'.107—dc21

                                  2002003643

Published by Paulist Press
997 Macarthur Boulevard
Mahwah, New Jersey 07430

www.paulistpress.com

Printed and bound in the
United States of America

CONTENTS

CHAPTER ONE

The Pentateuch and History

The Pentateuch is the foundational book for Judaism and Christianity, and some of the most fascinating questions about the Pentateuch are historical questions. These first five books of the Bible tell the story of the creation of the universe and the beginning of the chosen people. Through the stories and the laws that God gives the Israelites, we see their most basic beliefs about who God is, the relationship between God and human beings, what it means to be the chosen people, and the way people are to live with each other.

The theological importance of the Pentateuch is obvious, but do these books record actual historical events, or is it all legendary material written centuries later? And how much difference does it make? If much of the Pentateuch turns out to be stories that do not record real events, does that mean that its theological message is also invalid? These are the questions this book is concerned about.

The word "Pentateuch" is from Greek, and literally means "five scrolls." It refers to the five books of Genesis, Exodus, Leviticus, Numbers, and Deuteronomy. The Pentateuch is also known as the Torah, a Hebrew word meaning "instruction" or "law." Much of the material is, in fact, laws, but even the stories that are not explicitly giving laws are giving instruction in a broader sense. These five scrolls of instruction include some of the most familiar stories in the Bible, including the stories of creation, Noah's ark, the promises to Abraham, the exodus from Egypt, and the giving of the ten commandments to Moses. These stories are all part of one continuous narrative, beginning with the creation of the world and ending with the Israelite nation on the verge of taking possession of the land God promised them. Besides the well-known stories, the Pentateuch also includes lesser-known episodes and characters who show up only briefly. The reader of the Pentateuch encounters the most familiar and the most strange parts of the Bible.

The title of each book is descriptive of its contents. *Genesis* means "beginning," and this first book tells of the beginnings of the world and of the chosen people. God creates everything to be harmonious, but that harmony comes to an end when the first people disobey God. God tries to restore things by sending a flood to wipe out all evil and starting the human race over, but people continue sinning, so God sets apart one group of people, the descendants of Abraham, to be the chosen people. The chosen people are to become a great nation and take possession of the land of Canaan. They are to be a sign to the rest of the world of the perfect relationship God intended to have with all people. Genesis ends with the chosen people beginning to become large in number, but they are outside the promised land, having gone to Egypt during a famine.

Exodus describes the chosen people (now called the Israelites) departing from Egypt and beginning their journey back to the promised land. As the book begins, the Israelites have become so numerous that the Egyptians have tried to suppress them with forced labor. God calls Moses to lead the people out of slavery, which he does with miraculous assistance from God. As the people begin their journey through the desert, God appears to Moses on Mt. Sinai and gives him the ten commandments and other laws that will form the basis of a covenant between God and the chosen people.

Much of *Leviticus* is laws having to do with worship. Worship was under the control of Israelite priests, who, according to the Pentateuch, all had to be descendants of the tribe of Levi. During most of the book God is still speaking to Moses, and the book emphasizes laws on how to conduct sacrifices and other rituals, the ordination of priests, the concept of purity and impurity, and the calendar of religious feasts. Besides these laws, the book includes a small number of narratives about people following or failing to follow the laws.

The book of *Numbers* includes a census of the Israelite people during their desert journey. It also includes additional laws for the people to follow as well as descriptions of a failed attempt to enter the land of Canaan from the south, the Israelites' journey around to the eastern side of Canaan, their victories over kings who try to prevent their progress, and their arrival at the border of the promised land. The book also summarizes the entire journey of the Israelites from Egypt to the border of the promised land, with a list of all the places at which they camped.

The last book of the Pentateuch is *Deuteronomy,* a Greek word meaning "second law." This book repeats and summarizes many of the laws given in the earlier books. It is framed as the final speech of Moses to the people gathered on the eastern side of the Jordan River, ready to enter the promised land. He repeats many of the laws, although sometimes in a slightly different version from that in other books, and motivates the people to stay faithful to the covenant with God. Deuteronomy ends with the death of Moses and the people still outside the promised land.

In the Hebrew tradition, the titles of the books are different. Each title is the first word, or the most important word, of the first sentence of the book. Genesis is called *Bereshit,* the Hebrew word meaning "in the beginning." Exodus is *Elle Shemot,* "these are the names"; the book begins by listing the names of the twelve sons of Jacob, the ancestors of the twelve tribes of Israel. Leviticus is *Veyyiqra,* "and he called out," referring to the Lord speaking to Moses. Numbers is *Bemidbar,* "in the desert," since the book describes the journey of the Israelites through the desert. And Deuteronomy is *Haddebarim,* "the words," because this book reports the final words of Moses to the Israelites at the end of their journey.

There is much debate about when, how, and by whom these five books were written. The details of composition will be discussed in chapter 2, but one thing that most people agree on is that, after they were written, the books of the Pentateuch were the first books to become scripture. Clearly the books did not immediately achieve the status of sacred scripture when they were written, but over a period of decades and centuries they were accepted by Jewish religious leaders and by the community as a whole as the best expression of what is essential to Judaism. The Book of Ezra, describing events in the fifth century BCE, says that Ezra was a scribe "skilled in the law of Moses that the LORD God of Israel had given" (Ezra 7:6), and that he carried out a religious reform that included persuading the Jews to follow the laws given to Moses. As with any other book, there are questions about how much of Ezra is historical, but the fifth century seems to be the earliest time that the law of Moses is claimed as the foundational teaching for Judaism. It is most likely that the Pentateuch became authoritative in the fifth or fourth century, and other books became accepted as scripture later.

After becoming accepted as scripture, the Pentateuch continued to be the most influential part of the Hebrew Bible. In Judaism, the five books of the Torah are still the most sacred part of the Bible. Readings from the Torah are the central part of the synagogue service, and the events recounted in the Torah are commemorated in the major Jewish festivals. Later Jewish literature, including works in the Pseudepigrapha, the Mishnah, and the Talmud, is largely expansion and interpretation of the Torah.

The Pentateuch has also shaped Christianity. Many of Jesus' teachings are interpretations of laws of the Pentateuch. The gospels, especially Matthew, assume that the reader knows the Pentateuch; Matthew also draws several parallels between Moses and Jesus. Paul uses the story of Abraham and other parts of the Pentateuch to explain his teachings about Jesus and the law. Christian liturgy, including the Easter Vigil, makes extensive use of the Pentateuch, and Christian ethics uses the ten commandments and other laws from these books as a foundation for proper living.

The Pentateuch has also influenced another great religion, Islam, even though it is not itself considered scripture by Moslems. The Koran, the sacred book of Islam, includes stories of Moses, Abraham, and others that are variations of stories in the Pentateuch. Mohammed saw himself as restoring the authentic religion of Moses and Abraham, which he claimed Jews and Christians had corrupted.

These books have shaped later religious traditions so much that it is no wonder they have been the object of such intense study. Scholarly theories on how the Pentateuch was written were among the earliest efforts of the modern critical approach to the Bible. Archaeologists have searched for evidence confirming or contradicting events in the Pentateuch. Comparative religion sees many parallels between the stories in Genesis about creation and the flood and similar stories in other religions. Those who study the Bible as literature find subtle artistry in such stories as that of the sacrifice of Isaac, or of Joseph and his brothers.

The Pentateuch has also been the center of controversies over how to interpret the Bible. The creation story in Genesis is one of the most frequent areas of disagreement between the fundamentalist and the critical approach to the Bible, and questions about the degree to which the stories of Abraham, the exodus, and the beginnings of Israel are historical also bring out sharp disagreements over methodology. Before we can discover what the Pentateuch teaches, we have to decide what is the best method to use in discovering what it teaches.

Methodology

Ultimately, the purpose of the Pentateuch is theological; it is addressing foundational beliefs about God and human beings. But it is not a straightforward exposition of dogmas. Its teachings are expressed in a narrative and in laws covering every aspect of life. It assumes knowledge of people's customs more than twenty-five hundred years ago in a culture very different from the modern world.

Before getting to the Pentateuch's theological teaching, it is necessary to do some form of background study. The Bible is the most studied book there ever was, and, not surprisingly, there are disagreements over what type of study is most useful and what methods should be used in studying the Bible. A useful way to begin is to broadly divide the ways of studying the Bible into the literary and historical approaches.

The literary approach to the Bible is an attempt to discover how a story or other type of writing in the Bible functions as literature. For example, a literary study of the story of Adam and Eve in the Garden of Eden would ask how the characters (including God) are portrayed, how the conflict over disobeying God's command develops, how the conflict is resolved, how language, imagery, and word plays are used, and other questions about how the story is told. The literary study of other types of writing, such as poetry, collections of laws, or letters, would involve different particular questions, but such an approach could still be useful. In the last two decades there has been a great increase in literary studies of all parts of the Bible, making up for a long neglect.

This book, however, will focus on the historical approach. While the literary approach is valuable and necessary, anyone studying the Pentateuch also needs to have a clear understanding of the historical issues. The Pentateuch tells a story which, at least in parts, seems to present itself as a narration of actual events. It is natural to ask if the events are, in fact, historical. The story also takes place long ago and describes unfamiliar cultural practices, making it necessary to do historical background study just to have some idea of what the story is talking about. The historical study of the Pentateuch is not the only useful approach, and by itself it is not a complete approach, but it is a necessary approach.

In the historical approach, there are several types of questions we ask. First, did these events the Bible tells about actually happen? Historically, was there a person Noah who built an ark and saved himself and his family, along with a large number of animals, during a flood that covered the entire earth? Was there a group of Hebrew slaves in Egypt who escaped under the leadership of a person named Moses? Were they aided by miraculous divine intervention? The historical approach looks at the internal coherence of the stories themselves and any evidence outside the Bible that may support or contradict the biblical story.

A second type of question is, what background information about the social customs and religious practices of peoples in biblical times can help us understand what is going on in a story, even if we can't determine whether or not the story happened? When God asks Abraham to sacrifice his son Isaac, is this a request that would have shocked the people who heard the story in biblical times, or was human sacrifice common in that part of the world? When the Israelites built a golden calf to worship, why does the Pentateuch condemn the action so harshly? Do the laws in the Pentateuch make sense in an urban setting, a rural setting, a nomadic setting, or a combination of several settings?

And a third type of historical question is, what is the history of the composition of the story itself? Was the Pentateuch written by one person, Moses, or were there several authors involved? Was it written at one time, or did it gradually get put together over centuries? What sources might have been used, and was the writing of the Pentateuch influenced by similar stories from other people in the ancient Near East?

In answering these questions, we will use a *critical* approach. A critical approach is one that does not assume that any past answers have to be accepted. Whether the past answers are from church authorities, previous generations of scholars, current academic trends, or a desire to apply the Pentateuch's teachings to certain issues, the critical approach attempts to set them aside and come to the text with an openness to new answers and an openness to any methodology that might help interpret the text. In practice, of course, no one is entirely free of biases, but the critical approach consciously steps back from preconceived ideas of what the answers have to be.

In particular, a critical approach is different from a fundamentalist approach to the Bible, which says that the events narrated by the Bible must be historical and all of its teachings must be taken literally. In the abstract, the fundamentalist approach may sound appealing, especially for people looking for certainty in their religious beliefs. And there is something valuable about the fundamentalist attempt to follow the teachings of the Bible even when they are difficult or unpopular. But, in practice, no one is entirely a fundamentalist, nor would it be possible to be one. If everything in the Bible is literally historical, then did God create animals before people (Gen 1:24-27) or people before animals (Gen 2:7-20)? When Joseph's brothers threw him in the cistern and had him sold into slavery, did the Midianites take him to Egypt and sell him to Potiphar (Gen 37:36), or did the Midianites sell him to some Ishmaelites, who took him to Egypt and sold him to Potiphar (Gen 37:28; 39:1)? There are so many contradictions in the details of the biblical stories that the fundamentalist approach is always a selective approach, deciding which parts of the Bible to take literally.

The fundamentalist approach is also selective in deciding which laws must be followed literally. Rare is the fundamentalist who will say that the Pentateuch's laws on sex are culturally conditioned and need not be followed. But a complete fundamentalist would also refrain from wearing a shirt that is a blend of cotton and polyester (Lev 19:19), would never harvest an entire field or garden (Lev 19:9-10), and would almost certainly avoid driving a Mercury or a Saturn (Ex 23:13). No one, in fact, is a complete fundamentalist, for it is not a tenable approach to the Bible. Everyone who uses the Bible uses a critical approach with some parts of it. It is only a matter of whether one is critical with selective parts of the Bible or with all of it.

In using a critical approach with these historical questions, we will make use of any evidence that is available. That evidence will include other ancient texts that are not part of the Bible. Texts and inscriptions from Egypt, Mesopotamia, and Canaan may agree or disagree with the Bible's version of events. When there is agreement there is a good chance that the events are historical. When there is disagreement it is not always possible to tell whether the Bible or other writings are closer to history. Even when the writings are not about the same specific events as the Bible, they are often useful in giving us a general picture of the history of the time, or of customs that are similar to ones reported in the Bible, or of stories and myths that are similar to biblical stories.

Archaeological evidence is also useful for historical questions in some parts of the Bible. Much of the Pentateuch is about individuals or small groups traveling from place to place, people who would not have left behind many archaeological remains of their activities. But the evidence may tell us whether the setting of the stories seems genuine. If Genesis says that Abraham resided for a time in the land of the

Philistines (21:32-34), we can look for archaeological evidence of when the Philistines first appeared in the land of Canaan, and whether it is possible that there were Philistines around at the time Abraham is supposed to have lived.

History and Theology

A study of these historical issues inevitably leads to the question of how much it matters. If the exodus story is not based on a historical event, is our faith in a God who liberates people from oppression unfounded? Fundamentalists often use a "slippery slope" argument, that if we admit that one detail is not historical, then we are in danger of falling into the conclusion that none of it has any value. Most people would take a more moderate view, but it is a serious issue. Most of the Bible is about a God who acts in history. We learn who God is by seeing how historical events are shaped by God. But if those stories told as if they were historical events turn out to be unhistorical, how do we know we are believing the right things about God?

Ever since the critical study of the Bible began to raise questions about its historicity, scholars have disagreed on how much is theologically at stake. Much of the biblical archaeology work done by W. F. Albright and used by his followers sets out to prove that the Bible's major claims about the Israelites' ancestors, the exodus, and the conquest of the promised land were based on historical events, and therefore our faith in the God behind the events is well-founded. John Bright, in *A History of Israel*, concludes his chapter on the patriarchs by saying, "Although many gaps remain, enough has been said to establish confidence that the Bible's picture of the patriarchs is deeply rooted in history. Abraham, Isaac, and Jacob stand in the truest sense at the beginning of Israel's history and faith.... Abraham began far more than he knew. It is, therefore, not without sound historical reason that Christian and Jew alike hail him as the father of all faith."[1]

On the other hand, there have been many who have said that a negative judgment about the historicity of a character or event need not affect our judgment about its theological teaching. Gerhard von Rad, referring to the stories of Abraham claiming Sarah was his sister, says, "So it is no longer possible to discover what historical event lies behind the narrative of the jeopardizing of Sarah; we must, in fact, assume that the transfer of the material to Abraham and Sarah was only made subsequently. . . . Therefore one could say pointedly that the narrative is not 'historical'; but the experience that God miraculously preserves the promise beyond human failure was eminently historical for the community."[2] For von Rad, the validity of the theological teaching is, in fact, based on historical events; but it is based on the historical events surrounding the community that produced the text, and not necessarily the events narrated by the text.

Historical questions are interesting in their own right, but they are also theologically relevant. If there was a person named Abraham who lived a life substantially the same as what Genesis describes, then a knowledge of his historical world (whenever that may have been) will shed light on what it means to be the chosen people of God. If the story of Abraham is almost entirely the product of the much later monarchy or exile periods, then a knowledge of what issues the community faced in those historical periods will shed more light on who the people of God are. If an escape from slavery in Egypt involved only a small number of people, and the vast majority of the ancestors of the Israelites came from different backgrounds, then we should investigate what historical factors led the entire people to later adopt that story as their own. If the final form of the Pentateuch was completed after the Babylonian exile, then a knowledge of the history of the community in that period helps us understand the significance of, for example, the Pentateuch ending with the chosen people still outside the promised land.

A Summary of the History of Ancient Israel

Before beginning a historical study of the Pentateuch, it is necessary to be familiar with the outlines of the history of ancient Israel. In current scholarly discussion of ancient Israel there are many points where there is no consensus, and much disagreement about how much it is even possible to know. In the past, many histories written were not much more than paraphrases of the biblical story. Today there is a greater recognition that the biblical texts were produced much later than the events they describe and freely mix historical remembrances with legends and fiction, but there is disagreement on how much is based on historical events. The summary that follows is divided into five periods, although it must be kept in mind that the dates, especially for the early periods, are approximate.

Emergence, 1200–1000 BCE. Prior to 1200 the land now known as Palestine was part of a large Egyptian empire and was called Canaan. From archaeological evidence we know there were many large, fortified cities in Canaan. From letters and other texts we know that Egypt ruled Canaan through a system of semi-independent city states.[3] Each large city had its own king who had control over internal affairs but was dependent on the Egyptian military for stability. There was competition between the cities and there were occasional battles and threats from groups outside the cities, including gangs in the countryside called the Apiru, and nomadic people called Shasu farther out in the desert. After 1200, Egyptian control over Canaan lessened, and there was a gradual decline in the large cities; some of the cities were destroyed in battle and others lost population or were abandoned. At the same time, there were dozens of new settlements in the more remote hill country of Canaan. The new settlements were small, unfortified, agricultural villages. How and why this change took place is debated among scholars; there is also debate about whether the changes are connected to the exodus and conquest stories in the Bible.[4] In any case, a new, decentralized society emerged in Canaan.

Monarchy, 1000–587 BCE. The decentralized society of the new settlements came to an end as one king took control of the region. According to the Bible, Saul was the first king to take control. He was unsuccessful and was replaced by David, who was succeeded after his death by his son Solomon. The single kingdom, however, did not last, but split into two separate kingdoms. The southern kingdom was known as Judah; its capital was in Jerusalem and it was ruled by descendants of David. The northern kingdom was known as Israel; its capital was eventually in Samaria, and no single family ruled it permanently. The details of the biblical story of the beginning of the monarchy and division into two kingdoms have not been verified by external evidence, although there is evidence of the existence of the kingdoms. There is archaeological evidence of increased urbanization beginning in the ninth century;[5] an inscription from Dan (in northern Israel) from around 800 BCE refers to the "house of David" and the "king of Israel";[6] there are references in texts of neighboring nations to some individual kings, including Omri of Israel and Hezekiah of Judah.[7] Both of these kingdoms came to an end when empires from the east expanded toward the Mediterranean. Around 722 the Assyrian empire invaded and destroyed Israel, and invaded Judah but allowed Jerusalem and its king to survive. Around 587 the Babylonian empire invaded Judah, destroyed Jerusalem and the temple, and forced many of the people into exile.

Exile, 587–538 BCE. The Babylonian policy of forcing conquered people into exile was meant to destroy their ability to organize a revolt. For the people of Judah, it not only meant an end to their nation, but a threat to the survival of their religion as well. During the monarchy, religion and nationality were the same; if the religion were to survive, it would have to be redefined in a way that did not depend on having their own nation. During the exile, "Judaism" took shape as a religion separate from the nation of Judah, and its leaders emphasized those things that would express Jewish identity even though they were now a scattered people. Worship and food laws became more important as defining characteristics, and genealogies became important in expressing who was part of the community. Although biblical Judaism is most shaped by the exiles in Babylon, people from Judah were scattered over a much wider area. Some fled to Egypt, and many ended up scattered elsewhere in the eastern Mediterranean region.

Persian Period, 538–333 BCE. The end of the exile came when King Cyrus of Persia defeated the Babylonians and allowed the Jews to return to Judah. Cyrus had a strategy of being more supportive of local religions, and he often tried to persuade people that their local god had chosen him to be their ruler. Despite being allowed to return, only a small number of Jews did; Judah was still a place of poverty and instability, and many Jews had settled down to new lives in Babylon and elsewhere. Thus the problem that had existed in the exile, of maintaining the religious identity of a scattered people, continued in the Persian period. After Cyrus, the Persian empire continued to be closely involved in the local religions of the various peoples in the empire, sometimes in beneficial ways, such as by providing support for the rebuilding of the temple in Jerusalem, and sometimes in more burdensome ways, such as by imposing heavy taxes that the temple was responsible for collecting as tithes. The form of Judaism that the Pentateuch creates turns out to be one which would have been quite acceptable to the Persian rulers (e.g., the negative depiction of Egypt would fit Persia's desire to prevent Jews from joining Egypt in an uprising against the empire), so one question to be asked is how much influence Persia had on the making of the Pentateuch.

Hellenistic Period, 333–63 BCE. Eventually, when Alexander the Great defeated the Persians, a new empire came to power. Alexander, originally from Macedonia, had taken over his father's Greek kingdom and expanded it to the east. For the Jews it may not have made much difference politically, since it was yet another foreign empire ruling over them. But this time it was an empire from the west, so culturally it meant new influences on their religion. Greek literature and religion became known to more Jews, and in time the Greek language became their most commonly used language, especially for those Jews living outside of Palestine.

From this summary, it is clear that for most of the period the Old Testament covers there was no independent nation of Israel or Judah. Since religion in ancient times was so closely tied to nationalism, this means that the biblical period was a time of an evolving religion trying to define itself in a way that was relevant for changing social, political, and cultural circumstances. Studying the Bible historically means discovering just what those changing circumstances were and how they shaped the biblical text.

It will not be possible to definitively answer all of these historical questions. There is a lack of evidence about events that happened more than twenty-five hundred years ago, and the evidence that exists is interpreted differently by different scholars. Nonetheless, through the process of asking the questions and considering the evidence, we can come to a better understanding of the Pentateuch. We can get a sense of what the most likely historical background was, and if some parts of the Pentateuch seem not to be based on historical events, we can get some sense of why the stories developed the way they did. The historical issues are fascinating in themselves, and exploring them often leads to insights into the theological teachings of the Bible.

Chapter Two

How the Pentateuch Was Written

Nowhere in the Pentateuch itself is there any indication of who the author is or how the books were composed. The lack of an explicitly mentioned author is not unusual for biblical books. In ancient times books were often the result of a long process involving oral traditions being put into written form and written documents going through several stages before reaching the form in which we know them today. Whoever wrote the Pentateuch either was not one single person or did not see any need for readers to know his or her identity.

However, a tradition did develop that Moses wrote the Pentateuch. There are several reasons for associating the books with Moses. After Genesis, Moses is the main character in the story, and in places it does refer to Moses writing down the laws that God gave him (Ex 24:4; Dt 31:24). Later, the books of Ezra and Nehemiah refer to the "law of Moses" and the "book of Moses" as the basis for their religious reforms (Ezra 7:6; Neh 8:1; 13:1). The New Testament frequently refers to the law of Moses, and in some places speaks of Moses as if he were the writer of those laws. Mark has the Sadducees saying to Jesus, "Teacher, Moses wrote for us that, 'if a man's brother dies, leaving a wife but no child, the man shall marry the widow and raise up children for his brother'" (12:19; cf. Lk 20:28; the quote from Moses is actually a combination of Gen 38:8 and Dt 25:5). Luke and Acts refer to "Moses and the prophets," as the two major parts of scripture (Lk 16:29; 24:27; Acts 26:22). And Josephus, a Jewish writer who lived in the first century CE, speaks of Moses writing not just the laws in the Pentateuch, but all of its stories as well; for example, in his discussion of the creation story, he introduces sections with "Moses says," or similar phrases (*Antiquities of the Jews*, I.1, 2).

It is clear that by the first century CE Jews and Christians did think of Moses as the author of the Pentateuch in some sense. That view lasted for several centuries, and to this day is still held by a few conservative Jews and Christians. But there have long been questions about his precise role in putting together the Pentateuch, or whether he should be considered the author at all. There is the obvious fact that Moses dies at the end of the story, but that has been explained easily by saying he wrote the rest of it, and someone else added the part about his death later. Note, however, that even this simple case involves admitting the principle of multiple authors contributing different parts of the Pentateuch at different times.

More significantly, the twelfth-century Spanish Jew, Abraham Ibn Ezra, pointed to several passages that make more sense if they were written by someone else. Deuteronomy refers to the area east of the Jordan as "beyond the Jordan" (1:1), which is how it would be referred to by someone living west of the Jordan; yet the story has Moses die on the east side and never being west of the Jordan. In another place the Pentateuch says, "At that time the Canaanites were in the land" (Gen 12:6), as if written by someone living at a time when the Canaanites were no longer around, which would have been after the time of Moses. Ibn Ezra did not come right out and say what he concluded from these passages, but simply drew attention to them as a cryptic way of raising doubts about Mosaic authorship.

In the eighteenth and nineteenth centuries, more systematic attempts to explain the composition of the Pentateuch began. In 1753, Jean Astruc, a Frenchman, published a work in which he identified sources of diverse material in Genesis, based largely on the use of two different names for God in Hebrew, Yahweh and Elohim. (Although much of the development of the following theory is based on the different divine names, in fact the distinction applies only to Genesis and the first three chapters of Exodus; in Ex 3:13-15 the name Yahweh is revealed to Moses, and after that it can show up in any source.) Astruc did not reject a role for Moses, but said that Moses used these earlier sources when he wrote the Pentateuch. Over the next several decades, others took Astruc's basic idea, but said Moses had no role in writing the Pentateuch. Instead, the sources developed and were put together gradually, long after the time of Moses. Over time, the prevailing view among scholars came to be that there were four distinct sources, all written centuries after Moses, which were combined at a late date into the final form of the Pentateuch.

To get a sense of how these four sources are identified, consider the first two stories in Genesis. In Genesis 1:1–2:4, God is called Elohim. Elohim creates the universe in six days in an orderly way, with no opposition and no uncertainty about what to create. At the end, Elohim sets apart the seventh day to be a day of rest. Everything is in harmony, and everything is under Elohim's complete control.

In Genesis 2:4–3:24, we have another story about creation, but with very different characteristics. God is called Yahweh Elohim, and faces uncertainty and opposition. Yahweh Elohim wants to create a suitable partner for the man, but does so by trial and error, creating all the other animals, who turn out not to be suitable, before creating the woman, who turns out to be perfect. Then the story takes a turn that Yahweh Elohim seems not to have anticipated. The two people disobey the order not to eat the fruit of a certain tree, so, to punish them, Yahweh Elohim banishes them from the Garden of Eden and makes their life full of hard work and conflict. Unlike the first story with its certainty, this story is full of ambiguity about how much control God has, who is at fault for the disobedience, and what the future will be for creation.

Two different stories with different characteristics could mean anything by itself, but the significance is that the same pattern of characteristics shows up in other stories in the Pentateuch. There are stories like the first creation story in which God is called Elohim and is in complete control of the universe with no uncertainty about what to do. And, like the first story's day of rest being connected to the observance of the Sabbath, many of these stories are connected with religious observances. Genesis 17 is a typical example. God appears to Abraham, repeats the promise of a great number of descendants, and makes a covenant with Abraham, requiring that all his male descendants be circumcised. In this story, God is called Elohim (except for once in the first verse, which may have been the result of later putting it together with the previous passage); the main concern is a religious practice, circumcision; and God is in complete control, orderly, and has no uncertainty about the future of Abraham.

Likewise, there are stories like the second creation story, with God called Yahweh and portrayed more like a human character—not always in control, not anticipating what people might do, and often coming up with revised plans for the human race. Genesis 11:1-9 is an example. People try to build a tower to reach to the heavens. Yahweh comes down to earth and finds out about it, then decides it is not good for human beings to be able to become that god-like, so confuses their languages and scatters them over the earth. It is a story where people are able to go against God's will, and God needs to make a new plan for the future.

In addition to these two types of material, two other types were identified. One of these also calls God Elohim, but portrays God in a more distant way, communicating with people only through dreams or angels sent as messengers. This material has a particular concern with ethical issues. An example is Genesis 20. Abraham and Sarah travel to a city called Gerar, and Abraham, fearing that someone may kill him to steal his wife, claims that Sarah is his sister. Then Abimelech, the king of Gerar, takes Sarah without harming Abraham. God appears to Abimelech in a dream and warns him that he will be killed because he has taken another man's wife, so he returns Sarah to Abraham. This story is similar to the first creation story in that it calls God Elohim, but it has some different characteristics as well. It is concerned with an ethical issue, adultery, and God's way of interacting with people is indirect, through a dream.

And a fourth type of material was identified—the Book of Deuteronomy. Deuteronomy seems to have its own style of writing, different from other parts of the Pentateuch, and its versions of the laws are sometimes different from laws on the same topics elsewhere in the Pentateuch (e.g., Ex 12 says Passover is to be celebrated in each individual home, while Dt 16 says it is to be celebrated at one central location for the whole nation).

Identifying these different types of material led to the development of what became known as the "documentary hypothesis" for the composition of the Pentateuch. Julius Wellhausen, a German scripture scholar living in the second half of the nineteenth century and beginning of the twentieth century, is most often associated with the classic expression of the documentary hypothesis. Wellhausen was not the first person to come up with the idea, but his works were most influential in convincing the scholarly world of the validity of the theory. Wellhausen also made a thorough attempt to date each of the four sources and to explain how the events going on during Israel's history affected the shape of each of the sources. According to Wellhausen, the four sources and their dates are as follows.

Yahwist (J) Source. The earliest of the sources was written near the beginning of the Israelite monarchy. According to the Bible, King

David made Jerusalem his capital, probably around 1000 BCE, but did not build a temple. His son Solomon did build the temple in Jerusalem, so at that time a religious bureaucracy would have been established in Jerusalem, and one of its functions would have been to collect religious traditions and use them to write a national epic. For Wellhausen, sometime after Solomon (others have claimed even during Solomon's lifetime), this first source or national epic was written. This source called God Yahweh, portrayed God as a human-like character, and is often ambiguous in its theological message. Included in the J Source are the second creation story and the tower of Babel story. (The sources are often referred to by their one-letter abbreviations; in this case, the J is from the German spelling of Yahweh.)

Elohist (E) Source. After the reign of Solomon, the nation split into two separate kingdoms, a northern kingdom called Israel, and a southern kingdom called Judah. Jerusalem was the capital of the southern kingdom and the location of the temple, so when the northern kingdom separated, it established its own temples and religious bureaucracy, and eventually its own national epic. This northern epic, the Elohist source, calls God Elohim, is especially concerned with ethical issues, does not have God walking on earth like a person, has God communicating with people indirectly through dreams or angels or at most a voice from heaven, and is shaped by particular concerns of the northern kingdom. Examples of stories from the E Source are Genesis 20, the story of Abraham and Abimelech, and Genesis 35, about Jacob setting up an altar at Bethel (which was a city in the north) and eliminating the worship of other gods. To some extent the Elohist source is a reworking of the Yahwist source, since it does not come up with an entirely new epic, but includes additional stories about the main characters and events in the Yahwist source.

Deuteronomist (D) Source. Several parts of the Pentateuch contain collections of laws, but the collection in the Book of Deuteronomy seems to have developed separately from the other books in the Pentateuch. Not only are the vocabulary and style different, but the book repeats many laws that can be found in other books (e.g., the ten commandments are in both Ex 20 and Dt 5), and sometimes has different versions of the laws. Worship (e.g., the Passover celebration, any kind of sacrifice) is to be centralized. The role of prophets is emphasized, and Moses is described as the ideal prophet. The book's collection of laws is repeatedly called a covenant. An early version of the Deuteronomist source may have been part of a religious reform carried out by King Josiah of Judah in 622 BCE. That reform, during which a prophet had a prominent role in advising the king, centralized the worship in Jerusalem and was based on a book of laws called a covenant (2 Kgs 22–23).

Priestly (P) Source. After Israel was conquered by Assyria in 722 and Judah by Babylonia in 587, both the northern and southern kingdoms came to an end. The people of Judah were forced into exile in Babylon, and there, the priests who were their leaders added more material to the Pentateuch. The Priestly Source calls God Elohim, is concerned with worship, shows God in complete control and doing everything in an orderly, harmonious way, and also includes several genealogies. It is easy to see how these emphases fit the needs of the people in exile from their homeland and in the postexilic period, when most of the Jews remained scattered. They no longer had their nation to define who they were, so their way of worship would set them apart from the people among whom they were living. Jewish identity could also be preserved by keeping track of genealogies. And at a time when their whole world seemed to have been destroyed, they needed reassurance that God was, in fact, in control, and did have a plan for the chosen people. Examples of Priestly material include the first creation story and Exodus 12, the instructions on observing the Passover.

At some point after the exile, the final form of the Pentateuch took shape. According to Wellhausen, the Yahwist and the Elohist sources were combined into a single narrative during the monarchy. The Deuteronomist source was written later in the monarchy but remained a separate work until it was added to the end of the narrative. The Priestly source represents a reworking and expansion of the narrative after the exile.

In the redaction of these sources, sometimes two stories about the same event are both kept intact and simply placed one after the other—thus there are two separate creation stories. In other places, two stories about the same event are combined into a single story. The flood story in Gen 6–9 shows evidence of having originally been two separate stories. There are contradictions: in 6:19-20 God tells Noah to take two of every kind of animal into the ark, but in 7:2-3 he is to take seven pairs of clean animals, one pair of unclean animals, and seven pairs of the birds of the air. The number of days does not add up: in 7:11 and 8:13 it dates the beginning and end of the flood according to Noah's age, and covers a total period of ten and a half months; but several times in between those verses it mentions the number of days that passed, and the numbers add up to 361 days, somewhat longer than ten and a half months. Sometimes the story uses Yahweh as God's name, sometimes it uses Elohim, and there seems to be a lot of needless repetition of the instructions to Noah. The documentary hypothesis would explain these problems by saying that both the Yahwist source and the Priestly source had versions of the flood story, and the final redactor combined them into a single narrative, being more concerned to include elements of both than to perfectly harmonize the two.

Since Wellhausen's time scholars have proposed many variations of the documentary hypothesis. One type of variation is simply to take the same approach to the next level—perhaps within each of the four major sources one can discover slight differences in style, indicating that the sources themselves were composed from multiple sources. A J^1 and J^2 were proposed, and different stages within the P source. That type of analysis, though, can go on indefinitely, breaking the text into tinier and tinier fragments without adding anything to its interpretation, and is not much practiced today.

Another significant variation of the original theory has to do with the nature of D. Rather than seeing it primarily as a conclusion to the Pentateuch, Martin Noth saw it as an introduction to the books of Joshua, Judges, 1 and 2 Samuel, and 1 and 2 Kings. These six books, called the Former Prophets in the Hebrew Bible, are referred to as the Deuteronomic History by modern scholars, since their vocabulary and theology are similar to Deuteronomy's (e.g., on the covenant, the role of prophets, and centralized worship). Thus Noth spoke of a "Tetrateuch" (four books) rather than a Pentateuch, and treated the composition of D as part of a different process.[1]

More recently, some scholars have argued that the D source is responsible not only for Deuteronomy, but for other parts of the Pentateuch as well. For example, in Exodus 19–34 the covenant between Yahweh and the Israelites is the essential expression of their relationship, just as it is in D. The call of Moses in Exodus 3–4 is similar to prophetic calls, and thus associates Moses with the prophets, as D does. These and other similarities suggest that whoever wrote Deuteronomy may have also written parts of the other four books. Rolf Rendtorff takes this view, claiming that D was the main redactor of the entire Pentateuch, although P contributed some additional material later.[2]

There have also been questions about the existence of an E source. In practice, it is difficult to distinguish E material from J and P material, and many scholars today doubt that there was ever a separate, continuous E narrative.

There has been much debate about P as well. The predominant view is that P was composed after the exile, but several scholars, particularly from Israel, have argued that the material is from the monarchy, perhaps connected with a religious reform of King Hezekiah.[3] Also unresolved is whether the authors of P were also the final redactors of the Pentateuch, and whether the narrative and legal parts of P come from the same authors.

Another challenge to the hypothesis has to do with the dates of the sources. John Van Seters, who has done much work on J, argues that it is not from early in the monarchy, but from the exilic period. He sees J as the major shaper of the Pentateuch's story, and compares it to Greek historical epics from around the same times as the Jewish exile.[4] Some J stories do make more sense if they were written during or after the exile. Genesis 11, the story of the tower of Babel, is in part a criticism of Babylonian religion, which is the type of story one would expect from people living in exile there. Van Seters makes similar claims about the stories of Abraham; they would more easily fit a pastoral setting in the late monarchy or the exile than an earlier period. The exilic Yahwist should therefore be considered the main author of the Pentateuch, although there may have been later redactions, especially from the Priestly writers.

R. Norman Whybray has a view related to that of Rendtorff and Van Seters, that the Pentateuch is mainly the work of one exilic writer, but he goes a step further and says we should see the first comprehensive version as the final version. It does not make sense to speak of the traditional four sources as part of the process, or of several redactions being made after the story took its basic shape. Instead, the writer used a multitude of earlier stories that had not been put into one comprehensive narrative. This author also invented much new material. According to Whybray, scholars have not taken as much notice as they should of the fact that fiction is a major genre in the Old Testament.[5]

Besides these variations of the hypothesis, there has been much discussion of the approach itself. At the beginning of the twentieth century,

Hermann Gunkle, while accepting the existence of the sources, said that studying the oral traditions behind them was a better way to understand the Pentateuch; each individual story should be studied in light of the social situation that produced it, long before any of it was written down.[6] Later Gerhard von Rad took a similar approach, but rather than focusing on social situations, argued that the oral traditions originated in the worship of ancient Israel. He identified brief credal statements, such as Deuteronomy 26:5-9, which summarize the Pentateuch's story.

> A wandering Aramean was my ancestor; he went down into Egypt and lived there as an alien, few in number, and there he became a great nation, mighty and populous. When the Egyptians treated us harshly and afflicted us, by imposing hard labor on us, we cried to the LORD, the God of our ancestors; the LORD heard our voice and saw our affliction, our toil, and our oppression. The LORD brought us out of Egypt with a mighty hand and an outstretched arm, with a terrifying display of power, and with signs and wonders; and he brought us into this place and gave us this land, a land flowing with milk and honey.

Such statements were recited at worship and were gradually expanded into the Pentateuch as we know it.[7]

In recent years, the approach of the documentary hypothesis has been challenged by those who study the Bible as a work of literature. Robert Alter argues that it is more productive to study the final form of the text rather than its pre-history. It may be that sources were used, but we can never fully recover them, and whoever the final author or redactor was, that person did not mechanically paste together other sources, but wove them together with some artistic skill. We gain more by studying the final work of art rather than the hypothetical, partial sources.[8]

Wellhausen's documentary hypothesis has not survived in its original form. However, virtually all scholars today accept the basic idea behind it, that the Pentateuch is not the work of one single author writing at one time, but was composed over several centuries by people responding to different circumstances.

In this book I will not take a position on every disputed question, but I will argue that the Pentateuch is made up of three primary sources, the Deuteronomist, the Yahwist, and the Priestly. The

Deuteronomic material was written first, with the core of it connected to King Josiah's reform and more of it added during and after the exile. The Yahwist material preserves some laws and stories from the monarchy, but for the most part was written after the exile, and in some cases was influenced by the Deuteronomic writings. The Priestly material is the latest strand, and includes original laws and stories plus editorial additions to Deuteronomic and Yahwist material.

Specific reasons for these views will be given in the comments on each book, but there are some general characteristics of the Pentateuch that make more sense if it is primarily a postexilic work, except for the Deuteronomic material from late in the monarchy. One is that there is nothing in the Pentateuch, except for Deuteronomy 17, about establishing a king for Israel. For a foundational document about a people, written during a king's rule, to say nothing about the royal house is almost unimaginable. It would make sense, though, for such a document to have been written when those people no longer had their own king. A second general characteristic is that the Pentateuch is a story about a promise on the verge of being fulfilled: a nation and a land are promised to Abraham's descendants, and the story ends with them on the border, ready to take possession of the land. The story is addressed to people who are outside of the land, but have the chance to return and make it into a nation; the people were in that circumstance during the Persian period, not during the monarchy.

We will never know all the details of the process, but it is useful to ask the questions about the composition of the Pentateuch. Asking if a particular story was written during the exile can lead to insights into its meaning; asking if a collection of laws was associated with King Josiah's religious reform can lead to insights into their purpose. And the recognition that there are multiple viewpoints in the Pentateuch helps us understand its theology better. The God of the first creation story is all-powerful and creates a perfectly structured universe. The God of the second story creates by trial and error, is not all-powerful, and can be disobeyed. Those who gathered the material into the Pentateuch chose to include both stories despite the different views of God and contradictions in some of the details. The theological message is that God is too big to be captured by one story. We know the truth of who God is only by seeing from multiple viewpoints.

CHAPTER THREE

Genesis 1–11

Genesis 1–3 — Creation

Genesis 4–5 — From Creation to the Flood

Genesis 6:1–9:19 — The Flood Story

Genesis 9:20–11:32 — After the Flood

The stories in Genesis are among the most difficult stories in the Bible on which to use the historical approach. One reason is that many of the events do not sound like historical events at all. In Genesis there are more mythic elements then there are in most parts of the Bible. The word "myth" can be a misleading word. As applied to biblical and other ancient literature, it does not necessarily mean something is false, nor does it refer to stories that include miraculous elements. It refers to literature that explains the way the universe is by describing actions of gods and using figurative stories of people, animals, and other objects. It is true that ancient literature frequently mixes myth and history,[1] but note that certain occurrences in Genesis—a talking serpent, sex between divine and human beings, a person changed into a pillar of salt—are not typical of the Bible as a whole and are closer to mythological literature. With elements like these, can we apply the historical approach to Genesis in the same way we would apply it to, say, the Second Book of Kings?

Another difficulty is that no one knows for sure when these events are supposed to have occurred. No dates are given, and the main characters—Adam, Eve, Noah, Abraham, Sarah, and the others—are not mentioned in other writings from the ancient Near East. The only way to date these events is to work back from later events in the biblical story, but doing that is not easy. We know the kingdom of Judah ended around 587 BCE, and using the lengths of the reigns of the kings of Judah and Israel reported in 1 and 2 Kings we have an approximate idea of when David and Solomon supposedly reigned, sometime in the 900s. But there is contradictory information on the time before that. According to 1 Kings 6:1, 480 years went by from the time of the exodus from Egypt until Solomon began building the temple. Yet if we go through the events from the exodus until Solomon and add up the number of years claimed by the story to have passed between the events, it comes to more than 550 years. Then there is an unspecified period of time between the end of Genesis and the exodus events. And within Genesis the lengths of many of the characters lives are unbelievable—are they meant to be taken literally or symbolically? Adding to the problem is the fact that the ancient Greek version of the Old Testament (the Septuagint) and the Samaritan version of the Pentateuch have numbers different from the Hebrew version's. Many have tried various methods to solve these date problems (a seventeenth-century Irish bishop said that creation occurred on October 4, 4004 BCE). But the truth is that no one knows when the events in Genesis were supposed to have occurred, which makes it difficult to look for evidence of their historicity.

Despite these problems, it is useful to see what can be discovered from asking historical questions. For some parts of Genesis, the question of whether the events happened will be unanswerable. But the historical approach also asks about the history of the composition of the book and about background historical information that may shed light on the meaning of the stories.

Creation (Genesis 1–3)

The question of whether the creation of the universe occurred in the way Genesis describes it is not really a historical question, but a scientific one. Still, some comments are in order, simply because in popular culture, and sometimes even in politics, there is the impression that there is uncertainty on the scientific accuracy of Genesis. There may be uncertainty about the precise physical processes of the beginning of the universe and the beginning of life on earth, but there is no uncertainty on one point. Geology, biology, astrophysics, and any other natural science that touches on the issue leave no doubt that Genesis is not a literal description of how the universe began, and scripture scholars who use a critical approach agree that Genesis is not to be taken literally in the creation stories. The fact that this is even a question for some people may be a curious commentary on our society, but it is irrelevant for a critical study of the Bible.

The creation of the universe did not occur in the way Genesis describes it, but the historical approach can lead to other insights about these stories, particularly when it comes to how the stories were composed and the circumstances to which they were responding.

Genesis 1:1–2:4. As mentioned in the previous chapter, according to the documentary hypothesis, the first creation story is from the Priestly source, written during or after the exile. This helps us see how the story is emphasizing God's complete control over a universe that was orderly and had a purpose, especially at a time when the whole world seemed chaotic and many wondered if God really was in control. The story also connects creation to worship, with the day of rest on the seventh day corresponding to the observance of the Sabbath. Connecting worship to the major events in the Pentateuch's story (the exodus/Passover connection is another example) served to make worship more meaningful at a time when the nation had come to an end and worship had become more important for defining what it meant to be a Jew.

If the first creation story was written during or after the exile, we can also ask if it was influenced by Mesopotamian views of creation. In fact, a number of Mesopotamian texts have been discovered since the nineteenth century. They include several versions of a creation epic. The Babylonian creation story is called the *Enuma Elish*, for its first two words, "When on high." The story was probably written in the early second millennium BCE. It begins with nothing yet created and nothing in existence except Apsu, the father god, and Tiamat, the mother goddess.

> When on high the heaven had not been named,
> Firm ground below had not been called by name,
> Naught but primordial Apsu, their begetter,
> And Mummu-Tiamat, she who bore them all,
> Their waters commingling in a single body.[2]

Tiamat gives birth to other gods, who in turn give birth to more generations of gods. After some time the younger gods begin to disturb the older gods with their noise, and Apsu determines to destroy them all so he can have some peace. Tiamat, however, does not think they should destroy what they themselves have created. The younger gods hear about Apsu's desire to destroy them and they kill him before he can act. When Tiamat discovers that her husband Apsu has been murdered, she is furious and vows revenge against the younger gods. The younger gods are terrified of Tiamat's fury, and so they assemble to plan their strategy. One of them, Marduk, is chosen as the most skilled in battle. He is asked to fight Tiamat. Marduk agrees, but only on the condition that if he is victorious he will be made supreme ruler of all the gods.

Marduk defeats and slays Tiamat, and the other gods are saved from her vengeance. Marduk then creates the world from the carcass of Tiamat. He splits her body in half lengthwise; one half he uses to form the sky, the other half the firmament of the earth. He then gives the other gods positions in the sky as the stars.

> He constructed stations for the great gods,
> Fixing their astral likenesses as the images.
> He determined the year by designating the zones:
> He set up three constellations for each of the twelve months.[3]

Last of all, Marduk creates humans.

> Marduk spoke: "Blood I will mass and cause bones to be.
> I will establish a savage, 'man' shall be his name.
> Truly, savage man I will create.
> He will be charged with the service of the gods, that they
>   might be at ease."[4]

After finishing creation, Marduk calls an assembly of all the gods, where he gives them instructions for their roles in this new world.

The *Enuma Elish* is quite different from Genesis 1, but there are some striking similarities. Both have the same understanding of the shape of the universe—a fixed dome above, and a firmament below. Both begin with chaotic, unstructured waters before anything is created (the name Tiamat is even similar to the Hebrew word *tehom*, the deep, in Gen 1:2). The order in which things are created is the same: the dome above, then the firmament below, then the stars and other objects in the sky, and human beings last. (The *Enuma Elish*, however, does not mention the creation of plants and animals.) And both stories conclude with the creator god setting apart a special day for something different.

These similarities are too close to be mere coincidence. They show that the Babylonians and the authors of Genesis 1 shared some basic assumptions about creation and the universe. And some version of the *Enuma Elish* must have been known to the authors of Genesis 1, especially if it was written by the Priestly source during or after the exile. The Priestly source was influenced by, if it did not directly borrow from, the Babylonian creation story.

But the differences between the two stories are of more significance. First, there is only one god in the Genesis story. Despite being similar to the goddess Tiamat, the *tehom*, the deep in Genesis, is only unformed waters; it is not a competing god that has to be defeated in battle before God can create anything. And even though the stars in Genesis are similar to those in the *Enuma Elish*, having fixed positions on the dome and marking the seasons of the year, they are just created objects completely under the control of one God. The stars are not other gods to whom the chief god has to give positions of honor in order to make sure that they stay loyal to him. By paralleling the *Enuma Elish* but changing the other gods to objects without any power of their own, Genesis is emphasizing the control of one God over all forces in the universe.

Another difference is the emphasis Genesis gives to creation being good. Not only does the *Enuma Elish* never say creation is good, there is an implicit message that there is something fundamentally flawed about it—it resulted from conflict among the gods, and is made from the dead body of a defeated god. Related to this is another difference, the view of human beings. In the *Enuma Elish* people are made only to be slaves to the gods. In Genesis people are created in the image of God, and are given dominion over the rest of God's creation. If creation is good and people are made in God's image, then surely God will protect people, even in times like the exile that seem catastrophic.

The authors of Genesis 1 were aware of the *Enuma Elish* and shared some assumptions about the universe with it, but they deliberately told a story with a different message. They wanted a story that clearly differentiated Judaism from Babylonian religion. This was especially necessary during and after the exile as many Jews were adopting the customs and views of the people among whom they were scattered. They wanted a story that emphasized God's control, and a positive role for human beings. Basically, they wanted a story that would give them reason to hope for a future better than what they were living through in the exile.

Genesis 2:5–3:24. The second creation story does not have any parallels in other literature as close as Genesis 1 has, but there are general similarities to literature from other peoples. A story of an ideal state, followed by someone breaking a prohibition, leading to an imperfect state closer to reality, is common around the world, from the ancient Near East to Africa to North America.[5] Because the story pattern is so common, Genesis 2–3 may be based on a more ancient story that the Yahwist has adapted.

Joseph Blenkinsopp has pointed out that the story of Adam and Eve is never referred to elsewhere in the Bible before the exile, and that its vocabulary is closer to postexilic literature than to literature from the monarchy.[6] This is further evidence that the Yahwist source was not written until the exile or later, instead of during the monarchy as many scholars used to believe. In fact, Genesis 2–3 can be read as a commentary on the exile; the monarchy was the ideal state; the nation sinned by failing to follow the covenant with God, and, as a result, God expelled them into the broken world of the exile. Alternatively, it has been read as a commentary on David's reign. During David's rise to power and at the beginning of his reign, everything works out perfectly for him, but after his sin with Bathsheba one disaster follows another. In either case, the story is clearly not meant to be just a record of the earliest events in the world. It is meant to be a comment on events that happened at the time the text was written. By telling the story in mythological language and putting it at the beginning of creation, the Yahwist universalizes its message: it is about the exile, or it is about King David, but it is also about the experience of all of humanity.

However the story originated and whenever the Yahwist made it part of the national epic, as part of the Pentateuch it sets the stage for everything that follows. The perfectly harmonious relationships that exist at the beginning are broken, and Yahweh will try again and again to restore a good relationship with humanity.

From Creation to the Flood (Genesis 4–5)

Genesis 4:1-16. Following creation, the story continues with the two sons of Adam and Eve, Cain and Abel. Abel is a keeper of flocks, and Cain a tiller of the soil. When they both bring their offerings to God, God looks favorably on Abel's, but not on Cain's. In anger, Cain murders his brother Abel.

The origin of the story may be in ancient conflicts between herders and settled farmers. There has also been speculation that Cain represents the Kenites, a group of people closely associated with the Israelites in several incidents, and the story explains the relationship between the Israelites and Kenites (despite the different spellings in English, in Hebrew the names Cain and Kenite are almost identical, and in some passages are identical). This type of story, explaining the origin of some aspect of the present world, is called an "etiology," and is common in the Old Testament. Biblical etiologies, however, rarely serve just one purpose, but add several things to the narratives of which they are a part. In this case, the Cain and Abel story shows the consequences of the disobedience of Adam and Eve: now all relationships among people will have discord. It is also the first of many stories in the Pentateuch (and elsewhere in the Bible) of older and younger brothers. In all of these stories—Jacob and Esau (Gen 25–33), Perez and Zerah (Gen 38:27-30), Joseph and his brothers (Gen 37–50; Joseph is the second youngest of the twelve)—it is the younger brother who is chosen by God and who comes out ahead in the end. The stories express the national identity of the Israelites as a younger-son type of people. They had fewer natural advantages than their neighbors, but became successful because they were chosen by God.

Genesis 4:17-26. After the Cain and Abel story there is a list of the next generations. The list of Cain's descendants concludes with Jabal, the ancestor of those who dwell in tents and keep cattle, Jubal, the ancestor of all who play the lyre and the pipe, and Tubalcain, the ancestor of all who forge instruments of bronze and iron. This is followed by a report that Adam and Eve had another son, Seth, who had a son Enosh, and that "At that time people began to invoke the name of the Lord" (4:26). The origin of this list of generations is problematic. Two of the names in Cain's line (Enoch and Lamech) also appear in the genealogy in the following chapter, as descendants of Seth, and others (Cain and Methushael) are variant forms of names in that genealogy (Kenan and Methuselah). It is also inconsistent with the larger narrative; all of Cain's descendants will die in the flood, so they cannot be the ancestors of all who keep cattle, play the lyre and pipe, and forge metal instruments (although, strictly speaking, only with Jubal does the Hebrew say *all*). And the claim that the practice of invoking the name of Yahweh began at the time of Seth's son contradicts statements in the Book of Exodus that the name of Yahweh was not revealed until the time of Moses (Ex 3:13-15; 6:2-3).

Because there are these problems, the list of descendants here was probably originally a variant form of the list of the earliest generations that is found in the next chapter. The authors kept this variant form and rearranged it into two lines, so that in its present context it shows a contrast between the line of Cain and the line of Seth: with Cain came increased civilization and technology, but with Seth came worship of Yahweh. The contrast serves to get across the theological message that an increase in civilization and technology may seem like a positive thing, but if it comes without a proper relationship with God, then it will lead to a downfall. That idea is similar to what is found in several stories from the Yahwist source. In the Yahwist's version of creation, the sin of Adam and Eve was eating the fruit to become like gods. Becoming like gods may seem like a positive thing, but when outside of a proper relationship with the one God, it is not. Evil, for the Yahwist, is not something totally opposite to good; it is something good that is not used in the way God intends.

Some may be dissatisfied with this explanation for the contradictions in the genealogies. Those seeking a literal history in the genealogies may object that surely the authors were not so stupid that they didn't notice the contradictions; there must be some other explanation. Maybe by coincidence there were several people in the different genealogies who happened to have the same names; maybe when the authors say that Jubal was the ancestor of all who play lyre and pipe, they meant to say all people before the flood; maybe people began to invoke Yahweh, but then stopped, and so the revelation to Moses was like a new revelation. While these explanations are not impossible, the accumulation of them becomes too much of a twisting of the text. And resorting to what the author *meant* to say seems to be changing the meaning of what literal history is. Moreover, biblical and other ancient writers were not as bothered by outright contradictions as we are; one can compare the two New Testament genealogies of Jesus (Mt 1:1-17 and Lk 3:23-38, where the attempts to explain away the contradictions are even more farfetched).

Rather than trying to force on the text a historical meaning that the authors did not intend, it is more useful to consider the purposes that biblical and other ancient genealogies served. Genealogies were often created artificially to express a social connection. They were used to legitimize an inherited political or religious office. In the context of a larger narrative, they connect past events with people living at the time the story is told. The events of Genesis thus become more than just stories in the distant past; they become events that affect people in the present. In the case of Genesis 1–11, the genealogies also keep the story moving forward. This is especially necessary because so much of the story is about sin and a failure of humanity to live up to what God intended. To balance the sense of creation coming apart, the genealogies give a sense of life continuing, with one generation following another in orderly progression.

Genesis 5:1-32. Chapter five is a separate genealogy, taking the list down to the time of the flood. One striking thing about this genealogy is the length of the people's lives; most of them lived several hundred years, the longest lived being Methuselah, whose years numbered 969. There have been attempts to explain how these ages could be factual, e.g., that the environment was in better condition then or that diseases weren't as common.[7] It is more productive to note that attributing long lives to the earliest generations was common in the ancient Near East. One well-known document is a list of Sumerian kings, with reigns of 28,800 years, 36,000 years, and similarly long terms.[8] It is also worth noting that the genealogy in Genesis 5 is likely from the Priestly source, which had no story of disobedience and expulsion from paradise; thus these generations represent a phase when humankind was still close to the ideal state created by God.[9]

The Flood Story (Genesis 6:1–9:19)

The flood is a pivotal incident in the Pentateuch's story. It comes as the culmination of all the evil going on in the world since the expulsion from the Garden of Eden. It results in the destruction of what God created. It uses terrifying imagery of rising and uncontrollable waters, yet it all occurs in an orderly way, under God's control, and directed toward a purpose. The story is included for a theological reason—to say something about God's ongoing relationship with humanity, about God's desire to start creation over again after eliminating the corruption. It is also a story that can be profitably studied using literary methods.

But is there any value in studying the flood story using historical methods? Advances in the natural sciences since the seventeenth century have raised problems with considering this a story describing a real occurrence. There are still attempts to prove that it could be possible, but such attempts depend on bizarre scientific views invented solely for the purpose of proving that the Bible is literally true (e.g., the lack of geological evidence for the flood is because geological processes that shaped the earth's surface used to take place differently from what scientists have observed in recent centuries), or on ignoring the inherent implausibilities within the story (e.g., the amount of room needed on the ark to hold all species of animals, or how animals from every climate and habitat on earth could have survived a year in one place). An awareness that there are far more species of animals, and of greater diversity, in the world than previously realized; the lack of geological evidence of a single flood covering the entire earth; knowledge of the amount of water such a flood would have to involve, and other issues make it impossible to accept the story as literal. Those who look for some basis in an actual event now look for a local flood behind the story. For the most part, critical biblical scholarship today does not search for an actual flood behind the story in Genesis. There may have been such a local flood, but the Pentateuch does not give us enough information to know when or where to look for the evidence of it.

With regard to the composition of the flood story, most biblical scholars believe it is a composite of the Yahwist and Priestly sources (see the previous chapter). The existence of two versions tells us that it was a widely known story in ancient Israel, and that it was employed for a variety of theological purposes. It is possible to separate some of the Yahwist and Priestly elements and try to reconstruct the two versions, but we don't know how much of each version was left out or revised when the two were combined. Since flood stories are common in many ancient cultures, there may have been earlier oral or written versions on which J and P are based. However, outside of Genesis, Noah is not mentioned in the Bible until exilic or postexilic literature (Ezek 14:12-20, which doesn't connect him to the flood, and Is 54:9-10, which uses the flood as a metaphor for the exile), suggesting that the particulars of the Genesis story are not very ancient.

One puzzle about the composition of the flood story is the way it is introduced at the beginning of chapter six. The "sons of God" took human wives, and had offspring, the Nephilim, who were the heroes of old. Then God decided, "My spirit shall not abide in mortals forever, for they are flesh; their days shall be one hundred twenty years" (Gen 6:3).

Who these "sons of God" were, and the purpose of this passage, have been much debated. The passage is not well-integrated into either what precedes it or what follows it. Sex between divine and human beings is a mythological element, representing disruption of the proper order of the universe.[10] It does not represent any one particular type of sin, but simply the fact that there was great corruption (similar to Gen 19, where the people of Sodom desire to have sex with the visiting angels). Here, it introduces the evil that causes God to send the flood, but because it is so different in character from the rest of the story, it is probably a fragment of yet another version of the flood story; if both the Priestly and Yahwist sources had their own flood stories, it would not be surprising if other ancient Israelite versions existed as well. This fragment shows that the final redactors were more interested in preserving multiple traditions than in harmonizing them all into one tidy story.

The discovery of other ancient flood stories around the world also is relevant for the historical questions asked about the Genesis story. There are flood stories from the ancient Near East, stories of which the authors of Genesis may have been aware; and there are stories from North America, China, and other places, stories of which the authors of Genesis certainly were not aware. The existence of so many flood stories could lead one to believe that there must have been some world-wide event behind them, but a little reflection tells us that floods are the kind of catastrophic events that would easily develop into mythological stories, and it would not be unusual for stories to develop independently continents apart. A useful question is which other stories the Israelites were aware of, and whether they borrowed elements from the other stories, or perhaps developed the Genesis story to counter the theological beliefs expressed in other flood stories.

Three flood stories from the ancient Near East bear a resemblance to Genesis. In the third century BCE a Babylonian priest, Berossus, included a flood story in a longer historical work; only fragments of this work survive, but its flood story is based on a much earlier Sumerian story. Another Mesopotamian work, the *Epic of Atrahasis*, known from a seventeenth century BCE copy, tells of a flood sent by the gods to punish humans for their sins. And the most significant of the ancient Near Eastern flood stories is one episode in a longer work, the *Epic of Gilgamesh*. Several versions have been discovered; it probably dates originally from the third millennium BCE.

The *Epic of Gilgamesh* tells of the adventures of Gilgamesh and his friend Enkidu. Eventually Enkidu dies and, in his mourning, Gilgamesh asks why people must die and if it is possible to live forever. He finds out that there is one man, Utnapishtim, whom the gods have allowed to live forever, so he seeks him out to find out how this can be, and if immortality can also be achieved by others. Utnapishtim tells Gilgamesh why the gods have allowed him to live forever. Long ago the gods decided to send a flood upon the earth. No reason is given for the flood, but one of the gods, having apparently disagreed with the idea, secretly warned Utnapishtim. He told him to build a ship, giving exact instructions on its size, and to take the seed of all living things with him on it. Then the storms came, and the waters rose, killing people and covering the mountains. The flood was so terrifying that even the gods were frightened, and retreated to the highest heaven. When the storm ended, Utnapishtim's ship came to rest on a high mountain. He sent out a dove, but it returned, since it could find no resting place. Then he sent a swallow, and it also came back. Then he sent a raven, and the raven did not return, since the waters had diminished. Utnapishtim released the animals, came out of the ship, and offered a sacrifice to the gods. When the gods smelled the burning of the sacrifice, they came to Utnapishtim. Since it had not been their plan to allow someone to survive, they argued about what to do with him. They decided to allow him to be immortal, but required that he live far away, at the mouth of the rivers, so that other humans would not see that one had become immortal.

The *Epic of Gilgamesh* has a number of parallels to the story of Noah. In both, one person receives a divine warning about the flood, is given exact instructions on how to build a ship to survive, and is told to take the other animals with him. In both, everything is submerged by the waters of the flood. In both, the ship comes to rest on a high mountain. In both, three birds are sent out, and the third one does not return, indicating that the waters have receded. In both, the person comes out and offers a sacrifice and the gods smell the smoke of it. The similarities are too close to have happened by chance. That does not mean that the authors of Genesis were necessarily borrowing directly from the *Epic of Gilgamesh*, but it does mean that they were influenced by the same traditional story.

The differences in the Genesis version, however, reveal its theological message. In Genesis, the flood, destructive as it is, serves a positive purpose—to give creation a second chance to live righteously. In the *Epic of Gilgamesh*, the flood is simply an arbitrary act of the gods. In Genesis, the survival of Noah and his family is part of the one plan of the one God. In the *Epic of Gilgamesh*, the gods had not planned for anyone to survive, and Utnapishtim survived only because the gods were divided and one of them secretly warned him of the flood. In Genesis, the flood occurs exactly according to God's plan. In the *Epic of Gilgamesh*, the gods themselves become frightened by the flood, suggesting that there are in the universe chaotic forces that even the gods can't control. In Genesis, the flood concludes with God making a covenant with all of creation and promising never to send such a flood again. In the *Epic of Gilgamesh*, the result is only a private reward for one person, and the gods try to prevent it from affecting anyone else.

The comparison of the Genesis story with the *Epic of Gilgamesh* does not, of course, tell us whether any of it actually occurred. But it does highlight what the authors of Genesis wanted to teach through the flood story. It is a story that emphasizes there is one God, in control of all forces in the universe, who will use that control to try to restore humanity to righteousness. The world is not an arbitrary place where humanity might come to an end at any time for no reason at all.

After the Flood (Genesis 9:20–11:32)

Genesis 9:20-29. The story goes on to say that after the flood Noah
was the first person to plant a vineyard. On one occasion he drinks
some of the wine and becomes drunk, and his son Ham sees him naked
in his tent. The other two sons, Shem and Japheth, refuse to look at
him. When Noah finds out that Ham saw him naked, he curses Ham's
son Canaan, and blesses Shem and Japheth, saying that Canaan will be
a slave to them and Japheth will dwell among the tents of Shem.

As part of the larger narrative, the incident shows corruption con-
tinuing even after the flood, although it is not clear precisely what
Ham's sin is. The story also refers to the relationship between the
Israelites and the Canaanites in later times. Shem is the ancestor of the
Israelites, while Canaan is the ancestor of the Canaanites, the people
who, according to the biblical story, lived in the promised land before
the Israelites conquered it. The story is saying that God intends the
Israelites to rule over the Canaanites because of the depravity of the
Canaanites.

That much is clear, but it is not explained why Canaan is cursed for
Ham's sin. Josephus, the Jewish writer of the first century, said that
because Ham was so closely related to Noah, Noah did not want to
curse him, but cursed his descendants instead (*Antiquities*, I, VI, 3);
that, however, does not explain why only Canaan was cursed and not
the other sons of Ham. The story may come from a separate tradition in
which Shem, Japheth, and Canaan were the three sons of Noah. Even
though it is not perfectly integrated into the rest of the narrative, the
author includes it to show corruption continuing after the flood, and to
comment on the relationship between the Israelites and Canaanites.

Genesis 10. Chapter ten is often called the "table of nations." It is in
the form of a genealogy of the descendants of Noah's three sons
Japheth, Ham, and Shem, dividing the known peoples of the world into
three groups. In general, the descendants of Japheth are the people of
Asia Minor and Europe, the descendants of Ham the people of Africa,
and the descendants of Shem the people of Mesopotamia and Syria
(the English word Semite comes from the name Shem). For example,
under Japheth, Javan is the Greeks, Ashkenaz is the Sythians, and
Tarshish is probably in Spain (cf. Jonah 1:3). Under Ham, Mizraim is

Egypt, Cush is the Nubians, and Put is Lybia. Under Shem, Aram is the small nation northeast of Israel, frequently mentioned in biblical stories about the monarchy. There are exceptions to the general organization, and it is clear that the chapter represents political realities at the time it was composed, and not actual racial or linguistic groups. Specifically, it represents the way the people of Judah saw the world at the end of the monarchy; e.g., making Cush rather than Egypt the eldest son of Ham would make sense during the time when the kingdom of Cush ruled Egypt, from 711 to 593 BCE, and making Sidon the first born of Canaan without even mentioning its neighbor Tyre fits the period of Sidon's pre-eminence, from the beginning of the sixth until the fourth century.[11]

It may seem odd that the Canaanites and the Philistines are grouped with Africa, Canaan as a son of Ham and the Philistines as descendants of Mizraim (Egypt). In the Bible, both are described as living in Palestine, so it would seem to make more sense to make them descendants of Shem, or, in the case of the Philistines, of Japheth, since the Philistines had migrated to Palestine from the islands around Greece. However, for religious reasons, the genealogy is trying to sharpen the distinction between the Israelites and the Canaanites and Philistines. And there may be some historical basis for grouping them with Africa. Late in the monarchy, people in Palestine, including the Philistines, occasionally allied themselves with Egypt in order to resist the expanding Assyrian or Babylonian empires. And by the time the table was composed, Canaan no longer referred to a separate political entity, but to anyone living in Palestine who did not practice the normative form of Judaism that was developing.

Most of chapter ten is just the lists of names, but there is one bit of narrative. Nimrod is said to be the first to become a mighty warrior, and becomes a "mighty hunter before the Lord." He has a kingdom in Mesopotamia, and builds several cities there (10:8-12). There have been attempts to connect Nimrod to an actual historical figure. The Assyrian king Tukulti-Ninurta I, in the thirteenth century BCE, is a possibility; besides the similarity of his name, he established a kingdom greater than that of his predecessors. Another possibility is the Egyptian king Amenophis III, who claimed to have ruled as far as Mesopotamia;[12] that would explain why Nimrod is called son of Cush, since otherwise it would be strange to have an African as king in Mesopotamia. Another possibility is that Nimrod is not based on a human at all, but on the Mesopotamian god Ninurta, who was a warrior and a hunter. Whatever the origin, we should ask why it has been inserted into a section that is otherwise just a list of names. Most likely it is meant to counter some popular legend with which the exilic Jews were familiar. The passage goes out of its way to emphasize that Nimrod is "before the LORD" (stated twice in 10:9). During the exile there was the danger of Jews adopting Mesopotamian legends and religious beliefs. To preserve belief in only one God, the exilic writers incorporated some of these legends, but made them consistent with normative Yahwism. The treatment of Nimrod is similar to the way the exilic Second Isaiah treats the Persian king Cyrus, emphasizing that all of his power is from Yahweh (Is 45:1-4).[13]

Genesis 11:1-9. The final narrative passage in Genesis 1–11 is the story of the tower of Babel. Like other episodes, it serves several purposes. It is an etiology explaining why there are different languages in the world. It is a criticism of Babylonian religion; the tower the people build seems to be based on the ziggurat, a tower temple built in ancient Babylon. It is a story that represents evil in a mythological way; building a tower to the heavens is a crossing of the divine/human boundary, similar to the sin of Adam and Eve in trying to become like gods. According to the documentary hypothesis, the story is from the Yahwist source—God is called Yahweh and is portrayed in humanlike ways; people are able to challenge Yahweh's control; Yahweh comes down to earth and changes his plans for humanity. It may indicate that the Yahwist source is exilic in date; knowledge and criticism of Babylonian religion could date from any time, but would have been most likely during the exile.

As part of the larger narrative, this incident is a turning point in God's relationship with humanity. Up to now, God has tried to have a harmonious relationship with all of humanity. When things failed, God tried to start over with the flood. But now that people continue to go against God, God will no longer try to have the same perfect relationship with all people. There will be a new strategy: after this God will set apart one group of people to be the chosen people and attempt to establish a perfect relationship with them rather than with the entire human race. That story of the chosen people will begin in chapter twelve, but for now the story is still about the failure of humanity as a whole.

Genesis 11:10-32. The tower of Babel story is followed by a genealogy from Shem to Abram (Abraham). Some of this is a repetition of the table of nations in chapter 10, but it has a narrower concern, leading directly to the chosen people. Like other genealogies, it gives the story a sense of moving forward despite all the setbacks. The tower of Babel was another human failure. Nonetheless, God has a plan for humanity, and that plan will be accomplished.

The first eleven chapters of Genesis express some of Judaism's foundational beliefs about God, humanity, and the rest of creation. Although they are not history, studying them from the historical perspective does highlight their teachings. At several points these stories draw contrasts between Jewish religion and Babylonian religion. There is one God who is in control of the entire universe. That one God created people with a positive role in the universe and keeps trying to restore that positive role. These chapters set the stage for the rest of the Pentateuch, which will recount the development of God's relationship with the chosen people.

CHAPTER FOUR

Genesis 12–50

Genesis 12–20 — The Promises to Abraham

Genesis 21:1–25:18 — The Son Isaac

Genesis 25:19–36:43 — Jacob and Esau

Genesis 37–50 — Joseph and his Brothers

There is no formal break in Genesis between chapters 1–11 and chapters 12–50, and when one reads straight through, the story of Abraham and Sarah beginning in chapter 12 may at first seem like yet another episode of the early generations. Yet it soon becomes clear that the focus has shifted. This is not *an* episode about Abraham and Sarah, but a longer series of episodes about them and, later, their descendants. Moreover, the story is no longer interested in humanity as a whole, but only in the family of Abraham and Sarah. Thus chapters 1–11 can be called the "Primeval History," and chapters 12–50 a separate section, the "Ancestral Narrative."

The Ancestral Narrative begins with God telling Abram (Abraham) to leave his home and go to a new land. God promises to make him a great nation, to give him a large number of descendants, and says, "I will bless those who bless you, and the one who curses you I will curse; and in you all the families of the earth shall be blessed" (Gen 12:3). The rest of the Pentateuch will be about God fulfilling these promises: getting Abram (Abraham) to Canaan, the promised land; giving Abraham and Sarah descendants and making them into a nation; and blessing and cursing all the other nations through them. Abraham and Sarah are now the chosen people. God will no longer have the same relationship

40

with all people, but will have a unique relationship with this people set apart from all others.

Like any good story, this one will involve obstacles and delays before the promises are fulfilled, but by the end of Genesis they begin to be fulfilled. Abraham and Sarah will have a son, Isaac; Isaac and Rebekah will have a son, Jacob; and Jacob and his wives will have twelve sons, the ancestors of the twelve tribes of Israel. However, Genesis also ends with this last generation outside of Canaan, having gone to Egypt during a time of famine, so the promise to give them land will need to be fulfilled later in the story. The last part of the promise, the blessing and cursing of other nations, is the least tangible, but it does show that God's making Abraham and Sarah the chosen people does not mean ignoring the rest of the world; in some way, the rest of humanity will still be affected by what God does with the chosen people.

Historicity of the Ancestors

Before looking at individual episodes in Genesis 12–50, we will look at the general question of the historicity of the ancestors. Since Abraham, Sarah, Isaac, and the others are not mentioned in any contemporary texts, and since their lifestyle was not one that would have left archaeological evidence in the form of monuments or great buildings, the historical study of the ancestors has relied on indirect evidence. This indirect evidence, of course, is open to different interpretations, and too often is swayed by a priori assumptions about how credible the biblical text is on historical matters.

For centuries there have been theologians such as Origen and Augustine who said that not everything in Genesis is meant as literal history, but it was not until modern times that there has been serious and widespread doubt about the basic historicity of the ancestral stories. In large part, the doubt followed the studies of the composition of the Pentateuch, which concluded that the stories were written long after the events were supposed to have occurred. Julius Wellhausen, influential in the development of the documentary hypothesis, believed that because of the late date of the Pentateuch's sources, the stories could not be historically reliable. During the twentieth century there was a movement in the other direction among some scholars, such as

W. F. Albright and John Bright, who claimed that archaeological discoveries in the ancient Near East showed that the ancestors authentically fit the early second millennium. Today much of their evidence is disputed by other scholars, especially influenced by Thomas Thompson and John Van Seters since the 1970s, and there continues to be debate about the issue.

The first question to ask is when the ancestors supposedly lived. The biblical chronology, which says that the Israelites were in Egypt 430 years (Ex 12:40) and that another 480 years passed until Solomon built the temple (1 Kgs 6:1), can be used, giving a date in the 1800s for the last generation in Genesis. But as we saw in the previous chapter, there are contradictions within the biblical time frame. Therefore scholars have looked for extra-biblical evidence, and, according to some, this evidence also fits the early second millennium. Many of the **names** found in Genesis were common in this period: the name "Jacob" occurs in an eighteenth-century Mesopotamian text; names beginning with y in their original Semitic form, such as Isaac, Joseph, and Ishmael, are common in early second-millennium texts from Mari, but are less common in earlier and later periods. Many of the reported **customs** of the ancestors are also known from that period: Abraham's fear that his slave Eliezer would become his heir (Gen 15:1-4) seems to assume inheritance customs similar to those from Nuzi in the fifteenth century; the inheritance Jacob provides for his twelve sons, with all receiving an equal portion, follows the practice of the twentieth-century laws of Lipit-Ishtar, but not later laws, when firstborn sons or sons from a first wife received more. Also, the **lifestyle** of the ancestors, as wandering seminomadic breeders of small cattle, was a common one in the early second millennium.[1]

The use of this evidence, however, has been disputed. Some suggest that the evidence fits a later period or no single period. Based on the use of the names Jacob and Abram in the Late Bronze Age (1550–1200 BCE), some scholars have argued for a date in that period, shortly before Israel emerged.[2] The lifestyle of the characters in Genesis is also similar to that of the nomadic Shasu, mentioned frequently in Egyptian texts from the Late Bronze Age. Others have pointed out that the parallels in customs and lifestyle that exist between the ancestral stories and what is known from the early second millennium are not exact, and most of the customs are known outside of that period as well.

In the past most scholars saw the early second millennium as the most likely setting for the stories, but today most are more cautious about assigning them to any one setting.[3]

The stories of the ancestors may accurately preserve some customs and details from the early second millennium and the Late Bronze Age, but it would be a mistake to look for one single original setting for all of the stories. The stories developed over time, and in their oldest form would have been passed down orally. It is true that oral traditions can preserve old memories, but it would be unlikely that those stories would remain intact for over a thousand years. Also, since the people who became the Israelites came from diverse backgrounds, the ancestral stories probably combine traditions that originally came from various peoples, and were later all applied to Abraham, Sarah, and the others. The question of when the ancestors lived cannot be answered, because if the stories preserve historical memories, they are not memories of one family line. The authors of Genesis felt free to combine diverse traditions from different people and different historical settings into one continuous narrative, without great concern for smoothing out anachronisms. Some of the anachronisms—such as the Philistines being in Canaan at the same time as Abraham (Gen 21:32-34)—are obvious, and remind us that fitting all of the stories into one historical setting is more of an issue for modern readers than it was for the authors.

There is no one single setting for the stories, but it is useful to take account of the setting in which they were composed. According to older versions of the documentary hypothesis, the basics of the Ancestral Narrative came from early in the monarchy (the Yahwist source) with later additions during the monarchy and exile (the Elohist and Priestly sources). That view has become less accepted, and many scholars opt for a later date for most of the material. One reason is that none of the incidents in the lives of the ancestors are mentioned in any other place in the Hebrew Scriptures before the exile, with the exception of a few incidents in the story of Jacob mentioned in Hosea (12:1-5, 13). In the Hebrew Scriptures the names Isaac and Jacob do get used frequently as place names for the northern kingdom Israel, so, during the monarchy, there was some tradition of Isaac and Jacob as eponymous ancestors, but no evidence of the complete stories that we have in Genesis. Van Seters, in particular, argues that the stories reflect the time of

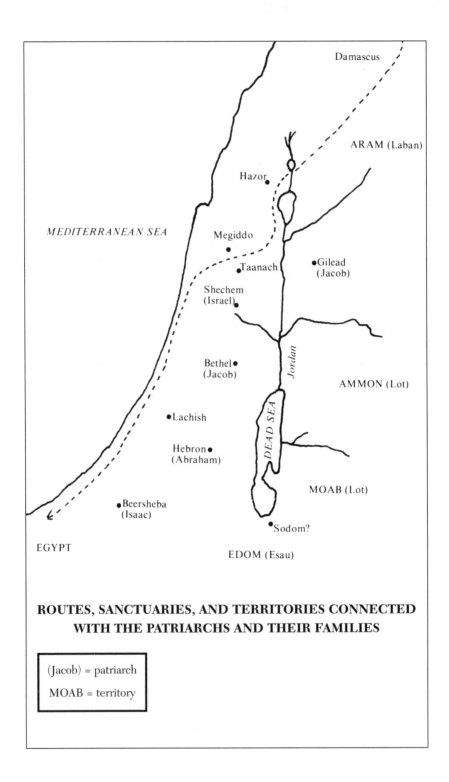

ROUTES, SANCTUARIES, AND TERRITORIES CONNECTED WITH THE PATRIARCHS AND THEIR FAMILIES

(Jacob) = patriarch

MOAB = territory

the Babylonian exile. The cities of Ur and Haran, from which Abraham and Sarah are said to have migrated, were important near the end of Babylon's rule; the promise of the land reflects the hope of returning from exile; Jacob's problems with Laban in Mesopotamia and the divine assistance he receives in becoming prosperous and returning are a paradigm for the Jews in exile.[4] That does not mean, of course, that the stories were invented out of whole cloth during the exile. Some traditional stories were adapted and combined with new material to become part of the national epic.

The traditions about Abraham, Isaac, and Jacob do seem to be centered in different geographic locations. Abraham travels to many places, but is based near Hebron, in the south (Gen 13:18; 23:17-20; 25:9-10). Isaac is also in the south, near Beersheba (Gen 26:23-33). And Jacob is in the north, near Shechem (Gen 33:18-20; 34) and Bethel (Gen 28:10-19; 35:1-15). It is possible that the core material about each one originated with groups from those areas. That would explain, for example, why Hosea, the eighth-century northern prophet, is familiar with parts of the Jacob story. As the religious traditions of the peoples who became Israel were united, the various traditions were combined into one narrative. Since the House of David, a dynasty from the Hebron area, ruled Judah, and religious authority became centralized in Jerusalem, the Abraham traditions were given priority, and he was made the ancestor of all the chosen people. Such a process involved the continued invention and accretion of stories about the ancestors in the late monarchy and exile, to fill in the gaps and to address concerns at the time of the Pentateuch's final composition.

Incidentally, the accretion of stories around Abraham and the other ancestors did not stop with the completion of the Pentateuch. The apocryphal *Book of Jubilees*, written in the second century BCE, credits Abraham with the ability to persuade crows not to eat the seeds that the farmers had planted and with inventing a machine to plant seeds more effectively (*Jubilees* 11:18-24). Josephus, in the first century CE, claims that Abraham introduced Babylonian mathematics and astronomy to the Egyptians (*Antiquities* I.8). Josephus was writing at a time when Jews wanted to prove that their civilization and learning were in no way inferior to those of the Greeks and Egyptians, so his remarks illustrate well how the stories invented about Abraham fit the time in which they were composed.

Understanding the composition of the Pentateuch clarifies the question of the historicity of the ancestors. Were there real people corresponding to Abraham, Sarah, and the other characters? Undoubtedly there were several such people, from several different periods, and some memories of them are preserved in the Ancestral Narrative. Was the Abraham of Genesis based on one historical figure from an identifiable period of time? No. The ancestors as portrayed in Genesis are literary creations.

J's invention

The Promises to Abraham (Genesis 12–20)

During the first several episodes of the Ancestral Narrative, God repeatedly promises Abraham and Sarah that they will have a large number of descendants and take possession of the land of Canaan, but those promises do not begin to be fulfilled for some time. Years pass before they have their son Isaac, and, not surprisingly, at times they doubt that God will deliver on the promise. Moreover, Abraham puts the fulfillment of the promises into jeopardy, twice almost giving away his wife Sarah, and once almost giving away the promised land to his nephew Lot.

yes The promise theme is not actually an intrinsic part of most of the episodes. Most of the stories could stand as independent episodes with their own purposes. The author has taken diverse traditions, probably about different people from different periods of time, and fashioned them into a long series of stories about Abraham and Sarah, adding in the process the promise and obstacle themes. The promise and delays and obstacles not only make the story more interesting, but they also *no* make it more relevant to Jews during and after the Babylonian exile, when efforts to re-establish Jewish life in Judah were going slowly.

Genesis 12. At the time of God's promise to Abraham, the family had already migrated from Ur in southern Mesopotamia to Haran, northwest along the fertile crescent. God tells him to go to Canaan, which he does, spending time in Shechem, Bethel, Ai, the Negev, and Hebron. He does not settle in the land, but builds altars and worships Yahweh in several places, establishing it as a sacred land.

In the midst of this initial sojourn, Abraham and Sarah go to Egypt because of a famine in Canaan. Afraid that the Egyptians will kill him to take his wife, Abraham pretends Sarah is his sister. When Pharaoh takes Sarah into the palace, God inflicts plagues upon him, and realizing that she is Abraham's wife, he returns her. This same incident will occur two more times, once with Abraham and Sarah (Gen 20) and once with Isaac and Rebekah (Gen 26:1-11). The separate stories may have been told by different groups within Israel, so the question is why the author has included all three. One reason is to show the chosen people's slowness to learn from their mistakes, which drives home the point that God did not choose them because they were intellectually or morally superior to other people. Specifically, this mistake involves putting the promise in jeopardy. It is also significant that the story is set in Egypt. In the Pentateuch, Egypt is the place where negative things happen, which reflects the views of Jews in Babylon during the exile. At that time there were some Jews who had fled to Egypt, but most of the exilic writings reject that approach to survival (cf. Jer 41–44), and see the Babylonian Jewish community as the authentic preserver of the tradition. *Oh yeah? Why?*

Genesis 13. During this initial sojourn, Abraham and his nephew Lot separate, because they have become so successful that their large flocks are causing overcrowding and conflicts. Abraham offers Lot his choice of land in which to dwell, and Lot chooses the Jordan plain to the east, leaving the promised land to Abraham. This incident is the beginning of the story of Lot's descendants, the Ammonites and Moabites, who lived east of the Jordan and Dead Sea during the Israelite monarchy and were seen as closely related to the Israelites. Depicting them as closely related does have a factual basis. Inscriptions discovered in the last two centuries show similarities between Ammonite and Moabite language and religion and those of the Israelites.[5] As part of the Ancestral Narrative, the story again shows Abraham putting the promise in jeopardy, raising questions about his worthiness to receive it. *BALONEY*

Genesis 14. The story of the battle of the kings is quite different from the rest of the episodes relating to Abraham. It is the only episode involving international affairs; it is the only episode in which Abraham is portrayed as a warrior; it is the only episode in which Abraham is called a "Hebrew"; and it is the only time Abraham has any contact with the city of Jerusalem—although even here the name Salem is used instead of Jerusalem. Because of these differences, the story is generally considered to have come from a separate, isolated source, rather than from one of the four sources of the documentary hypothesis. But when did the story originate, does it contain actual historical remembrances, and what is the purpose of including it here?

None of the kings in this story is mentioned in any other ancient sources. However, the names are similar to names known from the middle of the second millennium BCE; Arioch is probably the same name as an Arriwuka mentioned in the texts discovered at Mari. Albright and others have thus argued for an early setting for the story.[6] At the other extreme, Van Seters points out that the role of Melchizedek in the story parallels the role of the high priests in Jerusalem during the Hellenistic period, when a single person had political and religious authority, indicating that the story may be as late as the end of the fourth century, and its purpose is to justify the power the high priests were beginning to have.[7]

It is impossible to determine the origin of the story, but what can be said is that it illustrates the author's desire to include diverse material in the Ancestral Narrative. The purpose of the stories is not to give historical information, but to unite all of the people who became part of the Jewish community, by making all of their various traditions part of a common ancestry.

Genesis 15. God's reiteration of the promise, and Abraham's doubts, are recurrent themes. Now the promise is made more formal through a covenant-making ritual. The solemnity of it eases Abraham's doubts, at least for the time.

Abraham's concern that his slave will become his heir since he has no son has often been cited as evidence for a mid-second millennium setting for the ancestors, since the practice of adopting a slave is known from that time. Yet this story says nothing about adoption, and not enough is said about the inheritance issue to make it a useful clue for dating the ancestors. The phrase "Ur of the Chaldeans" indicates that in its present form the story is from no earlier than late in the monarchy, since Chaldea was not used as a term for Babylon until then. The sacrificial ritual is unusual, and has its closest parallel in Jeremiah 34:18-20, another indication of an origin in the late monarchy or exile.

The trance Abraham goes into is called *tardemah* in the Hebrew. This word was also used for the trance Adam was put into when God took his rib to make Eve (Gen 2:21). It shows the passive character of

Abraham in these events; it is God who is in complete control of the chosen people's fate.

Genesis 16. The story of the birth of Ishmael is another story about an ancestor of peoples related to the Israelites, and it also presents another obstacle to the promise being fulfilled, since it causes a conflict between Sarah and Hagar. The practice of a man having children through a female slave was known elsewhere in the ancient Near East. The law code of Hammurapi, from the eighteenth century, covers conflicts between the wife and the slave, and inheritance disputes between children of the wife and children of the slave.[8] Because there are similar concerns here, this story may have a setting in the second millennium. However, such practices were known of in later times, and Genesis also gives a different reason for Hagar having a child—she is to provide a child for the childless Sarah, not a child for Abraham's sake.

Genesis 17. Unlike the earlier expressions of the covenant between God and Abraham, in this story there is an obligation on Abraham's part, and not just a unilateral promise from God. Every male among the chosen people must now be circumcised. It is not known how common circumcision was in the ancient Near East. There is evidence of Egyptians practicing it from the third millennium BCE, but not of the Assyrians or Babylonians practicing it.[9] The Philistines, who came from outside of Canaan, are frequently called uncircumcised in the Hebrew Scriptures, but the Canaanites are not, so apparently Canaanites did practice it. Jeremiah says that Edom, Ammon, and Moab, nations near Judah, practiced it, in addition to Egypt (9:25). However, later Jewish texts indicate that the neighbors of Judah did not practice it; in the Book of Judith, from the second or first century BCE, Achior the Ammonite had not been circumcised (14:10), and Josephus says the Jews are the only people of Palestine who practice circumcision (*Against Apion* I.22).

Apparently circumcision was an early practice among the Canaanites and other groups from which the Israelites came, but began to be abandoned by others in the region after Assyrian and Babylonian rule. The Jews retained it because it helped set them apart from the people among whom they were scattered after the exile. By connecting circumcision to the covenant with Abraham, the story is saying the Jews' restoration in their land is dependent on keeping those customs that set them apart from other people. This story is from the Priestly source, which emphasizes those distinguishing characteristics more than the rest of the Pentateuch does. (There is evidence of an alternative tradition, that circumcision began with Moses, in Ex 4:24-26.)

Genesis 18–19. The visitors to Abraham and Sarah and the destruction of Sodom have been made one continuous episode by the author, but the two events are not intrinsically connected. As in other places in Genesis, the promise theme has been added to an originally independent story. Here the process of composition was more complicated than usual. The angels who visit Sodom are identified with the visitors to Abraham and Sarah who repeat the promise, but a conversation between God and Abraham has also been added, in which Abraham questions God about destroying the city if there are innocent people in it. This passage is meant to assure the reader that, despite the destruction of Sodom, God is not an indiscriminate killer who will destroy the innocent. In making this into one episode, the author did not try to smooth out every detail, as can be seen in the various ways the visitors are referred to: "the LORD" (18:1), "three men" (18:2), "the LORD" (18:13), "the men" (18:16), "the LORD" (18:17ff), "the men" and "the LORD" (18:22), and "the angels" only in chapter 19, in the Sodom part of the story.

The Sodom part of the episode is different from the rest not only in the way the visitors are referred to, but also in its use of mythological elements. Sex between divine and human beings is a mythological way of representing corruption, as in Genesis 6:1-4, the preface to the flood story. Lot's wife being turned into a pillar of salt is the only case in the Bible of a human being turned into an inanimate object, but in mythology it is a common punishment for a person looking upon the action of the gods. (Contrary to later interpretation, she was not punished for being indecisive, but for looking directly upon God's actions.) The Sodom incident, besides having mythic elements and being about destruction and the survival of one righteous family, parallels the flood story in another way. It is followed by a sexual impropriety—Lot's daughters having sex with him—which involves drinking too much wine, and by genealogical information with negative implications for those involved in the sexual impropriety. Moab and Ammon are the sons of Lot's daughters, and the ancestors of the nations Moab and

Ammon, which were closely related but rival nations of Israel. Like
Canaan at the end of the flood story, they are portrayed as inferior to
Israel because of the sexual decadence of their ancestors.

Later interpreters have used the Sodom incident as a condemnation of homosexuality, but that was surely not its original intent. It is not
a story about sex between men, but a story about sex between angels
and human beings of both genders. The crowd that comes to Lot's
house includes every person in the city, including the women and children (although some English translations are not clear on this), and in
the end the entire city—including the women and children—is punished. The story uses sex between divine and human beings as a mythological way of expressing evil. Other references to the story in the
Hebrew Sciptures show that it was associated with a variety of evils
(injustice in Is 1:10; 3:9; pride, complacency, and ignoring the poor in
Ezek 16:49), and was used more as a reminder of God's punishment
than as a condemnation of any particular sin.

Genesis 20. The author has included another story of Abraham pretending Sarah is his sister and almost giving her away. This story is set
in Gerar, in the Negev, rather than in Egypt, as the one in Genesis 12
was. Part of its purpose is to establish a claim to the land there, a theme
which will be developed later when Abraham makes a covenant with
Abimelech (Gen 21:22-34), and when Isaac settles in Gerar for a time
(Gen 26).

Traditionally this version of the incident has been considered part
of the Elohist source—it exhibits concern for ethical issues by having
Abraham explain that he was not really lying, and it has God acting
indirectly, through a dream. But it also can be used as evidence of
Deuteronomic influence in other parts of the Pentateuch besides the
Book of Deuteronomy. Abraham is called a prophet (20:7), the only
time that word is used of him; the importance of prophets is a common
theme in the Deuteronomic writings. Whatever the source of this
episode and the earlier version of it, the author used both to raise questions about Abraham's suitability to be the ancestor of the chosen people in this final incident before the birth of Isaac.

These first few episodes in the Ancestral Narrative are a collection
of diverse material that has been overlaid with a story of God making

promises to Abraham and obstacles to the promises being fulfilled. In its final form, the series of episodes allows the idea of the delay of the promise to become prominent. The doubts of Abraham and Sarah are not unreasonable, since many years have passed and they do not have their son yet. At the same time, Abraham himself is responsible for putting the promise in jeopardy. It is fitting that this section ends with a story that questions Abraham's worthiness.

The Son Isaac (Genesis 21:1–25:18)

After all the delays of the previous chapters, the birth of Isaac finally takes place, and a few episodes in his life are related. Isaac is the least developed of the patriarchs in Genesis, and serves more as a transitional figure between Abraham and Jacob. With the exception of the material in chapter 26, there does not seem to have been a collection of traditions about him as there was for the others; the first stories about him are really still stories about Abraham, and in the stories after the death of Abraham the focus shifts to Jacob. These stories have been created to provide a transition from Abraham to Jacob, and there is almost nothing in this section that shows evidence of being based on historical remembrances.

Genesis 21. The birth of Isaac is reported without any fanfare, and the story quickly moves to the problem of Ishmael's continued presence and the question of who will inherit the promise from Abraham. In this episode it is again clear that the author did not try to smooth out the inconsistencies among the various traditions about Abraham and Sarah that had been put together. By itself, this episode portrays Ishmael as a young child: he plays with Isaac; when he and Hagar are sent away, Abraham puts him on her back so she can carry him; when he and Hagar are in the wilderness, she places him under a shrub as if he were a vulnerable child. Yet, according to the overall chronology, Ishmael would have been fourteen years old when Isaac was born, and sixteen or seventeen when Hagar carried him on her back and put him under the shrub! Such inconsistencies did not concern the author.

Sarah's fear that Ishmael will share the inheritance has sometimes been connected with the laws of Hammurapi, which cover such conflicts, but, as mentioned earlier, this type of conflict was not limited to any one period, so it is not helpful for dating the story. Also, the resolution here does not depend on any legal tradition, but on a promise from God. The story shows God's concern for the welfare of Ishmael, but it also makes it clear that the descendants of Ishmael will not take the promised land away from the chosen people. During the exile in Babylon, Jews were concerned that the peoples living near Judah would be able to take possession of their land (cf. Ezek 11:14-21). This story would assure readers during the exile that God would preserve their land for them.

Genesis 22. The story of the sacrifice of Isaac is a literary masterpiece, but it also raises a historical question. This historical question is not whether the event actually occurred; we don't know for certain that Abraham and Isaac were historical people, and if they were, it is unlikely they were father and son. But what historical situation is the story responding to? There are several passages in the Hebrew Scriptures that mention human sacrifice, usually of young children. The Pentateuch condemns the practice (Lev 18:21; 20:1-5; Dt 12:31; 18:10). The Deuteronomic History and Jeremiah condemn it and claim that nearby nations and sometimes even Israelites practiced it, especially in times of national crisis (2 Kgs 3:27; 17:17; Jer 7:31; 19:5). There are laws in the Pentateuch which say that the firstborn male of all livestock belongs to the Lord and is to be offered in sacrifice, but in the case of humans an animal may be offered instead as a redemption (Ex 13:11-16; 34:20; Num 18:15). The story of Jephthah sacrificing his only daughter assumes that in early Israel it could be done, although not as a regular practice (Judg 11:29-40). Outside of Israel there are numerous references in texts to child sacrifice, and there is archaeological evidence from Carthage and elsewhere of child sacrifice precincts, with burial urns of infants. With all of the references to it and evidence of it occurring elsewhere, it is likely that child sacrifice did occur in ancient Israel, perhaps until late in the monarchy.[10]

The story may be based on an earlier story that said God no longer demanded human sacrifice, and composed around the same time Jeremiah and the Deuteronomic writings were condemning the practice. However, in its present context in the Pentateuch, it is more about the promise of descendants and land, and does not explicitly abolish human sacrifice. It is saying that Abraham, who in earlier stories seemed unworthy, is now worthy to receive the promise, because he was willing to give back the son who had been promised. NOPE!

Genesis 23. The series of Abraham and Sarah stories begins to wind down with the death of Sarah and the purchase of a field and burial cave. The story does not seem based on historical remembrances. The "Hittites" are out of place; the Hittite kingdom was a powerful kingdom to the north from about 1600 to 1200 BCE, but never ruled as far south as Palestine. When the Assyrians later ruled the region of Syria and Palestine they used the name, in the form "Hatti," for the whole region; probably influenced by that use, the Pentateuch occasionally uses Hittites in its lists of peoples living in the promised land before the Israelites (Gen 15:20; Ex 3:8; Dt 7:1). The name may also refer to some other, unrelated group that has been forgotten.

One purpose of this story is indicated by the high price for the purchase. The exact amount of money represented by 400 shekels of silver is impossible to determine, although it would certainly represent a large amount for Abraham's family. The story is saying that the chosen people must be willing to pay dearly to acquire what God has promised them. The fact that God has promised it doesn't mean it will be handed to them without cost. Such would have been the case after the exile, when returning to Judah meant great sacrifice and sometimes conflict over land ownership between descendants of the exiles and descendants of people who stayed in the land. Maybe - but settled people and bastards ???

Genesis 24. The story of finding a wife for Isaac is remarkably similar to the stories of Jacob and Moses finding their wives (Gen 29 and Ex 2:15-22). The literary pattern of these stories has been analyzed in depth by Robert Alter;[11] it is best to see this story as a literary creation rather than a report of facts.

The concern with finding wives from relatives in Mesopotamia does, however, reflect the concerns of the Jews living in exile. After the exile there was a desire to preserve Judaism by preventing intermarriage with foreigners. Moreover, the Jews who had been in exile in Babylon considered themselves the bearers of authentic Judaism; the negative attitude toward outsiders sometimes extended not just to foreign nations, but to other Jews who had remained in Judah during the exile. The books of Ezra and Nehemiah, describing the postexilic restoration, focus almost exclusively on returned exiles, who were in control of the temple and were better off economically than the people of the land. This story of Isaac's marriage is praising those Jews from exiled families who marry only among other exiled families.

Concern for marrying only within similar families is easy to criticize as being too exclusive and intolerant of others. However, during and after the exile Judaism was in danger of disappearing, and the steps taken to preserve it cannot be judged by the same standards that one would use to judge a secure and powerful community.

Genesis 25:1-18. The Abraham section ends with his death and a listing of other descendants he had, including from a wife Keturah, mentioned here somewhat unexpectedly for the first time. Like other genealogical information in Genesis, it expresses the political and social relationships that existed in the late monarchy and exile. Among these descendants are the Midianites, who will show up in several later stories. They are involved in selling Joseph into slavery in Egypt (Gen 37:28, 36), Moses spends time with them in the desert and marries one (Ex 2), and on the way to the promised land the Israelites fight battles against them (Num 31:1-12). The mix of positive and negative traditions about them, and the fact that they are portrayed as related to the Israelites, hints at a larger history that has been lost. The descendants of Ishmael also receive attention here. Their organization into twelve tribes parallels the way Israel will be portrayed, and suggests that at least part of Israel saw itself as a similar type of people.

These episodes about the beginning of Isaac's life and the end of the lives of Abraham and Sarah are used to strengthen the identity of the exilic Jews. One way of strengthening that identity is to preserve past traditions, including traditions of different groups within Judaism, even if combining them made an inconsistent story. In trying to hold Judaism together, the author is more concerned with preserving multiple traditions than with telling a story that is consistent in every last detail. The stories also raise hopes for the future, assuring the exiles that they will have their own land. God is portrayed as gradually fulfilling the promise to make them a nation, despite all the obstacles. And the stories address Jewish identity by discussing the relationship of

Israel to the surrounding peoples. During the exile, Israel along with its neighbors had all suffered under Babylonian rule, and so had reason to claim a relationship—and even an obligation—to be allies at times. Yet that did not erase the conflicts that occurred among them, or Israel's desire to express its uniqueness and superiority over the other nations.

Jacob and Esau (Genesis 25:19–36:43)

With the birth of Isaac's twin sons Esau and Jacob, the focus of the story shifts from Abraham to Jacob. The story begins with Rebekah having two sons in her womb, struggling against each other, and God revealing to her that the younger will triumph. They are born and grow up as contrasting individuals. The elder, Esau, is hairy, a man of the fields who is a skillful hunter. Jacob, the younger, is smooth, and a man who stays with the flocks at the tent. On one occasion Jacob acquires the rights of the first born by making Esau sell them to him for a bowl of stew, when Esau is famished after an unsuccessful hunt. Sometime later, when Isaac is on his deathbed and wants to give his final blessing to Esau, Rebekah and Jacob deceive him and Jacob gets the blessing instead. Then Jacob goes to Mesopotamia to get a wife from their relatives, and after years of delays returns a wealthy man. He makes peace with Esau, and the twelve sons of Jacob become the ancestors of the twelve tribes of Israel.

Much of the material in this section has to do with the relationship between Israel and the Edomites, whom the story identifies with the descendants of Esau. Edom was the nation southeast of Judah, and the two nations were frequently opposed to each other. According to the Deuteronomic History, Judah at times ruled over Edom, sometimes Edom broke free, and some territories shifted back and forth between Edom and Judah (2 Sam 8:13-14; 1 Kgs 11:14-22; 2 Kgs 8:20-22; 16:6). During the exile there was particular enmity between them, with Jews accusing Edom of cooperating with the Babylonians in destroying Judah (Ps 137; Jer 49:7-22). However, other parts of the Hebrew Scriptures recognize a close relationship between the two nations; Deuteronomy 23:7, after harsh words against the Ammonites and Moabites, says, "You shall not abhor any of the Edomites, for they are your kin." The narrative framework of Deuteronomy portrays Edom positively, and draws a parallel between God dispossessing the Canaanites to give the promised land to the Israelites and God dispossessing the Horites to give the Edomites their land (Dt 2:12). Jeremiah refers to Jews who lived in Edom after the fall of Judah (Jer 40:11). There is evidence of a religious connection, including poetic passages that speak of Yahweh coming from Edom (Dt 33:2; Judg 5:4; Hab 3:3). A late ninth- or early eighth-century inscription from a shrine at Kuntillet Ajrud, in the Negev, refers to "Yahweh of Teman" (a place in Edom). There has also been speculation that the Book of Job came from an Edomite setting (his home Uz may have been in Edom—Lam 4:21 uses it in parallelism with Edom; one of Job's friends is Eliphaz the Temanite). To be sure, there are also extremely hostile passages against Edom (Ps 137; Jer 49:7-22; and in Ob), but even in some of these there is the notion that Edom's misdeeds are worse because he is a brother of Israel (Ob 12; Am 1:11). As we will see, the Genesis story wavers between a negative and a positive portrayal of Esau, possibly indicating diverse sources of material, but preserving the ambiguity of Judah's relationship with its close neighbor. The Hebrew Scriptures do not have the simplistic "us against them" attitude toward Israel's neighbors that is sometimes assumed.

As in the other parts of the story, the material comes from different traditions, and not all of the details have been harmonized. Isaac is supposedly on his deathbed in chapter 27, but does not die until more than twenty years later in chapter 35. There is inconsistency on who Esau's wives are (26:34; 28:8-9; 36:2-3), and other indications that Esau is a composite of at least two different people. Despite being described as so different when they are introduced, later Jacob and Esau are living almost identical lifestyles (Gen 32–33). At times they are portrayed as enemies, but a summary statement near the end of the section not only describes their lifestyles as identical but also says that Jacob and Esau separated because they had too much combined livestock to live together (Gen 36:7), the exact same reason given for Abraham and Lot separating in chapter 13. Esau/Edom is a composite character, although Genesis is not the only book in which they are identical (cf. Dt 2:1-7, 12; Jer 49:7-8; Ob 6, 8, 18). The development of an Esau/Edom character probably occurred late in the monarchy alongside the development of traditions about the Israelite patriarchal characters, and the Esau/Edom character was made secondary to them.

Despite the diverse origins of the material, the author has woven it together to bring out the themes that have already been emphasized: the giving of the land to the chosen people, the etiology of certain sacred sites, and how the chosen people are to understand themselves. And again there are obstacles to the promise being fulfilled, in particular Jacob's conflicts with Esau and Laban.

Genesis 25:19-34. The conflict that will characterize Jacob's life begins while he is still in the womb, where he struggles with his twin brother Esau. God reveals to Rebekah that the two sons in her womb are two nations. The two nations turn out to be Israel and Edom, and the description of Esau as less civilized and not as intelligent is how the Israelites saw the nation of Edom. The description of Esau as red-skinned and the story of the red lentil stew are examples of etiologies for a place name. The word Edom is similar to the word for red (*adom*); probably the name comes from the reddish soil of the hill country of Edom, although the word is also similar to the word that simply means "person."

The birthright which Jacob gets for the stew is the larger share of inheritance that the elder son would receive. The practice of the older son inheriting more was common in the ancient Near East, and is mentioned in the laws of Hammurapi and texts from Mari, Nuzi, and Ugarit. Deuteronomy 21:15-17 prohibits a father from transferring the inheritance rights from the firstborn of a wife he does not like to the firstborn of the wife he prefers, but there are no laws in the Pentateuch that address the situation here, a son selling the rights to another son. This story of Esau selling his birthright for some lentil stew is not concerned with the legal issue, but with describing the relationship between the ancestor of the Edomites and the ancestor of the Israelites. Esau does come across as less intelligent than Jacob, but mixed with that is a sympathy for Esau. Among biblical peoples, hunger was a serious issue. Esau is not hungry in the sense of having skipped a meal, but hungry in the sense of being desperate to stay alive. Esau may not have gotten a good deal, but there is more sympathy for him than ridicule in this story.

Genesis 26. This is the only section in which Isaac is the main character. A variety of material about him has been put together, addressing some issues that have already been addressed in the Abraham stories, especially the issue of establishing a claim to the land, in a way that the returning exiles would identify with.

Isaac's going to Gerar and pretending that Rebekah is his sister is the third time a similar incident has occurred, the previous two being with Abraham and Sarah, once in Egypt and once in Gerar. This time God explicitly tells Isaac not to go the Egypt, but to stay in Canaan, the land his descendants will receive. This is another expression of the view during and after the exile that those Jews who had gone to Egypt had corrupted Judaism, and that the authentic faith was to be found among those who were exiles in Babylon and would return to Judah.

The claims to the land and water, which were also issues for the returning exiles, are established by an agreement with Abimelech, king of Gerar. The story of the agreement is similar to the story of Abraham making an agreement with Abimelech about water rights (Gen 21:22-34), and both stories also claim to be the origin of the name "Beer-sheba," meaning "well of seven," but also similar to "well of the oath." This material about Isaac probably developed out of stories originally about Abraham. The alternative version with Isaac as the main character was told by other groups within Israel. The author of Genesis has retained them, and used them to reinforce the message of God's promise of land to the chosen people.

Genesis 27. The story of Jacob deceiving his father Isaac in order to receive the blessing intended for Esau is one of the most entertaining in the Pentateuch, but also one of the most morally questionable. Is it right that the chosen people receive God's promises through deception? The story addresses theological issues regarding what it means to be the chosen people, and makes additional comments on their complex relationship with the Edomites.

In biblical times there was a great sensitivity to the power of words and gestures. When Isaac gives his blessing to Jacob, and then cannot take it back even when he realizes he has been deceived, it may seem like a superstitious belief in the magical power of blessings. But the issue is not that simple; in fact, the story reveals an awareness of the power of language to create. In the biblical view, God creates the world by speaking words, and human beings when speaking, especially in a solemn way, create a new situation that cannot be undone. It is not insignificant that in Hebrew the word *dabar* means both "word" and "action." The original readers of this story would not have found Isaac's inability to take back his blessing so strange. A similar example is in Joshua 9, where the Israelites make a covenant with the Gibeonites, and are bound to keep it even though it was made by deception.

Isaac cannot give his first blessing to Esau, but Esau is not completely doomed. Isaac tells him that he will live in an inferior land and will serve his brother, but also says, "When you break loose you shall break his yoke from your neck." The prediction reflects the back-and-forth relationship that existed between Judah and Edom during the monarchy.

The story's message about the chosen people is, first, that God is going to shape them outside the bounds of normal legal and social customs: In a society in which women had little power, it is Rebekah who controls events here. Second, the chosen people are not to consider themselves morally superior to their neighbors: Jacob's deception is not praiseworthy, but God did not choose them because they merited it. And third, the chosen people are a younger-son type of nation: Like other younger sons in the Hebrew Scriptures, Jacob was chosen and made successful by God.

Genesis 28–31. The extended narrative about Jacob going to Haran to find a wife incorporates several episodes. Its general purpose is the same as that of the story of Isaac getting his wife, to encourage Jews during and after the exile to associate primarily with other Jews from among the exiles. Various episodes that have been made part of the narrative serve other purposes: to show the sacredness of certain sites, to introduce the ancestors of the tribes of Israel, and to put down Laban. The material does not all flow smoothly. Two different reasons are given for Jacob leaving Canaan—to escape from Esau's murderous desires (27:41-45), and to avoid marrying a Canaanite woman (27:46–28:5). Esau's wives in 28:6-9 are not the same as his wives in 36:2-3, an indication that he is a composite of at least two characters.

Two sacred sites are part of the story, Bethel on Jacob's journey to Haran, and Mizpah on his return. Bethel is given more attention, with God appearing to Jacob in a dream and Jacob setting up a memorial stone (*masseba*) and naming the place Bethel (house or temple of El; Jacob will actually name the place Bethel again in 35:15). There was a settlement at Bethel at least as far back as 1800 BCE,[12] and there was a history of an Israelite shrine there. According to 1 Kings 12:26-32, Jeroboam, first king of the northern kingdom Israel, built temples at Dan and Bethel. The Deuteronomic History, however, condemns him for that, since it considers Jerusalem the only proper place for a temple and sacrifice. The eighth-century prophet Hosea condemned Bethel as well (Hos 4:15; 10:5), but Hosea was not entirely positive with regard to Jacob either (Hos 12:3-4). The story is at odds with other parts of the Bible in another way: setting up the *masseba* is condemned elsewhere in the Pentateuch (Lev 26:1; Dt 16:22). Since the name of the place honors the Canaanite god El, Bethel was probably the site of a Canaanite holy place that continued through the Israelite period. Although condemned late in the monarchy by the Deuteronomic movement, some positive traditions about the place continued and were used in Genesis. At the time Genesis was completed there was no particular reason for a polemic against Bethel, so the traditions of it as a sacred place were kept (in contrast to Shechem in Gen 34).

The story uses Jacob's time in Haran to develop his character as a crafty and competitive person. The account of Jacob's meeting his wife Rachel at the well follows the same story type as Isaac and Moses' marriages, and his success in raising goats uses elements of folklore. These parts of the story are literary creations and do not preserve historical remembrances.

This section also includes the birth of Jacob's first eleven sons and daughter (Benjamin is born later, after their return to Canaan), and the story gives etymologies of their names describing the situation of their births. The sons will become the ancestors of the tribes of Israel, and to some extent who their mothers are reflects the relationships of the tribes in later history (see next page, "The Sons and Daughter of Jacob"). Joseph is the son of the preferred wife Rachel, and he becomes the ancestor of the two powerful tribes in the northern kingdom, Ephraim and Manasseh. Two of the sons of Leah, the other wife, become ancestors of tribes that had special importance, Judah and Levi. The four sons of the slave women, Dan, Naphtali, Gad, and Asher, represent marginal tribes. (Dan probably came from the Sea Peoples and was related to the Philistines;[13] there was a Canaanite group called Asher before the beginnings of Israel.[14]) However, too much should not be read into the circumstances of their births. The story here makes no explicit claim that any of the tribes are to be more prominent than the others, nor does it make any explicit prediction of

The Sons and Daughter of Jacob

Leah	Bilhah	Zilpah	Rachel
Reuben			
Simeon			
Levi			
Judah			
	Dan		
	Naphtali		
		Gad	
		Asher	
Issachar			
Zebulun			
Dinah			
			Joseph
			Benjamin

The births of Reuben through Joseph are reported in Genesis 29:31–30:24; the birth of Benjamin in Genesis 35:16-18.

the futures of the tribes, as Genesis 49 does. And any discussion of the tribes has to be qualified with the reminder that little is known about them historically. There were certainly not twelve fixed tribes that united to form the monarchy. The Hebrew Scriptures themselves indicate some of the shifts in identities, with Levi ending up with no territory, Simeon absorbed by Judah, Dan moving from one territory to another, and Joseph representing two tribes. In addition, this story gives no great significance to birth order, which is surprising, with that having been such an issue for Jacob and Esau. It is clear that this is not based on a real historical family. Instead, the author wants to show that, although differing in power, on one level all of the "sons of Israel" are equal (in contrast to their relationship with the descendants of Esau and Ishmael, which is not one of equality). The idealized equality is akin to what the prophet Ezekiel portrayed during the exile (Ezek 48), although expressed in a very different way.

Genesis 32–33. The story of Jacob's return to the promised land and his meeting with Esau includes a nighttime encounter with a messenger from God, who changes Jacob's name to Israel. With his large family, secure possessions, and entrance into Canaan, Jacob is now prepared to take on his role as ancestor of the Israelites. One possible obstacle remains, his rivalry with Esau.

The meeting with Esau portrays Jacob as more conciliatory than in earlier parts of the story, because of his fear of Esau, and at the same time Esau is portrayed more positively, no longer intent on killing Jacob. There are a couple of unusual features of the meeting. One is that it takes place east of the Jordan River, whereas Esau/Edom is supposed to be associated with the land south of the Dead Sea. The other is that Jacob and Esau seem to be living identical lifestyles—seminomadic cattle herders with plenty of family and servants—whereas when they were introduced in chapter 25 their lifestyles were said to be entirely different. We may have stories originally about different people put together here, but the overall effect is to show the ambiguity of Israel's relationship with Edom. Edom is seen as less of a threat than the people living right in the land of Canaan, and is more of a rival than a continuing enemy. This fits the immediate needs of the returning exiles, who needed to establish a foothold within the land of Judah, and were less concerned with fighting outside nations.

Just before the meeting, while Jacob is encamped by the river Jabbok, the messenger of God comes in the night and wrestles with him. The incident combines several elements of folklore, including a supernatural being who guards a river crossing and one whose power disappears at daybreak; the power of a divine being's name; and the etiology of a dietary custom. The story was not invented by the author of Genesis, since a version of it is mentioned in Hosea 12:4. But it fits in well at this point. As a story of testing Jacob and giving him a new name, it shows Jacob worthy to become the ancestor of the Israelites. *honor stuff?*

Genesis 34. After offering a rather benign view of Esau, the story now presents a negative view of the inhabitants of the land of Canaan, specifically with the rape of Dinah at Shechem, where Jacob and his family have settled. The Shechemites are criticized for several things: their sexual depravity, both in the person Shechem himself and in the rest of the community for their lack of disapproval; their greed, as exemplified by their concern only for the economic advantages of inter-marriage with the Israelites; and their stupidity, in letting themselves be deceived and destroyed. The story is in part a humorous put-down of the Shechemites, and in part a warning to the returning exiles not to intermarry with the people of the land.

Jacob's sons are outraged not just because of a crime of violence, but because Dinah is now impure. The vocabulary repeatedly used to describe what was done to her refers to ritual impurity. The piel verb *timme'* (34:5, 13, 27) means "to make impure." It and its adjectival form are common in parts of the Hebrew Scriptures dealing with purity and ritual, with emphases on sexual activity that makes one impure (Lev 15:18; 18:23) and improper worship that causes impurity (Ezek 36:18, 25; 37:23; 2 Chron 36:14); the word is also used with sex as a metaphor for impure worship (Ezek 23:1-20). For the returning exiles, avoiding intermarriage and keeping their worship pure were part of the single effort to preserve Jewish identity.

The setting of the story in Shechem is also significant. Shechem was a massive city before the beginnings of Israel. There is archaeologi-cal evidence of urban buildings, including a large temple, from the twentieth to eighteenth centuries BCE,[15] and the Amarna letters, from the fourteenth century, show that Shechem's Canaanite king was the most powerful city king in central Palestine.[16] The size and importance of the city in those periods that are usually considered possible times for the patriarchal period make it impossible that two men could have killed all the able bodied men of the city, and unrealistic that the city would have fallen for Jacob's sons' ploy just to intermarry with the small clan of Jacob. The story does not go back to any pre-Israelite historical memories. However, the way Shechem appears here and in other bibli-cal stories is illuminating. Besides this one, two other major stories involving Shechem are Joshua 24, in which the Israelites renew their covenant with the Lord at Shechem after conquering the promised land, and Judges 9, in which Abimelech tries to become king of all of Israel from Shechem. While Joshua 24 recognizes Shechem as a sacred place, Judges 9 denigrates it as a power-grabbing place. The same two tendencies appear in briefer mentions of the city. In Genesis 12:6 it is the first place in Canaan at which Abraham stops, and is referred to as an already sacred place, but in 1 Kings 12:1-25 it is where the division of the monarchy takes place and where Jeroboam, first king of the northern kingdom, makes his residence.

The story of the rape of Dinah clearly emphasizes the negative side, and even takes a swipe at Shechem's tradition as a sacred place by emphasizing the ritual impurity of what happened. The story could have originated late in the monarchy as part of the efforts to centralize worship in Jerusalem, but it also serves the needs of those who wanted to preserve a strong Jerusalem-centered Jewish identity in the postexilic period. That a polemic against Shechem was needed for them is shown by the fact that the Samaritans eventually did build a rival temple on Mt. Gerazim at Shechem.

hmm! [handwritten marginal note]

Genesis 35. The material here seems to tie up events in Jacob's life, including an assurance that his family will get rid of foreign religious influence, the birth of his last son Benjamin, the death of Rachel, and the death of his father Isaac. In fact, however, Jacob will still be around through the Joseph story and will not die until the last chapter of Genesis. Again there are indications that the material about Jacob comes from multiple sources. God changes Jacob's name to Israel a second time (cf. Gen 32:28), and Jacob names Bethel a second time (cf. Gen 28:19). Isaac dies only now, despite being on his deathbed more than twenty years earlier (Gen 27) and having been absent from the story since then.

At the death of Isaac both Esau and Jacob come to bury him, just as both Ishmael and Isaac came to bury Abraham (Gen 25:9). Genesis is often sympathetic to these other brothers, Ishmael and Esau. Even though the promise is not passed on through them, they are among the descendants of Abraham, and part of "all nations of the world," who are blessed through Abraham.

Genesis 36. It is unusual to have so much genealogical information in the Bible for non-Israelites, but Genesis does portray the Edomites as more closely related to Israel than any other non-Israelite group. It is likely that some people from an Edomite background became part of Judah, even though Edom as a whole remained a separate nation. As noted at the beginning of this section, the Hebrew Scriptures indicate several connections between the two nations, besides making Edom the brother of Jacob.

Little is known about the history of Edom, and it is impossible to determine how much of this genealogy is derived from historical memories. Egyptian texts from the thirteenth century BCE mention the nomadic Shasu people living in the territory, but contrary to Genesis 36:31, give no indication of Edom being a monarchy before Israel.[17] There is archaeological evidence of urbanization in the eighth century.[18] Edom was at its most prosperous during the time of Assyrian rule; the stability provided by Assyria meant the Edomites no longer needed to spend their resources resisting domination by Judah. The religion of Edom included a chief god Qos, and like Israel in much of its history, the Edomites also worshiped the Canaanite god Baal. At the eighth-century shrine at Kuntillet Ajrud, mentioned above, there was an inscription mentioning "Yahweh of Teman"; this, along with the biblical passages describing Yahweh coming from Edom, may indicate that Yahweh was also worshiped in Edom. It seems that Israelite and Edomite religion had much in common.

Like other biblical genealogies, this one is probably artificial, expressing social and political relationships at the time it was developed. It must have been created by groups of Edomite background who became part of Judah, for others would have had little reason to create it.[19] The claim that there were kings in Edom before Israel is not supported by any other textual or archaeological evidence. It may be based on memories of local chieftains similar to the "judges" of Israel's tribal period, although some have argued that the claim is evidence that, for ideological reasons, Israel resisted kingship longer than the neighboring peoples.[20]

The stories about Jacob and Esau, from different origins, have been gathered together and made part of the Ancestral Narrative. These stories came from different groups within Israel. The Jacob stories are primarily from northern groups, especially those associated with the sacred site of Bethel, although in their final form the stories about Jacob are also used to denigrate another northern place that made claims to being sacred, Shechem. This shows that at the time Genesis was completed there was no pressing need to deny the traditions of Bethel as a sacred place, but there was a need to deny that status to Shechem because the people of Samaria were still treating it as a major sacred place in competition with Jerusalem.

Esau, the ancestor of the Edomites, is mainly portrayed from the point of view of Israel, but the material is influenced by Edomite traditions themselves, especially in the genealogy and also in the occasional positive portrayal of Esau. When we think of the groups that made up the Israelites, we have to remember that there was no fixed division between Judah and Edom. However, because at least two different characters have been combined in the Esau/Edom character, and because he is secondary to Jacob, it is more difficult to discern the origins of those traditions.

Joseph and His Brothers (Genesis 37–50)

The focus of the story now shifts from Jacob and Esau to Joseph, Jacob's eleventh son. The story of Joseph is different from the rest of Genesis, in that (except for chapter 38) it is a long, continuous narrative about one main character rather than a series of brief episodes. It is also unconcerned about the promises of land and a nation, and the origin of sacred sites. The differences have led to questions about its origin and how it should be classified as literature. Within the Pentateuch the Joseph story accomplishes two things. First, it takes the chosen people out of the promised land to Egypt, making it necessary to bring them back later in the Pentateuch. And second, there is a significant increase in the number of Abraham's descendants; by the time they go to Egypt the clan numbers around seventy people who are well on their way to fulfilling the promise of numerous descendants. These two elements do not depend on the substance of the Joseph story. Other than the sons of Jacob having children and migrating to Egypt, the story could be removed without changing the outline of the Pentateuch.

An important historical question is whether the story is based on actual migrations of Semitic people to Egypt. The existence of Semites in Egypt is well documented for many historical periods, both for groups migrating on their own and for slaves, usually captured in battle, brought to Egypt. During one period, approximately 1650–1540 BCE, there is evidence of a Semitic dynasty, known as the Hyksos ("foreign rulers"), ruling Egypt and being eventually expelled by the Egyptians.

It has been argued that the Hyksos period would have been a favorable time for Joseph rising to power and the rest of the family settling in Egypt. Moreover, the time of their rule is around the time in which many believe the ancestral stories are set. James Hoffmeier points out that many details in the story of Joseph fit the first half of the second millennium, and are evidence of an authentic Egyptian setting. The price Joseph's brothers receive for selling him into slavery is twenty shekels (Gen 37:28), which was the average price paid for slaves at that time, while in later times the price was higher. The position Potiphar gives Joseph, making him "overseer of his house" (Gen 39:4), corresponds to the position of several servants mentioned in Egyptian texts. Personal names in the story, including Potiphar, Asenath, and Zaphenath-paneah, are authentically Egyptian.[21]

There are, however, several problems with finding an authentic setting for the story. The general problem of dating the patriarchs has already been discussed. Identifying the Hyksos rulers as Semitic has been challenged.[22] In addition, Donald Redford argues that the details in the story fit a mid-first millennium setting rather than an early second millennium setting. The Egyptian names that occur, Potiphar, Asenath, and Zaphenath-paneah, are of types that occur in several periods, but were most common in the seventh and sixth centuries BCE. The titles used are not specifically Egyptian; "chief baker" (Gen 40:2) is attested in the seventh century Jerusalem court; the "guard" of which Potiphar is captain corresponds to the guard in Judah at the end of the monarchy. Some titles that are Egyptian are from a late period; the "overseers" Pharaoh appoints (Gen 41:34) correspond to a position in the Persian period (538–333 BCE). The type of tale that this is, of a wise man saving his people, was most common in Egypt in the first millennium, and its closest biblical parallels, such as the tales in Daniel 1–6, are late, from the Hellenistic period. Redford concludes that the origin of the Joseph story is in the late monarchy or exile, and that the story is not based on historical events.[23]

Another answer to the background of the Joseph story is that of Gerhard von Rad, that it is a wisdom novella from the time of King Solomon. Von Rad argued that there are no precise historical references in the story, and the author simply used what he knew or assumed about Egypt in his own time. Joseph is the ideal man of wisdom. He rises from misery to honor by living a virtuous life. He is a court official, embodying the traditional connection between wisdom and royalty. And, as in other wisdom literature, the story's views on God are not related to the covenant theology of the rest of the Hebrew Scriptures. During Solomon's reign there were close political and commercial ties between Israel and Egypt, and an interest in wisdom, and it was thus the most likely time for the composition of the story.[24] This explanation for the story has also been criticized. For one thing, the existence of a "Solomonic enlightenment" that would have produced such literature is doubted by scholars today. Also, as Thomas Thompson argues, Joseph is not so much an ideal wise man as a young man clever in achieving his own success, and the comparisons with wisdom literature are forced.[25]

    On the composition of the story the documentary hypothesis has often been invoked. Two separate versions of the story are most clear in chapter 37, where there is an outright contradiction over whether it is Midianites or the Ishmaelites who take Joseph to Egypt (cf. Gen 37:27, 28, 36; 39:1), and differences as to whether it is Rueben or Judah who tries to save him (cf. Gen 37:22, 26-27). The shortcomings of the documentary hypothesis are that the differences are less clear in the rest of the story, and that the story as a whole reads like such a well-constructed work of literature that it is hard to imagine that it could have been produced by patching together two or three originally separate stories. One can think of "the Joseph story" as a single work of literature beginning in chapter 39, with chapter 37 as a composite of two different introductions that serve to connect the story to the rest of the Ancestral Narrative. To be sure, the conclusion of the Joseph story assumes previous events in chapter 37—that Joseph's brothers caused him to be sold into slavery in Egypt—but it needn't assume the precise details of either of the versions of chapter 37. Thinking of chapter 37 as a separate composition also makes it easier to understand how the seemingly unrelated story of Judah and Tamar in chapter 38 could have been inserted into the Joseph story at that point.

Genesis 37. Unlike the rest of the Joseph story, chapter 37 existed in two distinct versions. Since the basic contents are necessary for what happens later in Egypt, one of the versions must have been part of the story all along, and in the process of the transmission of the story among different groups, an alternative introduction also developed. Scholars have traditionally considered the two versions to have been from the Yahwist and Elohist sources, with the Yahwist having Judah as the brother who does not want to kill Joseph and having the Ishmaelites taking Joseph to Egypt, and the Elohist having Rueben as the brother not wanting to kill him and the Midianites taking him to Egypt. There are difficulties with the documentary hypothesis, but one can safely say that there were two versions, woven together by the author into one narrative (see next page, "Two Versions of Joseph Being Taken to Egypt").

There are other indications in this chapter that the Joseph story existed independently, apart from the rest of the Ancestral Narrative. In 37:10 Joseph's father rebukes him for his dreams of becoming great, saying, "Shall we indeed come, I and your mother and your brothers, and bow to the ground before you?" Yet Joseph's mother Rachel is supposed to have already died (35:18-20). In 37:3 it is said that Jacob loved Joseph "more than any other of his children, because he was the son of his old age." Yet earlier in Genesis Joseph was born around the same time as his older siblings, and it was Benjamin who was the son of Jacob's old age (29:31–30:24; 35:18).

Genesis 38. The story of Judah and his family appears to be unrelated to the rest of the Joseph story. From a literary point of view one can see that it serves a purpose in the final form of the narrative, by providing a pause and a sense of time having passed before the events that take place in Egypt. Robert Alter has shown that in fact there are several careful connections made between chapter 38 and the rest of the story—e.g., when Joseph's brothers bring the bloodied coat to Jacob they say, "Please recognize" (37:32, Alter's translation), and Tamar uses the exact same words when she brings out Judah's signet and cord and staff (38:25).[26] Also, by focusing on Judah this chapter draws attention to his role in the rest of the story. Of all the characters, Judah is the one who changes the most—from scheming and deceitful in chapter 37, and irresponsible at the beginning of chapter 38, to acknowledging his sin against Tamar at the end of chapter 38, and sincerely repenting of his sin against Joseph and offering himself as a slave in chapter 44. Judah the character is a fitting representative for the postexilic nation of Judah, repenting of its past sins, and chapter 38 is key to making the Joseph story also a story about Judah. Nonetheless, appreciating these literary points is not to deny that chapter 38 had an origin separate from the rest of the Joseph story.

Two Versions of Joseph Being Taken to Egypt

When Jacob sends his son Joseph to his brothers, they see him coming and make plans to kill him.

A

Rueben heard, and he rescued him from their hand, and he said, "Let us not strike against flesh." Rueben said to them, "Do not shed blood. Throw him down into this pit in the wilderness, but do not set a hand upon him"—in order to rescue him from their hand and return him to his father. Joseph came to his brothers, and they took him and threw him into the pit. The pit was empty; there was no water in it.

Some Midianite traders passed by, and they pulled Joseph up from the pit. Then Rueben returned to the pit, and Joseph was not in it. He tore his clothes. He returned to his brothers and said, "The child is not there, and I, where will I go?"

The Midianites sold Joseph in Egypt to Potiphar, eunuch of Pharaoh, captain of the guards.

B

Joseph's brothers stripped his tunic from him, the long tunic he had on. They took him and threw him into the pit.

When they sat down to eat food they lifted up their eyes and saw a caravan of Ishmaelites coming from Gilead, and their camels were carrying gum, balm, and resin, taking it down to Egypt. Judah said to his brothers, "What profit is there if we kill our brother and conceal his blood? Let us sell him to the Ishmaelites and not have our hand on him, for he is our brother, our flesh." And his brothers listened. They sold Joseph to the Ishmaelites for twenty pieces of silver, and they took Joseph to Egypt.

They took Joseph's tunic, and they slaughtered a goat, and they dipped the tunic in the blood. Then they sent the long tunic and brought it to their father and said, "We found this. Please identify it—is it the tunic of your son or not?" He identified it and said, "My son's tunic! A vicious animal has devoured him—Joseph is certainly torn into pieces!" Jacob tore his clothes and put sackcloth on his loins and mourned his son many days. All his sons and daughters rose to comfort him, but he refused to be comforted. He said, "No, I will go down to my son mourning, to Sheol." And his father wept for him.

Joseph was taken down to Egypt, and Potiphar, eunuch of Pharaoh and captain of the guards, an Egyptian, purchased him from the Ishmaelites who brought him down there.

*These translations are the author's. Version **A** is Genesis 37:21-23a, 24, 28a, 29-30, 36. Version **B** is Genesis 37:23b-24a, 25-27, 28b, 31-35; 39:1. They are fairly literal translations of the Hebrew, but that is not meant to imply that these were the exact wordings of the original versions; the final author of the text would have eliminated some redundancies and added other phrases to weave them together. Earlier scholars often attributed **A** to the Elohist source and **B** to the Yahwist, but that is no longer certain.*

The story assumes the custom of "levirate" marriage, in which a brother of a man who dies childless is to marry the widow in order to produce offspring for the dead man. The law requiring this comes later in the Pentateuch (Dt 25:5-10), and it is not clear when the practice originated or how widely it was practiced. The point here is simply that Tamar makes sure the obligation is carried out, after Judah's failure to do so.

Marriage to Canaanite women is not explicitly condemned in the story, although there is an implicit disapproval, since it is connected to negative events. The story considers the nation Judah a people of mixed backgrounds, a fact that is evident elsewhere in the Hebrew Scriptures, especially with regard to its kings—the Book of Ruth tells the story of a Moabite woman who becomes an ancestor of David, and David and Solomon both have foreign wives.

The story reinforces some of the Pentateuch's regular themes. It is another story of younger and elder brothers; this time the one who is supposed to be born second is born first. It is a story in which God's plan for the chosen people moves forward despite the failings of the individuals involved, and through unorthodox means. It speaks to the scattered Jews after the exile about God preserving them through messy situations.

Genesis 39. The "spurned seductress" motif of the story of Joseph and Potiphar's wife was a common one in ancient Near Eastern literature. In particular, this incident is quite similar to the Egyptian "Story of Two Brothers," in which the wife of an elder brother tries to seduce his younger brother, and falsely accuses him when he refuses. In the Egyptian story, which was written centuries before the Pentateuch, the elder brother eventually finds out the truth and kills his wife, and the younger son exiles himself to a distant land, until he is brought back and becomes king of Egypt.[27] The Genesis story is using a well-known folktale motif, although it would be a mistake to reduce it to that. As is frequently the case in the Pentateuch, the authors have borrowed material from the surrounding peoples, but have used it for a different purpose. Here the purpose is to show an Israelite put into jeopardy in a foreign land for an unjust reason. This purpose shows up in several postexilic stories (Tobit, Esther, Dan 1–6), and such stories remained popular because of their continued relevance to people living under foreign rule.

Genesis 40–41. Joseph's rise to power in Egypt and his administration of the government grain program have often been compared to the historical situation in Egypt in the middle of the second millennium BCE. The rule of the Hyksos from around 1650 to 1540 has been mentioned above. Several texts from Egypt refer to a vizier, an official second only to the Pharaoh, and thus similar to Joseph.[28] One text discusses a king and his officials' concern over a seven-year drought and famine, but it refers to a much earlier period, the twenty-eighth century BCE.[29] It is likely that an original core Joseph story was based on some general knowledge of Egypt, but in its final form the story is more shaped by the theme of a Jew rising to a high position in a foreign court, a theme also found in Esther and Daniel 1–6. As in those stories, Joseph becomes successful, but since this is part of the larger narrative of the Pentateuch, it serves an additional purpose, preparing for the Israelites living in Egypt.

It is noteworthy that this part of the story shows no disapproval of Joseph having a foreign wife or of his two sons, who become the ancestors of the tribes Ephraim and Manasseh, having a foreign mother. That aspect must have belonged to a version of the story before it was incorporated into the Pentateuch. The author saw no need to remove it, although elsewhere there is a great concern about not marrying foreigners. Within the story itself it is part of Joseph's success, but it may also have seemed appropriate to an author from a southern background to have the two most powerful northern tribes have a foreign ancestor.

Genesis 42–45. The grain-buying journeys of Joseph's brothers and the eventual reunion are told in a long, drawn out way, and is clearly a literary creation meant to add suspense and raise questions about Joseph's character rather than report anything historical. Yet the author uses knowledge about Egypt to give it an authentic feel, as any good storyteller would. People did often go to Egypt to buy grain. Egypt did have legitimate concerns about spies and invaders coming into their land. Egyptians did sometimes allow refugees from elsewhere to settle in their land—a text from around 1220 BCE reports that nomadic Shasu from Edom were allowed to come into the Delta region when Edom became too dry,[30] and of course many Jews fled there after the Assyrian and Babylonian invasions (cf. Jer 42–44).

Joseph is now called "governor" over the land (42:6), a term not used earlier in the story. The Hebrew word *shallit* is used only here and in Ecclesiastes, a fairly late book; the identical Aramaic word is used several times in Ezra and Daniel 1–6, both written well after the exile. This part of the story is a late incorporation of the Joseph story into the Ancestral Narrative. The author is making it no longer a story about just Joseph, but about all of the family. Related to that purpose is the prominence of Judah. His speech in chapter 44 is a moving description of all that has happened, and completes his transformation into a repenting, self-sacrificing leader of the brothers. He is a model for the way the postexilic Jewish community was to see itself, after recognizing the past sins of the nation.

Genesis 46–47. The settlement of Jacob's family is told in a way that emphasizes how numerous and prosperous they have become, thus fulfilling part of the promise to Abraham, even as they are leaving the land promised to them. It sets the stage for the liberation that will occur in Exodus and the journey back to the promised land through the rest of the Pentateuch. Although this is presented as a successful conclusion to the Joseph story, in the background is the knowledge that this will lead to trouble for the chosen people. The core of the Joseph story may have been entirely positive with regard to him, but the way the author has incorporated it into the Pentateuch suggests that following him leads to short-term salvation at best.

To emphasize how numerous they have become, the author includes a genealogical list of the people who went to Egypt. Making this list part of the story leads to some chronological problems. Throughout the story there have been indications of how much time has passed (Gen 37:2; 41:46; 45:11), which adds up to twenty-two years from the time Joseph was taken to Egypt until the rest of the family comes. Within that same period Judah has married, had three sons, and then fathered Perez and Zerah after his third son reached marriageable age (Gen 38). These events must have taken at least twenty years, so Perez cannot be more than two years old at the time they come down to Egypt. But now in the list of people who come to Egypt, we find that Perez already has two children (Gen 46:12)! The list is clearly from a separate source, but it must have seemed appropriate to include it here because it shows the fulfillment of the promise of many descendants.

The settlement of the family is said to take place at Goshen, away from the other Egyptians, "because all shepherds are abhorrent to the Egyptians" (46:34). The statement may reflect the frequent conflicts

Egypt had with nomadic groups infiltrating its territory. The author is also maintaining that the Israelites stayed pure of Egyptian influence despite living among them for several generations. There is, however, a discrepancy between this and Exodus 12, where the Israelites are depicted as living among the Egyptians, so that they need to mark their doorposts as a sign to God to pass over their houses when striking dead the firstborn of the Egyptians, and they have Egyptian neighbors from whom they take silver and gold and clothing.

Genesis 48–49. With the family secure in Egypt, the story now wraps up the lives of Jacob and Joseph and turns to the future of the tribes. Chapter 48 is concerned with Ephraim and Manasseh, two tribes descended from Joseph. Having Jacob say that Ephraim and Manasseh are now to be considered his sons and that Joseph is to have a double portion provides an explanation for why the twelve tribes do not correspond exactly to the twelve sons of Jacob. This is also another story of a younger son, Ephraim, being favored over the elder, Manasseh, although both of them are to become great.

The testament of Jacob in chapter 49 consists of predictions of the futures of the twelve tribes, although Joseph is treated as a single tribe rather than two and the passage about him is in the form of a blessing on him as a person rather than a prediction about his descendants. Judah and Joseph, as the two most powerful groups in later Israelite history, receive the most attention. Some of the material here may come from early poetic traditions about the tribes, but other parts show influences of the monarchy and exile, or include vague predictions that probably come from a time when the historical tribes had long since disappeared.

Reuben, the firstborn, is said to be vigorous, but will no longer excel because of his instability and because he went up to his father's bed—a reference to his lying with Jacob's concubine Bilhah (Gen 35:22). This is the only explanation given so far for the firstborn not having a greater inheritance than the others, and it doesn't explain it very well. The theme of younger sons becoming more prominent is so common in the Hebrew Scriptures that the author felt no need to give more of an explanation. There is extra-biblical evidence of Reuben losing its territory. The Moabite Stone, from around 830 BCE, describes the king of Moab capturing cities that the Bible lists as belonging to Reuben (Josh 13:15-23).[31]

The testament condemns **Simeon** and **Levi** for their attack on Shechem (cf. Gen 34), and says they will be divided and scattered in the land. Elsewhere in the Hebrew Scriptures these groups do lose their land. For Simeon, the territory allotted is contained within the southern part of Judah (Josh 19:1-9) and was apparently absorbed by that tribe (Judg 1:3). The later history in Chronicles, however, has Simeonites living in the north as well (2 Chron 15:9; 34:6); the prediction here that Simeon will be scattered in Israel and Jacob—names for the north—reflects that later understanding of their fate. (The fact that Jacob refers to the land as "Jacob" shows how anachronistic the poem is.) For Levi, the lack of land is elsewhere explained more positively in terms of their becoming priests for the entire nation (Num 35:1-8; Josh 21). This poem is unusual in being so negative regarding Levi; its closest parallels are exilic criticisms of the Levites for leading the nation astray (Ezek 44:10; 48:11).

Judah's destiny is to rule over his brothers. He is compared to a lion, an image frequently used for kings. The passage originated sometime after the time of David and Solomon, when kings from the tribe of Judah did rule over all the others, and expresses a hope for a return to those days. Verse 10c is unclear. It literally reads, "until he comes to Shiloh," but many translations emend the text to make it more in keeping with the rest of the passage (e.g., "until tribute comes to him" in the NRSV). It is possible, though, that it refers to the destruction of the shrine at Shiloh, and is saying that the rule of Judah will last until a similar fate befalls the temple in Jerusalem. The prophet Jeremiah made a similar claim in his temple sermon (Jer 7:12-14).

The prediction that **Zebulun** will live by the sea contradicts other descriptions of the tribe's territory, which was inland (Josh 19:10-16). This may be simply an exaggeration of the scope of the territory, or it may be based on a memory that after the fall of the northern kingdom in 722 BCE, when Assyria exiled and scattered the people, a community of Israelites did thrive for a time in Phoenicia.

Issachar is depicted as strong but docile, and forced into slavery. The prediction is too vague to connect to any particular historical situation, and probably just reflects the knowledge that many Israelites spent time in forced labor under foreign rule.

Dan is said to be a judge, using a play on words with the Hebrew *din*, "judge." There is no reason to believe that the tribe of Dan had a reputation for better judgments than anyone else, and the use of a wordplay indicates that the passage comes from a time when actual historical memories of the tribe had been lost. The comparison to a snake is a general view of how Israel believed its ancestors lived before the monarchy, with no central authority to impose order.

For **Gad** another wordplay—the Hebrew *gdd*, "raid"—is used. The description of being raided and raiding back would fit most of the early Israelites. In the above-mentioned Moabite Stone, the king of Moab claims that he fought and defeated Ataroth, one of the cities of Gad (Num 32:34).[32]

The traditional territory of **Asher** was Mt. Carmel and the northwest coastal region of Israel. It is a fertile region, and the saying about it in Jacob's testament shows a knowledge of that fact, but no historical knowledge of the tribe.

The description of **Naphtali** also does not include any historical remembrances, but is an idealized picture of nature, of animals living in freedom. This is another general view that Israel had of its ancestors before the monarchy, of a people living freely.

The passage on **Joseph** is different from the others, in that it is a blessing on the person Joseph and not a prediction of how one of the tribes will live. This part of the poem may be much earlier than the rest; the imagery of being fruitful and receiving the blessings of breasts and womb has similarities to aspects of Canaanite fertility religion, possibly connecting Joseph with the worship of the goddess Asherah.[33] This early picture of Joseph suggests that the core of the Joseph story was related to a larger complex of legends about him going back to the Canaanite origins of early Israel. Other legends about him may have been lost, but it is interesting that the main surviving one is the story of his rise to power in Egypt. In this respect he parallels Daniel—the surviving stories about Daniel are about an Israelite reaching a position of authority in a foreign court (Dan 1–6), but there are indications of other legends about him in the Book of Ezekiel (14:12-20; 28:3), and there are legends of a Daniel in the Canaanite literature from Ugarit.[34] Both Joseph and Daniel were probably extensively developed characters in Canaanite and Israelite lore. By the time most of the Hebrew Scriptures were written, during and after the exile, the most relevant stories about each had to do with becoming successful in a foreign court, and those are the ones that have been preserved.

The description of **Benjamin** as a ravenous wolf is another side of the general picture Israel had of its ancestors. They were free and peaceful like the deer used to describe Naphtali, but they were also fierce and ruthless like the wolf describing Benjamin. Neither image is based on historical remembrances of how either tribe lived, but express different aspects of how Israel saw its past.

The material in chapters 48 and 49 transforms the story from one of a family to one of a collection of tribes. It does not yet portray them as a nation—that will take place in the rest of the Pentateuch—but it brings them to a transitional stage. To do that, the author has made use of some historical memories of where certain tribes lived and how they either became powerful or lost territory; some old legends related to tribal ancestors, such as the Joseph legends; and some general views of how the ancestors of Israel lived, views depicted through descriptions of tribes whose actual historical characteristics have been forgotten. Although very little here can be used to reconstruct the history of early Israel, it is a valuable illustration of how the Israel of the late monarchy and exile saw their past, and—more important—understood the identity they wanted to shape for the future. *doubtful*

Genesis 50. The events in chapter 50 conclude the Jacob and Joseph stories and stress that the sojourn in Egypt is only temporary, particularly by having Jacob's body taken back to Canaan to be buried, and Joseph making the family swear to do the same with his body. Once again there is evidence of diverse traditions being woven together. At some points it seems that Jacob's burial place is a tomb he dug himself at Atad, east of the Jordan, and at other points it is the field at Machpelah that Abraham bought and used previously.

When Joseph tells his family to return his bones to Canaan, he says he wants this done because it is the land promised to Abraham, Isaac, and Jacob. This is the only place in the entire Joseph story where he refers to or even exhibits any knowledge of the promise, another indication that the Joseph story was originally a separate entity. It is here that the Joseph story, finally, is fully incorporated into the Ancestral Narrative. He is now more than a younger brother who comes out ahead, more than a successful Israelite in a foreign court, more than a person who saves his family from famine. He is now an active participant in God's plan for the chosen people. *but he has been from the start!*

CHAPTER FIVE

Exodus 1:1–13:16

Exodus 1 — Oppression

Exodus 2–6 — Moses and His Mission

Exodus 7–11 — The Signs against Egypt

Exodus 12:1–13:16 — The Departure and Passover

The second book of the Pentateuch picks up the story where Genesis left off, but quickly skips ahead several generations and moves
to new circumstances for the descendants of Jacob. They are no longer
favored guests in Egypt, but slaves oppressed by a new pharaoh. Exodus 1–13 tells the story of a pharaoh's attempts to oppress the Israelites,
Moses' birth and escape, his meeting with God in the desert, his pleas
to a pharaoh to let the Israelites go, and their dramatic departure. Its
theological message is about God fulfilling promises, freeing people
from oppression, and shaping them into a nation with a common identity. These teachings would have resonated well for the scattered Jews
after the exile, who sometimes experienced oppression and sometimes
wondered if their community would survive, but who needed some
persuasion before they would give up whatever lives they had established and go back to Judah to rebuild a community there.

Because of the centrality of the exodus story, the historical issues it
raises have been among the most studied in the Bible. Indeed, since it
is now no longer a story of just one family, we can expect more concrete
results from historical investigations. The lack of evidence of Abraham
and his travels is not surprising, but the exodus story involves profound
effects on nations, and we are justified in expecting more evidence that
it either did or did not occur.

79

The general question—did such an event occur?—involves several related questions. First we will need to look at what was happening in Egypt during the range of time the exodus might have occurred, in order to evaluate the plausibility of the story. We can then try to determine the most likely date for the exodus, and see if there is evidence of Semitic slaves in Egypt who could have escaped and journeyed to Canaan at that time. If the story is not historical, we also need to ask how and why it became part of Israel's national origin epic, and how the tradition developed into its final form in the Pentateuch.

Egypt in the Late Bronze (1550–1200) and Iron Age I (1200–1000)

Following the expulsion of the Hyksos in 1540, a series of pharaohs, the 18th dynasty, ruled Egypt. During this time Egypt established an empire over Canaan, but there were threats to that rule. One was the Hittite kingdom to the north, which also had designs on Canaanite territory, and another was revolt by kings of the Canaanite cities. A collection of letters discovered at Tell el-Amarna in Egypt reveals some of what was going on in Canaan. The Amarna letters are fourteenth-century reports from Canaanite kings under Egyptian rule, often complaining about other local kings who are not as loyal to Egypt and are causing problems, such as raiding someone else's land. Several letters mention groups called the Apiru, gangs in the countryside outside of anyone's control, who raid farmland and are sometimes hired as mercenaries by one king against another. Some scholars suggest the Apiru may have been the ancestors of the Israelites, or joined forces with a newly arrived exodus group to overthrow the rulers of the cities to establish a new society in Canaan. Whether that did occur or not, the activities of the Apiru are an indication of the instability in Canaan in the centuries before Israel began.

It was during the Late Bronze age that there was an unusual religious movement in Egypt. During the reign of Akhenaten (1351–1334), there was officially the worship of only one god, the sun disk Aten. Although this was not pure monotheism as would later develop in Judaism, and it did not last after Akhenaten's reign, some have speculated that it could have been background for the monotheistic belief

Egyptian Rulers of the New Kingdom

The New Kingdom is the period of Egyptian history from ca. 1540 to 1070 BCE, during the rule of the pharaohs of the 18th–20th dynasties. If the exodus story is based on a historical event, it was probably from this period. Pharaohs mentioned in this chapter are in bold print. Dates are approximate.

18th Dynasty

Ahmose	1540–1515
Amenhotep I	1515–1494
Thutmose I	1494–1482
Thutmose II	1482–1479
Hatshepsut	1479–1458
Thutmose III	1479–1425
Amenhotep II	1425–1397
Thutmose IV	1397–1388
Amenhotep III	1388–1351
Akhenaten	**1351–1334**
Smenkhkare	1337–1334
Tutankhamun	1334–1323
Ay	1323–1319
Horemheb	1319–1292

19th Dynasty

Ramesses I	**1292–1290**
Seti I	**1290–1279**
Ramesses II	**1279–1213**
Merneptah	**1213–1203**
Amenmesse	1203–1200
Seti II	1200–1194
Siptah	1194–1186
Tawosret	1186–1185

20th Dynasty

Setnakht	1185–1183
Ramesses III	**1183–1152**
Ramesses IV	1152–1145
Ramesses V	1145–1142
Ramesses VI	1142–1134
Ramesses VII	1134–1126
Ramesses VIII	1126–1125
Ramesses IX	1125–1107
Ramesses X	1107–1103
Ramesses XI	1103–1070

Moses taught. Most, however, do not consider that a serious possibility. Akhenaten's emphasis on one god had more to do with rival factions among Egypt's priests than a theological conviction, and in any case monotheism did not develop in Israel until centuries later.

The 19th Egyptian dynasty began with Ramesses I, who ruled only briefly, followed by Seti I and Ramesses II. During this time Egypt attempted to strengthen its empire, with mixed results. Ramesses II (1279–1213) fought a major battle against the Hittites at Kadesh, and, although he failed to take Kadesh, he claimed victory; the long-term result was a stalemate between Egypt and the Hittites. Ramesses' failure to extend his empire led local Canaanite kings to believe they could break free from Egyptian rule, requiring Ramesses to carry out military campaigns to put down revolts. At home, Ramesses II undertook major building projects, including a new royal residence, which some believe was one of the projects worked on by the Hebrew slaves mentioned in Exodus.

Ramesses II was succeeded by his son Merneptah. Like his father, Merneptah campaigned in Canaan to put down revolts. In 1209 he put up a monument, the "Merneptah Stele," claiming victory in Canaan and listing several peoples he defeated. Included in the list is the name "Israel," the earliest mention of the name in any written source.[1] The Merneptah Stele is a significant source for the beginnings of Israel, but not necessarily for the exodus, since we do not know if the Israel referred to was an indigenous Canaanite group or had come in from elsewhere.

Over the next century and a half, Egypt lost its empire in Canaan. The military and economic decline cannot be attributed to one single cause. A series of droughts may have contributed to economic weakness. Ineffectual pharaohs may have led to a weaker army. The continued skirmishes with the nomadic Shasu and the instability and rivalry among Canaanite kings made it difficult for Egypt to exert any control outside its own borders. And, a group of people who had begun showing up earlier became even more of a problem for Egypt. These were the Sea Peoples.

"Sea Peoples" is a collective term used for groups migrating from the Aegean Sea region to other places in the eastern Mediterranean during the thirteenth and twelfth centuries, although why they needed to leave their homeland has not been completely explained. There are some reports of Egyptians encountering these Sea Peoples in the thirteenth century, but the larger scale encounters took place in the twelfth century. Ramesses III, in the twelfth century, put up an inscription celebrating his victory over invading Sea Peoples, and accompanying reliefs show not only warriors, but also oxcarts with women and children, indicating that the Sea Peoples were not just invading armies, but communities looking for a place to settle.[2] Ramesses III also claimed that he captured some of the Sea Peoples and settled them as soldiers in his fortresses in Canaan.[3] As Egyptian power declined, other Sea Peoples were undoubtedly able to settle in Canaan on their own.

The Sea Peoples are significant in early Israelite history for several reasons. One of the groups was the Philistines, who are a major enemy of the Israelites just before the monarchy in the books of Judges and 1 Samuel. Other groups of the Sea Peoples may have been part of the mix of peoples who became the Israelites (the tribe of Dan in particular). And, most relevant for the exodus story, the Sea Peoples contributed to the weakness of Egypt that would have made it easier for a group of escaped slaves to make their way to Canaan.

By the middle of the eleventh century the pharaohs could no longer claim a glorious empire in Canaan or a glorious administration at home. The lands formerly controlled by Egypt had fallen into the hands of others—nomadic peoples in the Sinai and south of the Dead Sea, the Philistines and other Sea Peoples in parts of Canaan, new settlements in the highlands of Canaan, and Canaanite kings in some of the Canaanite cities—with no one group yet dominant. The region was evolving, and conditions were right for small groups to find a new place for themselves and for new coalitions to form.

Historicity of the Exodus

As with other events, the first step in investigating the historicity of the exodus is to determine when it is supposed to have occurred. There is one place in the Bible that seems to give a direct answer: 1 Kings 6:1 says that Solomon built the temple in the fourth year of his reign, 480 years after the exodus. If Solomon reigned sometime in the middle of the tenth century BCE, then the exodus would have occurred in the middle or late fifteenth century. There are, however, several problems with that date. On the one hand, 480 is too *few* years when compared to other information in the Bible. The events that take place between the exodus and the building of the temple—the wandering in the wilderness, the conquest of the promised land, the rule of the judges, Samuel, Saul, and David—take more than 550 years. On the other hand, 480 is too *many* years if we look at extra-biblical evidence for when the beginning of Israel could have occurred. Archaeological evidence of changes in Canaan that correspond to the emergence of Israel (a decline in Canaanite city-states and the establishment of new villages in the highlands) dates from around 1200. Most who defend the historicity of the exodus argue for a date between 1300 and 1200 because details in the story, such as the building projects the Hebrew slaves worked on, and encountering Edomites and Moabites on their journey through the wilderness, more conveniently fit that period. Note, however, that accepting the historicity of the exodus in that period means denying the historicity of other parts of the Bible that maintain it was two or three centuries earlier. As remarked in chapter one, there is no such thing as a complete fundamentalist. Defending the literal truth of some parts of the Bible always means rejecting the literal truth of other parts.

It is sometimes argued, further, that the exodus must have occurred before 1209, because in that year Merneptah's monument refers to Israel as a group in Canaan.[4] If Israel was already in Canaan in 1209, then the exodus must have been several years earlier. The problem with this argument is that it assumes the exodus group and the Israel of the Merneptah Stele are the same people. In fact, the people who became the Israelites of the Bible came from diverse backgrounds, and there are reasons to believe that most came from within Canaan. It is more likely that the Israel of the Merneptah Stele was an indigenous Canaanite group (the name suggests they worshiped the Canaanite god El) whose name was later used by the larger nation of Israel. Once we recognize that the earliest use of the name Israel does not necessarily refer to the exodus group, we can consider dates after 1209 for the exodus event.

Similarly, it is argued that the exodus must have occurred before 1200 to give this group time to get to Canaan and cause the decline of the Canaanite cities and to establish the new settlements in the highlands.[5] Again, this assumes that the exodus group was primarily responsible for the changes that took place in Canaan, rather than a small group that became involved in those changes at some later point during the process. It is possible, and in fact more likely, that the changes in Canaan were primarily an internal upheaval, and not caused by former slaves wandering in from the desert.

A date between 1250 and 1050 BCE is the most likely time for an exodus event, if it did occur. This is a slightly later range of dates than that used by most who argue for a historical exodus, but it best takes account of what was going on both in Egypt and in Canaan. From the end of the thirteenth to the end of the eleventh centuries, conditions in Canaan were favorable for a group of outsiders coming in and finding a place in the evolving society. Considering circumstances in Egypt, a date late in this period is more likely than a date early in it. Individuals and small groups of slaves could have escaped at any time. However, as Egyptian power declined and the pharaohs became weaker late in the twelfth century or in the eleventh century, it would have become easier for a group of slaves large enough to develop a common identity to leave Egypt and to preserve legends about their escape.

If we accept this range of dates, the next question is, were there Semitic slaves in Egypt in the period of 1250–1050 BCE? Here the answer is clearly yes. Egyptian texts from this period (and others) refer frequently to slaves, especially slaves captured in battle. A letter from near the end of the thirteenth century asks for help in finding two escaped slaves, and treats this type of thing as a common occurrence.[6] There is no doubt that the general circumstances behind the exodus story are plausible in this period.

If it is plausible that something similar to the exodus *could* have occurred, the more difficult question is *did* it occur? Among scholars who argue in the affirmative are Kenneth Kitchen and James Hoffmeier. One point they make is that several details in the story seem to indicate an authentic Egyptian background. There are Egyptian **names** in the story. The name Moses is from a common suffix meaning son or child (as in Thutmose). The **cities** the Hebrew slaves are said to work on, Ramesses and Pithom, may correspond to actual cities the pharaohs built late in the thirteenth century. Ramesses II built a residence, Pi-Ramesses (House of Ramesses), near the Nile delta; the existence of a Pithom is less certain.[7] The **plagues** are similar to natural phenomena that occur in Egypt. Silt can turn the Nile a reddish color; the frog population can increase dramatically; locust invasions and darkness caused by sandstorms can occur. Some of the **vocabulary** used in the story derives from Egyptian words, including the basket (*tebah*) into which the child Moses is put, the word used for the Nile River (*yeor*), and the reeds (*suph*) along the Nile and at the sea the Israelites cross.[8] With all of these Egyptian details, it is argued, the story must go back to an actual event in Egypt.

While it is true that there are Egyptian details in the story, there is no reason an Israelite storyteller from a different time and place could not have known about them and sprinkled them into the story. Throughout biblical times, travel, trade, and influence were prevalent along the fertile crescent, from Egypt to Mesopotamia. Hoffmeier, arguing that the vocabulary indicates an authentic Egyptian background, says, "... it seems unlikely that a scribe during the late Judaean monarchy or the exilic period (or later) would have been familiar with these Egyptian terms."[9] Yet the very terms he has just cited *were* used by scribes of the late monarchy, exile, and later. From the exile, Ezekiel 29:3, 9 uses *yeor* for the Nile; well after the exile Jonah 2:5 uses *suph* for reeds; *tebah* is used in the story of Noah's ark, of uncertain date but with much more Babylonian than Egyptian influence (see chapter 3). It should also be remembered that since late in the monarchy there had been Jews living in Egypt, in correspondence with Jews elsewhere, so knowledge about Egyptian words, names, places, history, and natural phenomena would not have been unusual for a late biblical writer.

The city Ramesses in the story having almost the same name as the historical Pi-Ramesses is also not as significant as it might seem. The Pentateuch calls the area in Egypt where the Israelites lived "the land of Ramesses" back in the Joseph story (Gen 47:11), long before any Ramesses ruled Egypt. Kitchen's claim that Genesis 47:11 is different because there it is the narrator and not a character who calls it Ramesses is incorrect, since in Exodus 1:11 it is also the narrator and not a character who calls it Ramesses.[10] In both places, the author uses it as a legendary place name in Egypt, without necessarily having a precise idea of when or how the name came into being. In addition, there were several places in Egypt named after the Ramesses pharaohs,[11] so an Israelite storyteller may simply have used a name known to have once been common in that area (much as someone telling a story set in an unspecified place in the United States might call the place Springfield).

Those who argue against an actual event behind the exodus story point out that there is no reference to it in any Egyptian text. That is not necessarily decisive; Kitchen responds that Egyptian pharaohs did not celebrate losses, but would have been more likely to gloss over an embarrassing event like the exodus, and that no administrative records from Pi-Ramesses have survived anyway, so even if there was an Egypt-ian record of it, it has been lost.[12] This makes sense for a small group of slaves, but, as told in Exodus, the event is far more than a military defeat or an event affecting only one city. The whole nation is devas-tated by the plagues; the entire army is destroyed in the sea; the num-ber of escapees is well over a million. To some extent one can dismiss these as exaggerations, but it is central to the story that the conflict is all-consuming for the pharaohs. The lack of any mention in Egyptian sources means that if the exodus story is based on a historical event, it was an event much smaller than, and not involving significant parts of, the biblical story.

Many other elements of the story seem legendary. The episode of the two midwives outsmarting the pharaoh is an entertaining folktale, and can hardly be historical. The story of Moses' birth and rescue has similarities to other "exposed baby" stories. It is often compared to the story of Sargon of Akkad, in which Sargon's mother puts him in a basket sealed with pitch and puts it in the river; he is rescued and raised by someone else, and he becomes a great king.[13] The story of how Moses meets his wife (Ex 2:16-21) is a literary creation, following the same pattern as the stories of Isaac and Jacob meeting their wives (Gen 24; 29). With so many nonhistorical elements, one needs to be cautious about using selective details to prove the event's historicity.

It is not possible that the exodus event occurred on the scale or in all of the details of the biblical story, but it is possible that it is based on some historical event. An exodus tradition did develop in Israel, so the occurrence of *some* event is a reasonable explanation for that tradition developing. A small group of Semitic slaves may have escaped from Egypt sometime between 1250 and 1050 BCE, perhaps aided by nat-ural phenomena. Eventually they made their way to Canaan and were able to find a place in which to settle because the control of Egypt and the Canaanite kings was declining. Over time they developed a life sim-ilar to that of other settlers in the hill country of Canaan, who came from various backgrounds—nomadic groups, the Sea Peoples, the Apiru, but most from the declining Canaanite cities. The people of this decentralized society of the hill country occasionally formed coalitions against the Philistines or Canaanite kings who were still around or against each other, but were not united as a nation until a monarchy developed around the year 1000.

The exodus group was only a minority in this new society, but their story was remembered and, some time later, in a very elaborated and theologically interpreted form, became the story of origins for the nation. How that happened is impossible to determine, but a look at the development of the tradition will provide some insights.

The Development of the Exodus Tradition

The final form of the exodus story dates from after the exile, but versions of it existed during the monarchy. Indeed, for it to be accepted as the national epic there must have been some awareness of it as an old story. Unlike the Ancestral Narrative of Genesis, there is evidence of an exodus tradition being widely known before the exile. A look at the pre-exilic references sheds some light on the development of the tradition.

The victory hymn in Exodus 15 is often considered very early Hebrew poetry, based on its linguistic similarities to Ugaritic poetry.[14] How early is much debated. Some of its language may suggest a pre-monarchic date, but since it presupposes the conquest tradition and either the building of the temple or the existence of some Israelite holy place (15:17), a date around the beginning of the monarchy is more likely. The hymn is thus often used as evidence of the exodus story being early, but it must be noted that the hymn itself does not refer to any escape from slavery in Egypt, or to Moses, and it uses much mythological language of a great battle between Yahweh and the forces of evil, making it difficult to determine what actual events it envisions. The hymn tells us that during the monarchy, probably fairly early, there was a tradition expressed in mythological form of Yahweh defeating Egypt in a battle by a sea, allowing Israel to establish a nation in Canaan.

There are several references in prophetic books to Israel coming up from Egypt. It is notoriously difficult to date passages in prophetic books. Besides the obvious additions of whole sections to some books, such as Second and Third Isaiah, individual passages went through decades of transmission before being compiled into the books we know. Caution is needed in claiming that certain passages are pre-exilic references to the exodus. Nonetheless, there are enough references to show that from the end of the eighth century people were aware of some version of the exodus story.

The Book of Amos refers to God bringing the Israelites up from Egypt (2:10; 3:1; 9:7). The book also refers to a pestilence of Egypt (4:10; *deber bederek mitsrayim*, literally, "a pestilence in the way/on the road of Egypt"), although it does not connect it to the exodus story and mentions no other details of that story. Hosea also speaks of Israel coming up from Egypt in its youth (2:15; 8:13; 9:3; 11:1). The only details it adds are that it was a prophet who led them out (12:13), and that the Lord knew them in the wilderness (13:4-6). The "prophet" is commonly assumed to be Moses, but since the only clear connections of Moses to the exodus tradition come from later, there is no reason to believe Hosea had Moses in mind. In Isaiah, two possible pre-exilic references are 10:24-27 and 11:11-16. In both, a parallel is drawn between God rescuing the people from the Assyrians in the future and God rescuing them from Egypt in the past. A divine intervention at the sea and a return from a place of exile are mentioned, but as in Amos and Hosea, Moses is never mentioned. Of course, one can speculate that the prophets knew the whole story but had no need to repeat any of it. Still, by themselves, all the books tell us is that there was a tradition of Israelites coming from Egypt, and it was sometimes connected with an event at the sea.

The Deuteronomic History (Joshua through 2 Kings), parts of which were written late in the monarchy, does mention Moses and an exodus event several times, but rarely together. Moses is almost always mentioned as the giver of laws (e.g., Josh 8:30-35; Judg 3:4; 1 Kgs 2:1-3), and, in the Book of Joshua, as Joshua's predecessor (Josh 1). He is mentioned in passing in Judges 4:11, where his father-in-law is identified as Hobab, a Kenite, contrary to the Pentateuch (except for Num 10:29), where his father-in-law is a Midianite named either Jethro or Reuel. In addition, there is one reference to the bronze serpent Moses made (2 Kgs 18:4; cf. Num 21:4-9). The Deuteronomic History also says several times that God brought Israel up from oppression in Egypt (e.g., Judg 2:1, 12; 1 Sam 2:27; 1 Kgs 6:1). Significantly, there are only three places in the Deuteronomic History where Moses and an exodus from Egypt are connected, and each of these—Joshua 24, 1 Samuel 12, and 1 Kings 8—is clearly part of the late expansion of the Deuteronomic History. There were traditions about a person Moses during the monarchy, and traditions about an exodus from Egypt during the monarchy, but the references to them in the Deuteronomic History suggest that making Moses the leader of the exodus story was a late development. This does not mean that there was ever a fully developed exodus story without Moses, just that the earliest, briefly expressed tradition that Israelites had come out of oppression in Egypt was not connected to Moses.

One other possible pre-exilic reference to an exodus event is Micah 6:4-5 (Mic 7:15 also refers to the exodus story, but is in a section that was almost certainly added after the fall of Judah). If this passage is in fact from the time of the prophet, at the end of the eighth century, it would be the only one of the prophetic references that mentions Moses, Aaron, and Miriam in connection with the exodus. However, the victory hymn in Exodus 15, all of the other prophetic references, and the Deuteronomic History apart from its late additions, are consistent in not connecting Moses with an exodus event. The consistency of the other references makes it likely that Micah 6:4-5 is a late addition to that book, although it is possible that it represents the earliest connection of Moses to the exodus.

If, as seen above, a historical exodus event could have involved only a minority of the people who became Israelites, why did the exodus tradition expand into such a developed story, and eventually become accepted as the foundational story for everyone? There are several possibilities. During the monarchy their story would have been appealing to the other groups, since the ancestors of most of the others had been under Egyptian rule. Descendants of the exodus group may have become the political and religious rulers during the monarchy and made their story the national story. And by the time the Pentateuch was being finished, the story fit the needs of those who were shaping Judaism's future. It made an ideal metaphor for a return from exile (cf. Is 43:14-21), and it depicted Egypt as an evil place, in line with those who wanted the Babylonian Jewish community rather than Jews who had fled to Egypt to be the ones to define their faith (cf. Jer 42). The exodus story, whatever history was behind it, became the paradigmatic story that the authors of the Pentateuch used to rebuild Judaism after the exile.[15]

Oppression (Exodus 1)

The opening chapter of Exodus connects the Ancestral Narrative to the Moses and exodus story. It is, necessarily, somewhat vague, since these traditions were not originally part of one story. It does not say how much time has passed (see the comment on Ex 12:40 below), or who the new king is, and while the cities it mentions may correspond to real Egyptian cities, they cannot be positively identified. Because it is connecting various traditions and using folkloric elements, some of the details do not seem logical. Killing the male children is not consistent with fearing that the slave labor force will leave the country, but simply sets the stage for the legend of Moses' birth.

Some have speculated that the "new king...who did not know Joseph" is based on a historical event, the expulsion of the Hyksos from Egypt, around 1540 BCE. That, however, would put the exodus much earlier than it could have occurred. The king's turning against the Israelites is necessary to get the story started, and it also sends the message that when Joseph brought the family to Egypt he was accomplishing only a short-term rescue from the famine. In the long term, going to Egypt leads to trouble, a message we see in other exilic literature as well (Jer 42–44).

Moses and His Mission (Exodus 2–6)

The stories of Moses' birth, his life in Midian, and the beginning of his mission are packed with folklore, theological reflection, and traditions about groups within and related to Israel. Although the events described are not historical, the stories raise historical questions about the development of Israelite religion, including the understanding of the name Yahweh, the emphasis on Yahweh's role as a liberator, the role of a person Moses in early Israelite religion, and possible Midianite influence in early Israelite religion.

Exodus 2. The motif of the exposed baby is a common one in stories of heroes. The similarity to the legend of Sargon has been mentioned above, although it need not imply direct dependence. Here, the threat to the child Moses is made part of the oppression of the Israelites, but it is not a perfect fit—a king wouldn't want to kill off his slave population, and in any case it disappears from the story after this. The fact that the Moses story and the oppression traditions do not fit together well is a further indication that a Moses legend and a tradition of oppression in Egypt were originally separate.

The Birth of Sargon

The story of King Sargon is a typical story of a child exposed at birth who grows up to become a great leader. The story of Moses' birth (Ex 2) is similar in several details. This needn't imply a direct dependence; it may simply mean that the author of Exodus 2 used commonly known literary elements.

Sargon, the mighty king, king of Agade am I.

My mother, the high priestess, conceived me, in secret she bore me.
She set me in a basket of rushes, with bitumen she sealed my lid.
She cast me into the river which rose not over me.
The river bore me up and carried me to Akki, the drawer of water.
Akki, the drawer of water, lifted me out as he dipped his ewer.
Akki, the drawer of water, took me as his son and reared me.
Akki, the drawer of water, appointed me as his gardener.
While I was a gardener, Ishtar granted me her love,   *king*
and for four and … years I exercised kingship.

(ANET 119; lines 1, 5-13)

The story is told with a great deal of irony—Moses' mother saving him by literally following the king's order to throw him into the river, the king's daughter rescuing Moses and paying his own mother to nurse him—which not only makes it more entertaining, but also shows the theological reflection that went into the story. The evil king is defeated by ironic outcomes, not by visible divine intervention. Indeed, God is not even mentioned in this part of the story. The God who is not visible but who nonetheless controls events in indirect ways is found in other postexilic Jewish literature, such as Esther, addressed to Jews under foreign rule and without visible signs of their God. *Also Joseph story*

Moses' father-in-law is called Reuel when he first appears (Ex 2:18), but in other places is called Jethro (Ex 3:1; 4:18; etc.) or Hobab

(Num 10:29; Judg 4:11—where he is a Kenite). According to the documentary hypothesis, the multiple names can be explained by different sources using different names—Jethro in the Elohist and Reuel or Hobab in the Yahwist. Whether that is correct or not, the ultimate explanation for these multiple names is that as Israelite religion developed and Moses became a central figure, more groups within Israel claimed that their ancestor had a connection to him. As in other places in the Pentateuch, the author has not eliminated the inconsistencies, but has acknowledged the existence of several claims.

Exodus 3–4. The call of Moses is similar to the calls of prophets and other biblical heroes (cf. Jer 1:4-10; Judg 6:11-18). The similarity raises the question of Deuteronomic influence on the passage, and may be an example of the D source being responsible for parts of the Pentateuch outside of Deuteronomy. Or, as Van Seters argues, the exilic Yahwist author was drawing on the previously written Deuteronomic History and prophetic books.[16] The passage is also key to more traditional uses of the documentary hypothesis, especially regarding the Elohist source. Source critics usually see this passage as a combination of J and E, although they disagree on which verses came from which source.[17] One of the most obvious differences between the Elohist and Yahwist sources was that the Yahwist called God Yahweh from the beginning, but the Elohist called God Yahweh only after this revelation to Moses, having used Elohim before. But God is still called Elohim hundreds of times in the Pentateuch after this passage, which lessens its impact in differentiating the sources.

Like many people called by God, Moses objects at first. One of these objections is about God's name, in 3:13-15.

> But Moses said to God, "If I come to the Israelites and say to them, 'The God of your ancestors has sent me to you,' and they ask me, 'What is his name?' what shall I say to them?" God said to Moses, "I am who I am." He said further, "Thus you shall say to the Israelites, 'I am has sent me to you.'" God also said to Moses, "Thus you shall say to the Israelites, 'The LORD, the God of your ancestors, the God of Abraham, the God of Isaac, and the God of Jacob, has sent me to you':
> This is my name forever,
> and this is my title for all generations."

The words translated, "I am who I am," read in Hebrew, *ehyeh asher ehyeh* (*ehyeh* = I am or I will be; *asher* = who, which, or what). It can be read as a refusal to give a name, as an affirmation of God's presence, and as an explanation for the origin of the name Yahweh (the interpretations are not mutually exclusive). In biblical times the name of a person carried great power, and knowing the name meant knowing the essence of a person. Divine beings may refuse to reveal their names, since no human can truly know a divine being (e.g., the angel who announces Samson's birth in Judg 13:17-18). God is thus telling Moses here that he must be satisfied not knowing who God is.

At the same time, the encounter emphasizes that God has always been present for the ancestors of the Israelites, and will continue to be present by rescuing the Israelites from slavery. Therefore the name "I am" can be taken as an affirmation that God is the one who is always present.

The pronunciation "Yahweh" is actually a scholarly reconstruction. In the original Hebrew text of the Bible, only consonants were written, so the name was written *yhwh*. It was not until the fifth century CE and later that vowels were added to the Hebrew text, and by that time there was a long custom of not pronouncing the name, as a way of acknowledging that the name is not like human names. Instead, "Adonai" (LORD) was substituted. Hebrew texts retained the consonants *yhwh*, but inserted the vowels of Adonai to remind the reader to say the latter. Thus the original pronunciation of the name was lost. The reconstructed pronunciation of Yahweh is fairly certain, as it fits the pattern of other Hebrew names and words. (The name "Jehovah," used by some, developed out of a mistaken reading of the consonants of *yhwh* with the vowels of Adonai, as if it were a single word.)

The phrase *ehyeh asher ehyeh*, of course, is not identical to the name Yahweh, but linguists believe there may be a genuine connection. The word *ehyeh* is the first person singular imperfect of the verb "to be," and can mean "I am" or "I will be." Yahweh is a word that probably comes from the same verb, but at an earlier stage of the language. Based on parallels with Amorite, another ancient Semitic language, the word Yahweh would be a causative form, meaning "the one who causes to be/creates."[18]

This tradition of the name Yahweh being revealed in the mountains around Midian raises the question of where and when worship of Yahweh began. There are indications that a god Yahweh was worshiped south of the Dead Sea or in the Sinai before the beginning of Israel. Egyptian texts from the fifteenth century and later often mention the nomadic Shasu groups, and sometimes refer to a group "Shasu-Yhw," along with other Shasu groups in the region south of the Dead Sea.[19] This may indicate that some of the Shasu worshiped a Yahweh at least three centuries earlier than Israel emerged in the land of Canaan. The Pentateuch also preserves a tradition of Moses' Midianite father-in-law offering sacrifice to Yahweh (Ex 18:12), and there are early poetic passages that depict the Israelites' God as a divine warrior coming from Seir, Mt. Paran, Edom, or Teman, all places south of the Dead Sea (Dt 33:2; Judg 5:4-5; Hab 3:3). The location of Sinai itself is disputed (see chapter 6), but it may well have been considered a place south of the Dead Sea rather than where it has been traditionally located in the Sinai peninsula. The evidence is suggestive of Yahwism originating among desert people south of what later became Israel and Judah, but as yet there is no definitive proof.

The earliest use of the name Yahweh for a god is not known, but it is well-attested for the Israelite God in the earliest available evidence. It is used in early biblical poetry, such as Exodus 15 and Judges 5. It is used by Israel's neighbors: the ninth-century Moabite stone refers to Moab defeating an Israelite city in battle, saying, "I took from there the vessels of Yahweh."[20] It is true that the Israelites did not worship Yahweh exclusively until after the exile, but the evidence shows that from an early date Yahweh was their chief god.

Besides his concern about the divine name, another of Moses' objections is that he is not able to speak well, and this provides an opportunity to introduce Aaron, his brother and spokesperson, into the story. Aaron's role is ambiguous in the Pentateuch. At times he is portrayed positively, as Moses' helper and, in passages traditionally assigned to the Priestly source, as the first in the line of priests for the nation (e.g. Ex 28–30). But there are also stories that are hostile to him, such as that of the golden calf in Exodus 32 and his opposition to Moses in Numbers 12. The various materials may reflect rivalries among different groups of religious leaders in later history.

Despite his objections, Moses does return to Egypt to take up his mission. There is a curious incident on the way, though, when God tries to kill him, and relents only when Moses' wife Zipporah circumcises *good*

their son, saying, "A bridegroom of blood by circumcision" (4:24-26). This may be a fragment of a story about circumcision originating in the Midianite desert, perhaps as part of the traditions of Yahwism originating somewhere in the south. It may preserve an old custom of circumcision being done before marriage, rather than eight days after birth (Gen 17). "A bridegroom of blood" would thus denote a male who is qualified for marriage, and the placement of the incident here would make some sense if the son Gershom is now going to be among Hebrews and is presumably of marriageable age by now (although a later story, Ex 18:1-4, has Zipporah and Gershom staying in Midian during Moses' return to Egypt).

Exodus 5. Moses and Aaron's first efforts to free the Israelites end in failure. Not only does the pharaoh refuse to let them leave, but the Israelites themselves turn against Moses and Aaron when the pharaoh imposes harsher conditions on them. The theme of reluctance to leave is a constant one in Exodus, with the idea that even though things may be bad, trying to leave will just make the situation worse. The message is addressed to Jews of the Babylonian exile who were reluctant to return to Judah. The message of liberation recognizes that one of the obstacles to liberation is people's unwillingness to leave behind the status quo.

Exodus 6. The beginning of chapter 6 ties together the exodus story and the revelation of the name of Yahweh with the Ancestral Narrative. The author occasionally provides summaries like this to bring out the larger story line of the promises to Abraham. It is noteworthy that the author does not hesitate to contradict other parts of the story—the claim that the earlier ancestors did not know the name Yahweh ignores the fact that in Genesis God does tell them the name (Gen 15:7), and numerous times they do call God Yahweh (Gen 14:22; 15:2, 8; 16:5; etc.). One can try to explain away contradictions like this, but the simple fact is that internal consistency was not the highest priority for the final author. In this case, a higher priority was to emphasize the new revelation of Yahweh, the God of the southern desert who liberates the oppressed.

The genealogy provides a pause in the narrative before the plagues against Egypt. Like other biblical genealogies, its purpose is to address later political, social, or religious circumstances. And, like other genealogies, it does not fit perfectly into the narrative. In this geneal-

i.e., sources,

editor

ogy, Aaron and Moses are only in the third generation after the descent to Egypt, which is far less time than other parts of the story assume; according to Exodus 12:40, 430 years passed from the time of the descent until the exodus.

The beginning of this genealogy is almost identical to the list in Genesis 46 of Jacob's descendants who went to Egypt, but with Levi it proceeds to several generations of his descendants and never returns to the rest of Jacob's sons. The focus is on the line of Aaron (Moses is barely mentioned), indicating that the genealogy comes from a Priestly tradition which considered Aaron's leadership most important.

One other name that gets attention is Korah, claimed to be a cousin of Aaron and Moses. This Korah shows up several other places, in the Bible and elsewhere. In Numbers 16 he leads a revolt against Moses and Aaron, and God punishes him by opening up the earth and swallowing him and his followers. Numbers 26:11, however, points out that the "sons of Korah" did not die in that incident. More positively, several psalms are entitled "of the Korahites" (Pss 42; 44–49; 84; 85; 87). Archaeological findings provide further evidence of a religious group by that name operating in southern Judah; at a temple at Arad during the monarchy there was an inscription with the name "sons of Korah."[21] The name Korah is also listed as an Edomite clan (Gen 36:14, 16, 18), suggesting that the Korahites are another case of the blending of Edomite and Judahite people and religion in southern Judah. The negative stories about Korah stem from late in the monarchy or the exile when one official priesthood developed and tried to eliminate rival groups. *probably*

The Signs against Egypt (Exodus 7–11)

Moses and Aaron's first audience with Pharaoh has ended in failure, and now begins a long series of meetings in which they repeat their request to leave the country, and Pharaoh continues to refuse. But now at each meeting a sign occurs, meant to show Pharaoh the power of Yahweh and convince him that it is useless to resist. The cycle of meetings and signs is told in a repetitive style, which builds tension for the anticipated moment when Pharaoh will finally break. *oral storytelling*

The signs have traditionally been called plagues, although that is not the word Exodus itself usually uses (the places in which Exodus does use words meaning plague are 9:14, which uses *maggepah*, "blow," and 11:1, which uses *nega*, "plague"). The story introduces them as "signs and wonders" (7:3, 9), which include not just the traditional plagues but also the changing of the staff into a serpent. In analyzing the signs and plagues, it is useful to consider the serpent incident as part of the other signs.

The question of whether the signs and plagues were historical events has already been touched on in a general way. The exodus story as a whole developed late in the monarchy, at the earliest, and if it is based on a historical event it is much exaggerated. No Egyptian source mentions any series of signs resembling these, and there is no indirect evidence of the kinds of catastrophes that these would have caused.

Those who argue for some historical basis to the plagues point out that they are similar to natural phenomena in Egypt: sediment can turn the Nile a reddish color that may look like blood, locusts could be a problem throughout the ancient Near East, etc. Hoffmeier goes further, and says that the first six follow a natural order. The river turning red and killing the fish would drive the frogs away to the land; after that it would cause the gnats and flies to increase; their increase would bring disease to the cattle and kill them; and these same insects would then bite the humans and cause the boils. The remaining plagues would not be directly caused by the first, but the darkness would be affected: it could be caused by a natural sandstorm, but in this case the sandstorm would be much worse than a normal one because of the previous destruction, making the darkness all the darker.[22]

There are several problems with such an approach. Rationalizing the text in order to prove that it could be historically accurate ends up ignoring the plain sense of the text. The story does not describe the plagues all happening as one continuous event, but as discrete events, each one beginning only when Moses and Aaron say so. It also ignores the scale (e.g., even the water in vessels turns to blood) and selectivity (the Israelites are not affected by them) of the plagues. Those who seek to explain the plagues with a natural phenomenon approach may acknowledge there is some exaggeration in the story, but even if the plagues occurred on a more modest scale, if all of them occurred around the same time the impact would have been so devastating that there would be some other evidence of it.

A better explanation is that the author had some familiarity with Egyptian natural phenomena (which would have been the case at any point in Israelite and Jewish history), and combined that with imagery chosen for its symbolic significance. All of the signs use imagery of judgment, but in the first seven signs (counting the serpent) there is also an association with ritual impurity. The next three do not refer to impurity, but use judgment and apocalyptic imagery. The final, the death of the firstborn, is a symbolic forced sacrifice to avert the afflictions (see next page, "The Plagues against Egypt"). This scheme of seven signs of impurity, followed by three signs of judgment, followed by child sacrifice does not overshadow the more general picture of all of the signs being about Yahweh's power and a judgment on the Egyptians. Rather, it is another layer the final author has included to show Egypt as a defiled and condemned place, where even the child sacrifice is not effective (it will be followed by the defeat at the sea).

When and how the sign and plague tradition developed is a difficult question, but there are some indications. Amos 4:10 refers to a pestilence in Egypt, but, as discussed above, it is not necessarily a reference to this story. Similarly, Deuteronomy refers to "diseases of Egypt," but these afflicted Israel as well as Egypt, while the plagues of this story afflict only Egypt (Dt 7:15; 28:60). There are other references to God bringing Israel out of Egypt with "signs and wonders" (Jer 32:20-21; Dt 4:34). These indicate the story was taking more shape; influenced by the pestilence and disease ideas, a series of plagues became part of the expanded story.

Once a story of a series of signs and plagues developed, how was it expressed in written form? Besides Exodus, two other written versions have survived, Psalms 78 and 105. These have fewer and different plagues, and in a different order (e.g., Ps 78 has a plague of frost; Ps 105 has the darkness first). The differences are sometimes dismissed as poetic license, but that misses the point. As the story developed it was seen as something that *could* be varied by poetic license, unlike, for example, an archival record of the reigns of kings. Even in biblical times the story was not treated as a historical record, which meant the authors of the Pentateuch felt free to shape it as they wished.

The documentary hypothesis can be used to explain the development of the Pentateuch's version of the plagues. Typically, source critics posit a Yahwist version, combined with a more fragmentary Elohist version, which was then expanded by a Priestly version. The Yahwist would emphasize the role of Moses and have him issue a threat, which God would carry out; an example of a Yahwist sign would be the death of the cattle (9:1-7). The Priestly source would give Aaron a prominent role,

The Plagues against Egypt

Seven Signs of Impurity

Staff becomes Serpent	Ex 7:8-13	cf. Lev 11:42
Water becomes Blood	Ex 7:14-25	cf. Lev 15:19-33; 17:10-13
Dead Frogs	Ex 8:1-15 (Heb 7:26–8:11)	cf. Lev 11:39-40; Dt 14:21
Gnats	Ex 8:16-19 (Heb 8:12-15)	cf. Lev 11:20-23
Flies	Ex 8:20-32 (Heb 8:16-26)	cf. Lev 11:20-23
Death of Livestock	Ex 9:1-7	cf. Lev 11:39-40; Dt 14:21
Skin Disease	Ex 9:8-12	cf. Lev 13–14

Three Signs of Judgment

Hail and Fire	Ex 9:13-35	cf. Is 28:2,17; 29:6; Joel 2:3, 30; etc.
Locusts	Ex 10:1-20	cf. Joel 1:4; Am 7:1-2
Darkness	Ex 10:21-29	cf. Ezek 32:7-8; Am 5:18-20; Joel 2:31; *Balaam Text*

A Forced Child Sacrifice

Death of the Firstborn	Ex 11; 12:29-30	cf. 2 Kgs 3:27; *Balaam Text*

include a contest with the Egyptian magicians, and have Moses and/or Aaron do some action to cause the sign; an example of a Priestly sign would be the gnats (8:16-19). Several signs would include elements from more than one source, and, as in other applications of the documentary hypothesis, scholars disagree on the details of what came from what source.

Other critics use variations of the documentary hypothesis. Propp sees the Elohist, not the Yahwist, as responsible for most of the non-Priestly material.[23] Whybray does not deny the existence of sources, but sees the final version as primarily the work of one author, and the differences among the signs as intentional stylistic variations.[24] There is no doubt that multiple written versions did exist (we know that from Pss 78 and 105), but there will continue to be debate about the traces that remain of them. And whatever sources may have been used, the final author applied a great deal of creativity in arranging them, especially in the grouping of the seven signs of impurity and the three signs of judgment.

Exodus 7:1-13. The signs begin with general instructions from God about the "signs and wonders," followed by the first sign, Aaron changing his staff into a serpent. This first sign also begins the contest with the Egyptian magicians—they are able to duplicate the trick, but Aaron's serpent swallows up theirs, foreshadowing his ultimate victory. The association with impurity also begins here, since serpents are unclean, along with all things that crawl on their belly (Lev 11:42).

The story has been vague about how much time has passed, but now we are told that Moses is eighty years old and Aaron is eighty-three. That may seem surprisingly old, but the numbers were artificially created to make Moses 120 at the time of his death, at the end of the forty-year journey through the wilderness (Dt 34:7). Moses' lifespan of 120 years fits the limit set in Genesis 6:3, but Aaron will surpass the limit, living to 123 (Num 33:39).

Exodus 7:14-25. The changing of the water into blood continues the theme of the defilement of Egypt. The mere presence of blood does not cause impurity, but eating the blood of an animal makes a person unclean (Lev 17:10-16), so the detail that it was even in the vessels makes this a cause of impurity. The contest with the Egyptian magicians continues, leading to a possible inconsistency—how could the magicians turn water into blood if Moses had already done it to all of the water? A common explanation is that there were two versions of this plague, one in which Moses turned all the water red (7:19) and one in which he just turned the Nile red (7:20-21). Another explanation is that the magicians turned to red the water for which people had dug in the ground after Moses' action. In any case, it shows that the final author was not concerned about such details, because the story was not understood as a historical record.

Exodus 8:1-15 (7:26–8:11 in the Hebrew text). The plague of frogs may seem more humorous than threatening, but it continues the theme of the series. The contest with the Egyptian magicians is still equal— they are able to call up frogs as well. And the frogs cause impurity by leaving behind their dead carcasses (Lev 11:39-40). It is uncertain if the author considered frogs themselves unclean. Later Jewish tradition did not (*Mishnah Tohoroth* 5:1,4), but at the time the Pentateuch was composed they may have been considered among the creatures that live in the water but do not have fins or scales, which were unclean (Lev 11:9-12). In any case, by including the detail that their carcasses were left behind—a detail not mentioned for gnats, flies, or locusts—the author makes this into a sign of impurity.

Exodus 8:16-19 (8:12-15 in the Hebrew text). The Hebrew word *kinnim* is usually translated gnats, although it might refer to mosquitoes or even lice. It is probably meant as a general word for small annoying flying insects. This time the Egyptian magicians are unable to duplicate the sign, meaning that the contest has taken a turn and will soon come to an end. The impurity continues, as winged insects, with a few exceptions, were considered unclean (Lev 11:20-23).

Exodus 8:20-32 (8:16-20 in the Hebrew text). The plague of flies is not much different from the plague of gnats; Psalm 105:31 treats them as a single plague. But here some new elements are introduced. As a reason the Israelites must leave, Moses claims that their sacrifices would be offensive to the Egyptians, who would stone them. The remark is probably aimed at postexilic Jews who needed to be persuaded to return to Judah. The author is reminding them of the hostility they occasionally faced from the foreigners among whom they lived. Also unusual is Pharaoh's request, "Pray for me." It is an ambiguous request. It may be part of an insincere attempt to make Moses think he has relented, or the author may be suggesting the motif of the foreign king who is at first an enemy but then becomes convinced of the power of Yahweh, a motif that was popular in postexilic tales such as Esther and Daniel 1–6.

Exodus 9:1-7. The death of the livestock causes more defilement, like the dead frogs. The claim that "all" the livestock died (9:6) may seem to contradict later parts of the story, where some are still around (9:20; 11:5), but is probably just an example of hyperbole. The inclusion of camels is anachronistic, and another indication of the late date of the story's composition.

Exodus 9:8-12. With the plague of skin disease, the contest with the Egyptian magicians ends. Not only do they not duplicate the sign, but they themselves are afflicted. The Hebrew word *shehin* is traditionally translated "boil," although words for skin diseases are not always precise in the Bible. In Leviticus, a single *shehin* is not necessarily impure, but if the priest judges that it is spreading, it is impure (Lev 13:18-23). Here, the author uses the same word (*prh*, "spreading") as Leviticus does for the impure kind of boil. Like the blood and the frogs, the sign is not intrinsically impure, but the author has made it so by including a key detail.

This will be the last of the signs associated with impurity. After seven such signs Egypt is fully defiled, and even though these signs did not strike the Israelites, it is still an unfit place for them to live. From this point on, the emphasis will be on the judgment against Egypt.

Exodus 9:13-35. The next sign is introduced with a longer speech from Yahweh, warning of plagues more intense than the previous ones. A new word is also used to describe them—*maggepah*, "blow, plague." Violent hailstorms are rare in Egypt. If the author was aware of that fact, he may have intended this plague to be all the more terrifying because of its unfamiliarity. The mention of fire (9:23, 24) makes this more than a bad storm; it is now described with the language of divine judgment. The prophets use thunder, hail, and fire to describe God's judgment (Is 28:2, 17; 29:6; Joel 2:3, 30). The imagery of this plague, and that of the next two, makes it clear that the time of Egypt's judgment is at hand.

Exodus 10:1-20. Locust plagues occurred throughout the ancient Near East, causing devastation over wide areas. Invading armies were compared to locusts (Judg 6:5; 7:12), and prophets used the image for God's judgment (Joel 1:4; Am 7:1-2). Unlike most insects, locusts were not considered unclean (Lev 11:22), so the symbolism here is strictly about the judgment against Egypt.

Exodus 10:21-29. Those who seek a naturalistic explanation for the plagues usually use a sandstorm to explain the darkness,[25] although if that were the case one would expect the sandstorm itself to be the plague. More likely, the author uses darkness because it was so frequently associated with the day of the Lord and divine judgment (Ezek 32:7-8; Am 5:18-20; Joel 2:31).

The *Balaam Text*, a seventh-century BCE text discovered in 1967 at Deir Alla, east of the Jordan River, also uses a plague of darkness for the gods punishing people.[26] The text is significant because of its connections to the Hebrew Scriptures. The prophet whom the gods summon to discuss the darkness is Balaam son of Beor, the same character who is unable to curse the Israelites in Numbers 22–24 and is mentioned several other places in the Bible (Neh 13:2; Mic 6:5; Rev 2:14). The gods are called *shaddayyin*, a plural form of one of the biblical names for God, Shaddai (Gen 17:1; Ex 6:3; Num 24:4, 16; Job 5:17). Although there is some uncertainty because of the fragmentary state of the text, in the *Balaam Text* the plague of darkness is apparently ended by a child sacrifice, similar to the darkness of the last plague being followed by the forced child sacrifices of the Egyptians. Of course, it is not possible to know if the authors of the Pentateuch were familiar with the story in the *Balaam Text*, but it does show that the plague story uses mythological ideas of judgment that were current in the region.

Exodus 11. The final plague, the death of the firstborn, is announced, but won't actually occur until later, at the Israelites' departure. The idea of child sacrifice averting affliction is well-known from the Bible (e.g., 2 Kgs 3:27) and elsewhere. Even though this does mark the end of the plagues, it is not the end of God's judgment on Egypt, and it is not a chosen sacrifice. But it is characteristic of the exodus story as a whole. Pharaoh has never been in control of anything—from the Hebrew midwives to his own hardness of heart that was caused by Yahweh—so it fits the logic of the story that the Egyptians' child sacrifice is not their own action that ends the disasters, but an even greater disaster being inflicted on them.

Another theme brought up here is the "despoiling of Egypt." The Israelites will receive objects of gold and silver from their Egyptian neighbors. The idea of this was introduced in Moses' original call (3:21-22), and will be accomplished at their departure (12:35-36). It is not consistent with other parts of the story, where the Israelites live separately and do not have Egyptian neighbors (8:22; 9:26). It is also hard to understand why Egyptians would give away wealth to escaping slaves. This addition may have been connected with later parts of the story, where jewelry is necessary (e.g., the golden calf in Ex 32), or may have been influenced by the fact that returning exiles had more wealth than Jews who had stayed in Judah after the Babylonian conquest (Ezra 1:2-4; Neh 5:1-13).[27] The way the author has incorporated it into the story emphasizes Yahweh's complete control over the Egyptians.

The plagues against Egypt are not finished, but the story takes a turn here to introduce the Passover ritual. The signs and wonders have demonstrated Yahweh's control over the forces of nature and over Pharaoh and Egypt. This examination of them shows that, while they have some similarity to natural phenomena, they are not presented as historical occurrences, but as a symbolic demonstration of Yahweh's power, borrowing imagery from the prophets and from the developing rules of ritual impurity. This part of the story probably began to take shape late in the monarchy, when prophetic announcements of judgment and stories like that in the *Balaam Text* were popular. The theme of impurity in the first seven signs was added. As can be seen in the stories of the blood, frogs, and boils, the impurity is not intrinsic, but is brought out only by including certain details. In the other written versions of the plagues, Pss 78 and 105, the impurity theme is absent. In the postexilic period, when notions of purity and separation from the impure became more important for Jews struggling to preserve their identity, the author added the impurity theme to the plague story to depict Egypt as a defiled place, unfit for Jews to live in.

The Departure and Passover (Exodus 12:1–13:16)

At what we might expect to be the climax of the story—the Israelites preparing to leave and Moses threatening the devastating plague of the death of the firstborn of all Egyptians—there is a pause, with detailed instructions on how this event is to be carried out and how it is to be commemorated in the future. All along, the exodus story has been told in a way that is very unlike historical records, but now it becomes even more so, and directly discusses the rituals that would unify the exilic Jewish community. First, there are instructions on selecting, slaughtering, roasting, and eating a lamb or kid, with exact dates and method of cooking, and instructions to splash its blood on the doorposts of their houses, as a sign to God to pass over their houses and strike dead only the firstborn of the Egyptians. Then, there are instructions on eating unleavened bread for seven days. The Israelites follow the instructions, God kills the firstborn of the Egyptians, and the Israelites depart and begin their journey through the wilderness. God gives further instructions on commemorating the event in the future, along with instructions on sacrificing the firstborn male of all livestock.

There has been a broad consensus among scholars that the Passover and Unleavened Bread were originally two separate festivals. The Passover had its roots in springtime rituals of seminomadic shepherds, celebrating the birth of new lambs and warding off danger during the move to new pastures. Spring is a time of new life but also of danger, so the sacrifice of a lamb or kid both expresses gratitude to God and seeks protection from the "destroyer" who would kill the young and vulnerable. The Unleavened Bread, in contrast, is believed to have been an agricultural festival of settled groups in pre-Israelite Canaan, marking the new barley harvest. The bread without leaven marks the end of the old and the beginning of a new, purified year. According to this theory, these two festivals were combined as the different groups joined together to form the nation Israel.

This reconstruction of the development of Passover has not gone unchallenged. Van Seters questions the antiquity of the tradition. He argues that the ritual of putting blood on the doorposts among ancient nomadic tribes was appropriate only for settling at a new place, not for departing from an old place. Furthermore, the description of the blood ritual is actually derived from rituals in exilic priestly circles, such as the one in Ezekiel 45:18-25, which instructs splashing blood on the temple doorposts in preparation for celebrating the Passover.[28]

An additional development was centralizing the Passover celebration in Jerusalem. While Exodus treats it as a family celebration in individual households, the instructions in Deuteronomy 16 treat it as a pilgrimage festival at one central location. The change was related to King Josiah's centralizing religious reform late in the seventh century (2 Kgs 22–23). The Pentateuch preserves both versions in what can be called a constructive ambiguity, for it allows an ideal view of a strong, Jerusalem-centered religion, and the practical need for a scattered people practicing a household-centered religion.

One element in the text, the exact dates for celebrating the Passover, is clearly postexilic. A letter written to an Egyptian Jewish community in 491 BCE gives instructions on when to celebrate the Passover.[29] The letter reveals that there was no fixed tradition for the date of Passover that scattered Jews would have known about. It also reveals a desire to unify, by common rituals, Jews living in different places. Postexilic Jewish leaders used the Pentateuch, religious rituals, and other means to preserve the identity of a people who no longer had their own nation.

In addition to the other developments, at some point the feast became connected to the exodus event, although it is impossible to say exactly when. Late in the monarchy and during the exile, as the exodus story took on a more prominent place in the community's self-identity, it would have been natural to celebrate it in some way. Passover emerged as the way to celebrate the exodus, perhaps because there was already a tradition of the exodus taking place in the spring, or perhaps because some details of the celebration—unleavened bread, bitter herbs—fit well in a story of hasty departure.

Exodus 12. The instructions for the Passover and departure from Egypt are told in a solemn and dramatic way, and it is obvious the author used a great deal of literary skill in constructing this part of the story. Nonetheless, most scholars see evidence of at least two sources being combined here. Typically, the initial instructions God gives Moses are attributed to the Priestly source, with the repetitions and additional information attributed to the Yahwist, Elohist, or Deuteronomist.[30] Concern with ritual is characteristic of the Priestly source, so significant contributions from priestly circles is likely, even if there is no agreement on the details.

Another concern of priestly circles was the liturgical calendar. The Passover is to be celebrated in the first month of the year, in the spring. There is evidence that earlier in Israelite history the new year began in the fall. A tenth century BCE agricultural calendar discovered at Gezer lists the months, beginning with fall,[31] and the liturgical instructions in Exodus 23:14-17 and 34:18-23 describe the fall ingathering festival as occurring at the turn of the year. But by the time of the exile this was replaced by a calendar with the year beginning in the spring (e.g., in Jer 36:22 the ninth month is in the winter). Also, the old Canaanite names (Abib for the spring month) were replaced by ordinal numbers and eventually Babylonian names (Nisan for Abib). The emphasis here on this being the first month may indicate that it was still a recent innovation.[32]

The number of people who depart from Egypt, six hundred thousand men, plus women, children, and a mixed crowd, is of course an exaggeration. If an exodus did occur it would have been a very small group, but later tradition wanted to create a unified identity for the people, which included the claim that all of Israel had the same origins. The number may have some symbolic significance (twelve tribes, times fifty thousand men per tribe) but mainly it is just meant to be a large number that could be a whole nation.

The number of years the Israelites are said to have been in Egypt, 430, is not consistent with other parts of the story. Moses and Aaron were supposedly only the third generation after Jacob's family came down to Egypt (Ex 6:16-20). Earlier, God had told Abraham that his descendants would be oppressed in Egypt for four hundred years (Gen 15:13), which could be consistent if there were only thirty years of not being oppressed, but the beginning of Exodus gives the impression of a much longer period of time before the oppression began. Clearly the author and readers were aware that these numbers were artificial, and were not concerned with the lack of consistency.

Exodus 13:1-16. Instructions on the dedication of the firstborn male to Yahweh are now given; this requires some explanation, since it is not part of the Passover celebration. Sacrifice of the first fruits of the harvest and firstborn livestock are frequently mentioned in the Hebrew Scriptures, and the basic idea of such sacrifices is common in many religious traditions. The biblical law in Numbers 18:15-20 states that, "The first issue of the womb of all creatures, human and animal, which is offered to the LORD" shall belong to the priests. But for humans and unclean animals, instead of actually sacrificing them, people redeem them, i.e., pay five shekels. (Note that the object of sacrifice or redemption is a female's firstborn male, rather than a male's firstborn son, which is the definition of firstborn when it comes to inheritance.) There is no connection with the exodus or Passover, but other passages do make a connection. In Numbers 3:13, Yahweh tells Moses, "When I killed all the firstborn in the land of Egypt, I consecrated for my own all the firstborn in Israel, both human and animal; they shall be mine." The liturgical instructions in Exodus 34:18-20 and Deuteronomy 15:19–16:8 put the instructions on dedication of the firstborn right after and before the instructions on Unleavened Bread and Passover, respectively, although no explicit connection is made. Now the connection is made most explicit: God killed the firstborn of the Egyptians and saved the Israelites, so as a sign of that event the Israelites are to sacrifice the firstborn male of livestock and redeem the human males.

Sacrifice of firstborn male livestock originally had nothing to do with the exodus, but as the exodus took on a more central role in Judaism, other practices were interpreted in terms of it. Including the instruction here and relating it to the exodus is thus similar to what was done with the Passover and Unleavened Bread festivals, but of course since births occur at unpredictable times it could not be made part of an annual celebration with a fixed date. The exodus adds another layer of interpretation to the sacrifice of the firstborn, and at the same time the sacrifice of the firstborn helps interpret the exodus story—it draws attention to the death of Egypt's firstborn as sacrifice, and not just punishment. *really?*

The Passover and escape bring to an end the chosen people's time in Egypt, and in time would be commemorated as a major festival in Judaism. But getting out of Egypt is only the first step for the chosen people. The journey that this escape begins will shape the chosen people into a nation, and will reveal to them who this God is who has entered their lives.

CHAPTER SIX

Exodus 13:17–40:38

Exodus 13:17–15:21 — Crossing the Sea

Exodus 15:22–18:27 — Journey to Mt. Sinai

Exodus 19–24 — The Covenant at Mt. Sinai

Exodus 25–31 — The Cult

Exodus 32–34 — The Golden Calf and Remaking the Covenant

Exodus 35–40 — Implementing the Cult

The Pentateuch's story continues with the Israelites beginning their journey, miraculously crossing the sea, reaching Mt. Sinai, and receiving the laws from God. The giving of the laws at Mt. Sinai actually continues beyond the Book of Exodus—through all of Leviticus and up to Numbers 10, when the Israelites finally depart and continue their journey through the wilderness. These laws are part of a covenant, a formalized relationship between Yahweh and the Israelites. The covenant forms the Israelites into a nation, both by establishing rules on how they are to treat each other and by establishing a relationship between them and their national god. The historical issues in this part of the story include the geography of the journey, the location of Mt. Sinai, the historical setting of particular laws, the influence of international treaties on the covenant form, and the development of traditions about Mt. Sinai and their relationship to the exodus story.

The Geography of the Journey and the Location of Mt. Sinai

In the past, scholars spent great effort trying to determine the exact route of the exodus. But despite the many place names in the text,

110

there was never any agreement on the issue. With a growing recognition that the story was written centuries after the events were supposed to have occurred and that there is little history behind it, the question has become less important. There have been recent attempts, such as those by Kenneth Kitchen and James Hoffmeier, to identify and locate the places mentioned here at the beginning of the journey, but they have been only partly successful. Succoth, for example, probably corresponds to the Egyptian Tjeku, but Tjeku was a military zone at the time the exodus is supposed to have occurred,[1] so it would make little sense for the Israelites to go there while they avoided the "way of the Philistines" because they didn't want to encounter war. The exilic author of the story may have known a few place names in Egypt, but we will never be able to draw a map of the route of the exodus.

Just as the route of the exodus cannot be determined, the exact location of Mt. Sinai is unknown. The story simply does not give enough information. The issue is also complicated by the fact that the place is occasionally called Mt. Horeb. The different names are sometimes explained by using the documentary hypothesis—that the Yahwist used Sinai and the Elohist and Deuteronomist used Horeb—but that begs the question of *why* different sources would use different names. We do not know whether Sinai and Horeb were always two different names for the same place or were originally two different places.

The traditional location of Mt. Sinai is Jebel Musa in the southern Sinai Peninsula. That identification dates only from the fourth century CE, and it is not known what it was based on. Another location that has often been suggested is somewhere in northwest Arabia. There are good reasons favoring both locations, but it should be remembered that the issue is not just where a historical event involving Moses and the laws might have occurred, but where the Bible depicts that event as occurring. If there was such a historical event, it occurred at a particular place that was at one time known. However, what we have in the Bible, even if based on some event, is a story that was influenced by multiple traditions and centuries of development, and whose authors may not have had a precise location in mind.

A reason favoring a location in the southern Sinai (either Jebel Musa or another nearby mountain) is that it would be consistent with an exodus route that goes through the southern Sinai. Although we do not know what the exact route would have been, the story reports that they avoided the "way of the land of the Philistines," and instead went

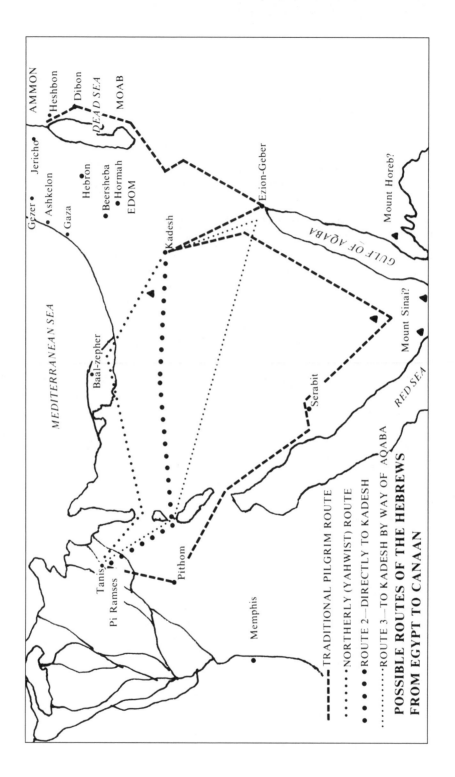

AMMON
Heshbon
Dibon
DEAD SEA
MOAB

Jericho
Gezer
Ashkelon
Gaza
Hebron
Beersheba
Hormah
EDOM

Kadesh

Ezion-Geber

Mount Horeb?

GULF OF AQABA

MEDITERRANEAN SEA

Baal-zepher

Mount Sinai?

Serabit

RED SEA

Tanis
Pi Ramses

Pithom

Memphis

----- TRADITIONAL PILGRIM ROUTE
.... NORTHERLY (YAHWIST) ROUTE
● ● ● ● ROUTE 2—DIRECTLY TO KADESH
·········· ROUTE 3—TO KADESH BY WAY OF AQABA

**POSSIBLE ROUTES OF THE HEBREWS
FROM EGYPT TO CANAAN**

through the wilderness (Ex 13:17). The implication is that they went far enough south in the wilderness to avoid Egyptian garrisons; this would have brought them near Jebel Musa. A second, admittedly weaker, reason is that there may have been an authentic basis for the eventual acceptance of this traditional location.

A location in northwest Arabia is favored by the fact that the events at Mt. Sinai take place in Midianite territory. Although Midian sometimes refers to a wide-ranging area, most of the time it refers to northwest Arabia, and there was a city there in biblical times named "Madian" (the earlier spelling of Midian). A second reason is that before the acceptance of the Jebel Musa tradition, many Jews and Christians apparently believed Mt. Sinai was in northwest Arabia, including Paul (Gal 4:25, although his meaning is disputed). Finally, in some of the early poetic texts, Sinai is associated with the mountainous region south of the Dead Sea: "The LORD came from Sinai, and dawned from Seir upon us; he shone forth from Mt. Paran" (Dt 33:2); "LORD, when you went out from Seir, when you marched from the region of Edom . . . the mountains quaked before the LORD, the One of Sinai" (Judg 5:4-5).

None of these reasons can answer the question definitively, since the geographic information given is not specific enough. And that vagueness is itself significant. God is not tied to one place, so the biblical authors were content to leave the place of this momentous meeting with God imprecise.

Laws and Covenants

From this point on, the Pentateuch, or Torah, includes several collections of laws. In chapter one it was pointed out that the word "torah," often translated "law," has a broader meaning of instruction or teaching. That obviously applies to the narrative parts of the Pentateuch, but even in the collections of laws the material is different from that in a modern law code. To be sure, some of it is made up of statements on behavior to be avoided and sanctions against those who break the law. But there is also much that goes beyond that, including general moral guidelines with no mention of punishments for not following them, liturgical instructions, dietary rules, building codes, and instructions on proper attitudes. The "laws" of the Pentateuch cover every aspect of life, and not exclusively in a legalistic way.

Influenced by Albrecht Alt, scholars often divide the laws into two types, apodictic and casuistic.[2] Apodictic laws are general statements of how to act, without concern for different circumstances or provisions for punishing violations. "You shall not murder" (Ex 20:13) is an apodictic law. Casuistic, or case laws, cover specific circumstances, and provide for remedies or punishments. An example is Exodus 22:5: "When someone causes a field or vineyard to be grazed over, or lets livestock loose to graze in someone else's field, restitution shall be made from the best in the owner's field or vineyard." Not all of the Pentateuch's laws easily fit into these categories, but they are a start in recognizing that different types of laws served different functions.

The laws of the Pentateuch developed out of the legal practices of ancient Israel. Many biblical passages refer to judgments made at city gates (Am 5:10-15; Prov 22:22; etc.); evidently people could bring their cases to respected elders stationed there. Over time legal traditions developed, and some were probably written down in early collections. In addition, other movements passed on their traditions: wisdom, on proper character and how to lead a good life; prophetic, on ethical behavior and the right relationship with God; and cultic, on worship practices. The Pentateuch brings together the laws and teachings of all these movements.

Collections of laws from other places in the ancient Near East have been discovered, revealing that Israel's laws were not unique. The most famous of these is the law code of Hammurapi, a Babylonian king of the eighteenth century BCE. These are casuistic laws, and many of them parallel biblical laws, such as laws on oxen who gore, and "eye for an eye . . . tooth for a tooth" laws (see next page, "Laws from Hammurapi's Code").[3]

While there are many parallels in individual laws, what is unique about the Pentateuch is that its laws are framed in a narrative, and the narrative is about a covenant between Yahweh and the Israelites, with the laws being the stipulations of that covenant. There were earlier covenants in the Pentateuch—with Noah, with Abraham, Isaac, and Jacob—but the Sinai covenant and the repeated version of it in Deuteronomy are far more extensive. A covenant is a formalized relationship, and can either be in the form of a unilateral promise (e.g., to

Laws from Hammurapi's Code

The casuistic laws in the Pentateuch are similar to laws from the ancient Near East. Compare the following laws from Hammurapi's Code (18th century BCE) to the laws in the Pentateuch. Note that many of the details are similar, although Hammurapi's Code makes more distinctions among classes of people in its application of the law.

If a nobleman has destroyed the eye of a member of the aristocracy, they shall destroy his eye. If he has broken another nobleman's bone, they shall break his bone. If he has destroyed the eye of a commoner or broken the bone of a commoner, he shall pay one mina of silver. If he has destroyed the eye of a nobleman's slave or broken the bone of a nobleman's slave, he shall pay one-half his value. If a nobleman has knocked out the tooth of a nobleman of his own rank, they shall knock out his tooth. (Hammurapi, 196-200; ANET 175)

> Anyone who maims another shall suffer the same injury in return: fracture for fracture, eye for eye, tooth for tooth; the injury inflicted is the injury to be suffered. (Lev 24:19-20)

> When a slaveowner strikes a male or female slave with a rod and the slave dies immediately, the owner shall be punished. But if the slave survives a day or two, there is no punishment; for the slave is the owner's property. (Ex 21:20-21)

If an ox, when it was walking along the street, gored a nobleman to death, that case is not subject to claim. If a nobleman's ox was a gorer and his city council made it known to him that it was a gorer, but he did not pad its horns or tie up his ox, and that ox gored to death a member of the aristocracy, he shall give one-half mina of silver. If it was a nobleman's slave, he shall give one-third mina of silver. (Hammurapi, 250-252; ANET 176)

> When an ox gores a man or a woman to death, the ox shall be stoned, and its flesh shall not be eaten; but the owner of the ox shall not be liable. If the ox has been accustomed to gore in the past, and its owner has been warned but has not restrained it, and it kills a man or a woman, the ox shall be stoned, and its owner also shall be put to death. (Ex 21:28-29)

Noah), or, as in this case, have obligations on both sides. In the Sinai covenant, Yahweh is to be Israel's national god and protector, and Israel is to follow these laws.

George Mendenhall and others have compared this covenant to international treaties, particularly Hittite treaties of the fourteenth and thirteenth centuries BCE, and Assyrian treaties of the eighth and seventh centuries, between powerful empires and smaller vassal states.[4] These treaties typically followed a form that included, among other elements, a review of the historical relationship between the two parties, a list of obligations on both sides, provisions for a public reading and deposit of the text, and blessing and curses for those who do or do not keep the treaty. The covenant between Yahweh and the Israelites is similar to such treaties, especially the way it is presented in Deuteronomy, and to a lesser extent here in Exodus. Many scholars object that the similarities have been overstated, but, at the very least, the way such treaties were composed had some influence on how the Israelites thought of their formal relationship with Yahweh.

The Development of the Sinai Tradition

For many decades scholars have discussed the possibility that the exodus and Sinai traditions were originally independent. One of the most influential proponents of this view was Gerhard von Rad, whose approach was to look for the earliest form of traditions in brief credal statements that were used in worship and later expanded into the biblical narratives. One such credal statement was Deuteronomy 26:5-9, which begins, "A wandering Aramean was my ancestor; he went down into Egypt and lived there as an alien, few in number, and there he became a great nation, mighty and populous." It goes on to recount their oppression, and God bringing them out with signs and wonders and bringing them to the promised land. Von Rad noted that while this recited the core of the Pentateuch's story, it did not include the giving of the laws on Mt. Sinai. Therefore, the Sinai tradition must have been a separate one, held by different groups among the tribes that became Israel. The separate traditions were then combined by the Yahwist in the tenth century.[5]

Today few would accept the entire explanation of von Rad. There is no reason to believe that Deuteronomy 26:5-9 is any older than the rest of the Pentateuch; the idea that biblical narratives are expansions of *not me* earlier credal statements is questionable; and most would date the Yah- wist later than the tenth century. Moreover, some scholars, particularly Mendenhall, claimed that the similarity to international treaties points to a unity of the exodus and Sinai traditions. The exodus story consti- tutes the historical relationship between the two parties and is the rea- son the Israelites should accept this covenant.[6] Mendenhall's approach has not convinced everyone. While the Deuteronomy version of the biblical covenant may be similar to international treaties, here in Exo- dus it is less so. And even if there was some intentional modeling after the treaties, that would most likely have been done by the final author, and does not represent an original unity of the traditions.

We saw in the previous chapter that the exodus tradition developed slowly, and that Moses' part in it probably did not develop until the late monarchy. Since Moses is primarily seen as a lawgiver, the lateness of his part in the exodus story suggests that connection of the exodus and the laws on Mt. Sinai is equally late.

If the Sinai tradition was independent of the exodus, there is still the question of when and how it developed. There are very few pre- exilic references to Sinai or Horeb. The early poetic passages men- tioned above refer to Sinai as a holy mountain of God, but do not con- nect it with law-giving or an exodus (Judg 5:5; Dt 33:2; Ps 68:8,17). In the Deuteronomic History there is the story of Elijah visiting Mt. Horeb and encountering God (1 Kgs 19:8), but again there is no men- tion of the mountain having a connection with an exodus or a giving of laws. It is not until after the exile (Neh 9:13; Ps 106:19; Mal 4:4) or in late additions to the Deuteronomic History (1 Kgs 8:9) that Sinai and Horeb are connected to an exodus and a giving of laws.

Most likely the tradition of Sinai as a holy mountain existed early in Israelite history, possibly before the monarchy, and was associated with other southern places, although the references to the mountain's loca- tion are vague. Sinai did not become a prominent tradition during the monarchy, because Mt. Zion, where the temple was located, became the most important holy mountain of God. However, since the tradition that Sinai was holy was not forgotten, it became an ideal mountain for the exilic authors of the Pentateuch to use. Being somewhere in the south it would fit into a journey from Egypt to Canaan, and being out- side the nation it showed that their covenant with Yahweh was not tied to one place.

Crossing the Sea (Exodus 13:17–15:21)

The Israelites have left Egypt, but they are not yet free, as the Pharaoh changes his mind and pursues them. Their escape reaches its climax with the crossing of the sea and the destruction of Pharaoh's army. The historical issues include the question of what "sea" they cross, and whether the miraculous parting of the sea is related to some natural phenomenon. It is helpful, though, to first look at the composition of the text.

The end of chapter 13 through chapter 14 is a prose narration of the Israelites' journey to the sea, Pharaoh's decision to pursue them, and God rescuing them by dividing the water and returning it when the Egyptian army attempts to follow. Chapter 15 poetically describes similar, but not identical, events, and is usually considered one of the most ancient pieces of writing in the Hebrew Scriptures, probably from around 1000 BCE. The mythological imagery in chapter 15 makes it impossible to say exactly what, if any, historical events it meant to describe. Exodus 13–14 historicizes the poem by fitting it into the prose narrative of the rest of the exodus events, and itself probably went through phases of composition. Many critics see a Yahwist version with a strong wind from God drying up the sea, and a Priestly version with God instructing Moses to raise his staff to separate the sea.[7]

A much debated question is what body of water the Israelites cross. Traditionally it was said to be the Red Sea, but that comes from the Septuagint, a Greek translation done around 200 BCE. The Hebrew texts calls it *yam suph*, "a sea of reeds" (Ex 13:18; 15:4, 22), although most times, and always in chapter 14, it is simply called "the sea." The Hebrew word *yam* can be used for bodies of water smaller than what the English "sea" is usually used for, and sometimes even means "river" (e.g., Is 19:5, referring to the Nile). The story never uses the definite article with *yam suph*, unlike the normal Hebrew usage when using the proper name of a body of water. To complicate things, *yam suph* is also used for the Gulf of Aqaba, on the east side of the Sinai Peninsula (1 Kgs 9:26). Most likely, in the early mythological poem in chapter 15, *yam suph* is just a description of the body of water as a marshy place, and not a proper name. The later prose version of the story just calls it "the sea" most of the time, without a precise place in mind, but repeats *yam suph* twice (13:18; 15:22) to tie it in to the older poem.

The Defeat of Egypt at the Sea

Exodus 15 is an early poem about Yahweh sending his weapon the Sea against the Egyptian army; Exodus 14 incorporates the story into the escape from slavery in Egypt. A comparison of the two shows how Exodus 14 has adapted the poem.

	Exodus 15	Exodus 14
Narrative setting	None	Escape from Egypt
Location	Near an unspecified sea	"The sea" near the Egyptian border
Sequence of events	Egyptian army attacks Israel; Yahweh sends Sea as a weapon; Egyptian army is destroyed; Philistia, Edom, Moab, and Canaan fear; Israel is given its land and sanctuary.	Israel arrives at the sea; Egyptian army pursues; Yahweh instructs Moses; Moses raises arms and divides waters; Israel crosses the sea on dry ground; Egypt pursues; Moses raises arm and waters return and cover Egypt.
Who causes	Yahweh	Yahweh and Moses

The other issue is whether an event like the crossing of the sea could have been caused by a natural phenomenon. It is well known that strong winds can temporarily dry up the marshy areas around the Gulf of Suez and the Nile delta. It is possible that a group of escaped slaves could have crossed such an area, and that soldiers following some time later could have been prevented from overtaking them by the returning waters. What we have in Exodus 14 and 15 would then be much exaggerated versions of the event. Such a scenario is not impossible, but it is also possible that the tradition stems from common mythological imagery of the sea as a force of destruction, rather than any actual event. Elsewhere in the Bible Yahweh defeats and rules over the sea, just as in Ugaritic mythology Baal defeats the sea god Yamm. Exodus 15 adapts that imagery to have Yahweh already controlling the sea, and using the sea as a weapon against Egypt, and Exodus 14 then historicizes it and makes it part of the exodus events. If there was some real event involving crossing a marshy area, the way of telling it has been so strongly shaped by the mythological imagery that it is impossible to reconstruct any such event.

Exodus 13:17-22. The "way of the land of the Philistines" refers to the road along the Mediterranean Sea, which would have been more heavily guarded than the more roundabout way through the wilderness. The longer journey is necessary for the story, since it will be during the forty years in the wilderness that Israel will be formed into a nation. At this point the author also connects the exodus story to the earlier ancestors, by having Moses bring the bones of Joseph to be buried in Canaan (cf. Gen 50:25; Josh 24:32).

Exodus 14. The prose version of the crossing of the sea locates Israel's camp "in front of Pi-hahiroth, between Migdol and the sea, in front of Baal-zephon." Unfortunately, none of these places are known with certainty. If Pi-hahiroth comes from an authentic Egyptian name, it would be "House of *hhrt*," i.e., the temple of an Egyptian goddess, but no such temple is known.[8] If it is taken as a Hebrew term, it could mean "mouth of the canals," as a descriptive term and not a proper name at all.[9] Migdol is the Hebrew word for tower, and could have been part of any number of place names. Baal-zephon is "Lord of the North," or "Lord of Mt. Zaphon," a title sometimes used for the Ugaritic god Baal, who was also known in Egypt, although no particular place with this name can be positively identified.[10] Thus, we cannot map out an exodus route from this information.

In this version of the crossing, Moses controls the water by raising his hand, and the water is divided, forming walls on either side between which the Israelites pass, and then the water returns to destroy the Egyptian army when they try to follow. These particulars are worth noting, because the poetic version in chapter 15 describes a different event at the sea.

Exodus 15:1-21. Studies several decades ago by W. F. Albright, Frank M. Cross, and David N. Freedman concluded that, based on linguistic comparisons to Ugaritic poetry, this poem dated from the twelfth or thirteenth century BCE.[11] Their linguistic arguments have been widely accepted, but many point out that the end of the poem, which speaks of Yahweh giving the people their inheritance and establishing his sanctuary, refers to the conquest of Canaan and building of the temple, and thus the poem must be from the time of Solomon at the earliest.[12] The sanctuary is not named, but it does appear to be a specific place, and could be some other early Israelite holy place (Shiloh, Gilgal, etc.).[13] An additional consideration is that the people who sing this victory song see themselves as distinct from and comparable to Philistia, Edom, Moab, and Canaan. From what we know of the emergence of Israel in Canaan, that would not have been likely before the eleventh century. Also, those who date the poem earlier must dismiss Philistia as a later anachronistic addition, but methodologically it is better not to dismiss data just because it does not fit the theory. Combining the linguistic evidence with possible historical contexts, a date around the beginning of the monarchy (tenth century BCE) is most likely.

Even though most agree that chapter 15 dates from earlier than chapter 14, and even though the fully developed exodus story dates from much later than chapter 15, there is still a tendency to read the poem through the lens of the prose version in chapter 14 and the exodus story as a whole—that was, after all, the intent of the final author. But, taken by itself, the poem in chapter 15 describes quite different events. Moses has no role in the poem; the destruction of the Egyptian army is entirely the work of Yahweh. And Israel never crosses any sea; there are no divided waters for Israel to pass through. Instead, while Egypt is pursuing Israel, presumably on land, Yahweh sends the sea as a weapon to destroy them. The description of the sea, as waters piling up and being blown in by the wind to cover the army (15:8-10), sounds more like a tidal wave than the parting of waters of chapter 14. Probably no particular natural phenomenon is meant, but simply a poetic portrayal of the sea as a force of destruction. It is similar to poetic descriptions of Yahweh battling the sea (e.g., Hab 3:8, 15), and to Ugaritic mythology of Baal battling the sea god Yamm, except that here the sea is under Yahweh's control as a weapon, and the enemy is Egypt.

Nor does the poem connect this event to an escape from slavery in Egypt. It is set at an unspecified time when Egypt is powerful and

Israel is vulnerable. It is also set at an unspecified place. Yahweh sends "the sea" against Egypt, and Egypt's officers sink in "a sea of reeds," but there is no indication of where this battle takes place. If one were to speculate on a historical background, then an event around the time of the poem's composition would be the pharaoh Shoshenq's tenth-century invasion of Judah and Israel (1 Kgs 14:25-28). Despite capturing many towns, Shoshenq eventually withdrew without retaining control of Palestine,[14] so the Israelites would have interpreted the outcome as Yahweh rescuing them from Egypt. Still, the language of the poem is too mythological to state with certainty what its historical background might have been. It is enough to note that there are other more plausible possibilities than an escape from slavery at the border of Egypt.

What can be concluded is that this poem about Yahweh the divine warrior rescuing his people from the Egyptian army by sending his weapon the sea against them existed early in the monarchy. Later in the monarchy and during the exile, as the exodus and Moses traditions developed, the poem became attached to the story, and was reread as the climax of Israel's escape from slavery in Egypt. In the fully developed story, Moses is given a role, dividing the waters for Israel to pass through. This last feature, dividing the waters, may have been modeled after the already existing story of Israel entering the promised land by dividing the waters of the Jordan River (Josh 3).[15]

Journey to Mt. Sinai (Exodus 15:22–18:27)

Between the escape at sea and the meeting with God at Mt. Sinai, several incidents occur that set out the themes for the entire journey, especially obstacles and murmuring against Moses, Aaron, and God. These incidents also allow time between the climactic escape and the theologically momentous meeting at Sinai, to prepare the Israelites (and the reader) for what Sinai will mean. The incidents themselves show some knowledge of desert life, and they may have some background in legends told by desert people.

The murmuring theme deserves attention because it is so common in the Pentateuch. The Israelites complain against their leaders and God, sometimes with good cause and sometimes without, and say that they would rather be back in Egypt. The complaints may be surprising at this point in the story, right after the miraculous escape at the sea. But it must be remembered that the story is aimed at exilic Jews. Given the chance to return to Judah after Cyrus conquered Babylon, most chose not to—why leave behind the predictable lives they had established in Babylon, even if it was in exile from their homeland, and start over again in an uncertain Judah? The journey through the wilderness is a metaphor for the risk of re-establishing Jewish life in Judah. There will be obstacles, and people will complain, but whether the complaints are justified or not, God will continue to protect the people.

This part of the journey, from the sea to Sinai, anticipates both the obstacles the people will face—lack of food and water, lack of faith in their leaders, battles with hostile groups—and the way of life that will guide their future—the Sabbath and other laws, a legal system. Within the story, these events are a preparation for the rest of the journey, after the people receive the laws at Sinai. For the readers, it is a preparation for the return from exile and re-establishment in Judah of Judaism, based on the laws of the Pentateuch.

Exodus 15:22-27. The first obstacle is no pure water to drink, which is easily overcome by God giving Moses wood to put into the water to purify it. The word "Marah" means "bitter," so this incident is in the form of an etiology of a place name, but no such place near the border of Egypt is known. Nor does the story tell the particular type of wood used, so it is unlikely it comes from folklore on surviving in the desert. Rather, it is a generic story of God giving a holy man the power over water—and thus over life—much like Elisha purifying water by putting salt in it (2 Kgs 2:19-22). The story emphasizes the Israelites' separation from Egypt, by having drinkable water and by avoiding the diseases God sent on the Egyptians. And it prepares for the next major event, the giving of the law on Mt. Sinai, by having Moses tell the people they will be saved from threats like this if they follow that law.

Exodus 16. The Israelites continue to complain against Moses and Aaron, and God continues to provide for them, this time with quail and manna. The availability of quail and manna is related to natural occurrences. Migrating birds often land exhausted in the Sinai Peninsula and are easily caught. The manna described here is probably a secretion from insects on tamarisk trees, which is present in the morning but quickly dissolves in the sun. The story is based on natural desert experiences, but has been transformed into a story of God miraculously providing food. It also uses a popular etymology to explain a name; "manna" sounds like the Hebrew *man hu*, "What is it?" The combination of desert knowledge, popular folklore, and attributing events to God's intervention is typical of the stories about the journey through the wilderness.

The instructions not to gather any manna on the Sabbath seems out of place, since God has not yet given the laws on not working on the Sabbath. The story was probably originally told in other contexts that assumed the Sabbath law, but the author has no problem using it here. It is a preparation for the laws to come, similar to the instructions Moses gave after purifying the water (Ex 15:25-26). God is providing in the wilderness, but more important than the food is the way of life God will provide in the laws.

In fact, there is a slightly different version of the incident that occurs after the giving of the law. In Numbers 11, after departing from Sinai the Israelites are already receiving manna but complain about it, so God sends quail, but gets angry at their disbelief and so causes it to spoil and kill some of them while they are still eating it. Psalm 78:21-31 tells of the same incident, although there it seems to be both the manna and the quail that kill the people. The story was widely used. Here, so soon after the departure from Egypt, the author downplays the punishment aspect, except for a rather mild rebuke of those who gather manna on the Sabbath. God is preparing them at this point, and is more tolerant of their failings than later in the Pentateuch.

Exodus 17:1-7. This story of Moses striking the rock to produce water when the people are thirsty is repeated in an almost identical form in Numbers 20:1-13. Like the manna and quail story, there is a pre-Sinai version and a post-Sinai version, emphasizing different things. A significant detail in this version is that the rock is "at Horeb," i.e., Mt. Sinai. If the story were strict history that would raise problems, since the people have not come that far on the journey. But the author did not intend it as strict history. Rather, it is another symbolic preparation for the giving of the law. The water flowing from Horeb is the life-giving quality of the law; water imagery is similarly used by exilic and postexilic prophets for the rebuilt temple and the city of Jerusalem (Ezek 47:1-12; Zech 14:8).

and the Torah

The story also adds an etiology of place names, Massah meaning "test," and Meribah meaning "contention." The locations cannot be identified (the version of the story in Num 20 has Meribah by Kadesh, in the Negev), but the connection between springs and quarreling is natural in regions where water is scarce. The fact that two names are given for one place is another indication that the story existed in various forms. Other references to the story sometimes mention only Massah (Dt 6:16), sometimes only Meribah (Num 20:13; Dt 32:51), and sometimes both (Ps 95:8).

Exodus 17:8-16. The victory over Amalek is the first of many battles the Israelites will fight on their journey to the promised land. Like other incidents between the sea and Sinai, this is a preparation for the rest of the journey.

According to other biblical passages, Amalek was an Edomite tribe (Gen 36:12), frequently at war with Israel during the journey through the wilderness (Num 14:39-45), the tribal period (Judg 6:3), and early in the monarchy (1 Sam 30:1-20), after which Amalek disappears from the scene. It is possible that the use of Amalek in these stories goes back to premonarchic memories of conflicts between Amalek and a group in southern Judah who became part of Israel, and the stories have been made part of all of Israel's experience.[16] However, well after the exile in the fictitious Book of Esther we still see the descendants of Amalek used as stereotypical archenemies of the Jews (Esth 3:1; Haman is a descendant of Agag, the Amalekite king whom Saul fought; cf. 1 Sam 15), so it is impossible to determine what history, if any, is behind this incident.

Joshua appears here for the first time in the Pentateuch. Eventually he will become Moses' successor, and his portrayal here is a preparation for his later role. He is successful, but dependent on Moses' actions (raising his arms to give him victory), and therefore not as great as Moses.

Exodus 18. The final events before arriving at Mt. Sinai involve Moses' father-in-law Jethro. As mentioned earlier, he is called by various names (Reuel, Hobab), indicating that different groups claimed connections to Moses. This incident is also at odds with an earlier part of the story. When Moses returned to Egypt from Midian he took his wife and son with him (Ex 4:20, 24-26). Now, they have stayed with Jethro, and there is a second son, Eliezer. Clearly, the story took various forms before being finalized during the exile. *4-15*

A noteworthy feature here is that Jethro, a Midianite, offers sacrifice and professes faith in Yahweh. This has led to much speculation that worship of Yahweh existed among Midianite or other southern groups before the beginning of Israel (see comments on Ex 3–4 in chapter 5). There are good reasons to believe that Yahwism originated somewhere in the south, but since this story dates from several centuries after the beginning of Israel, it cannot be used as proof of a specifically Midianite origin. The most that can be said is that the exilic author did not consider it strange for a non-Israelite in the south to worship Yahweh. Indeed, there is no reason we should consider it strange either. If both Israel and Judah, two separate nations, could include Yahweh among their gods, it is not surprising that other groups could as well. And we already saw in Genesis the close relationship the Pentateuch's authors claimed with southern groups: Midian was a son of Abraham (Gen 25:2) and Edom was a son of Isaac (Gen 25:21-26). The inscription from Kuntillet Ajrud shows that Yahweh was worshiped in Teman, a place in Edom. For nationalistic reasons, of course, some parts of the Bible claim an exclusive relationship between Yahweh and the Israelites, but other parts of the Bible, along with extra-biblical evidence, suggest the existence of Yahwism elsewhere.

The second event involving Jethro is his advice to Moses to delegate the judging responsibilities. Like Moses' earlier instructions not to gather manna on the Sabbath (Ex 16:22-30), there is a slight problem here, in that Moses says he is making known the statutes and instructions of the Lord (18:16), but those statutes and instructions will not be given until the people reach Mt. Sinai in the next chapter. Most likely this incident is based on a story originally set later in the Pentateuch. There are other stories of Moses delegating his powers (Num 11:16-30; Dt 1:9-18), and, as with the Sabbath instructions, the author created a similar story to show a preparation for what will happen later in the journey. Such preparations may seem unnecessary or anachronistic for modern readers, but they would have had a logic for the exilic readers of the Pentateuch. After all, these readers had a legal system and a system of worship including observance of the Sabbath before the Pentateuch became the formal authoritative expression of all of that.

The Covenant at Mt. Sinai (Exodus 19–24)

Exodus 19. The description of the meeting on Mt. Sinai uses common theophany imagery, and also shows a concern for purity. The thunder, lightning, and clouds are similar to other biblical passages where God appears, often on a mountain, with terrifying signs (Judg 5:4-5; Ps 18:7-15). The need to wash their clothes and avoid sexual activity reflects the increased emphasis on ritual purity during the exile.

There are indications that material from more than one source went into this passage. Verses 3-8 are probably from a covenant renewal ceremony. Moses and the people speak as if the commandments have already been given, and they are now accepting them. And the reminder of what God has done in the past, as a motivation for keeping the covenant, would be typical of such a ceremony.

Exodus 20:1-21. The ten commandments, or decalogue, also appear in Deuteronomy 5:6-21 in an almost identical form. In neither place are they called the "ten commandments," although elsewhere they are called, literally, the "ten words" (Ex 34:28; Dt 4:13; 10:4). There are different ways of counting what the ten are. In the Catholic and Lutheran traditions, 20:2-6, on having no other gods and not making images, is a single commandment, and 20:17, on not coveting a neighbor's wife or any other item, is two. In Jewish and the other Protestant traditions, 20:2-6 is two commandments, and 20:17 one.

There is no consensus on the origin of the decalogue. While many of its teachings could have come from any historical period, the form in which we have them gives the most emphasis to two issues regarding worship, making images and keeping the Sabbath, both of which had taken on more importance during the exile (cf. Is 40:18-20; Ezek 22:26; 23:38). The commandments that are stated briefly, against murder, adultery, stealing, and false witness, are similar to prophetic lists of sins, even using the same vocabulary (Hos 4:2; Jer 7:8-10). There is also the use of some of the key precepts of the wisdom tradition, especially in honoring parents and not coveting. The compilation of the decalogue was a matter of bringing together these essentials of worship, prophetic teachings on sin, and wisdom teachings on proper character. It is thus misleading to call them laws. They are torah—instructions on all aspects of life.

You shall have no other gods before me. The first commandment does not yet constitute monotheism, but is an insistence that the Israelites not have dealings with other gods. It is a requirement of their covenant that their relationship with Yahweh be exclusive, without saying anything about whether other gods exist or not. This "Yahweh only" covenant was an idea that grew with the prophets and Deuteronomic movement late in the monarchy, and would eventually become monotheistic.

You shall not make for yourself an idol... We know from archaeological evidence and prophetic denunciations that images were commonly used in Israelite worship and homes before the exile. Even after the exile, images were sometimes used; an early fourth-century coin from Judah has a picture of a deity on it.[17] The Hebrew word used here, *pesel*, is used both for images representing Yahweh (Judg 17:3; 18:31) and for images of other gods (Jer 10:1-16; 2 Kgs 21:7). It is not known when Israelite religion developed the idea that Yahweh cannot be represented by images. The theology is related to that of Exodus 3:14, where Yahweh tells Moses, "I am who I am." Just as God cannot be identified by a name, so any image is also too limiting.

You shall not lift up the name of the LORD your God in vain. "Lifting up the name" may have originally applied to taking an oath by Yahweh's name, so this commandment would have been directed against false oaths. But here it is stated in a broader way, and reflects the growing belief that the name was too sacred to use casually. Later in the Old Testament period the practice developed of not pronouncing the name at all.

Remember the Sabbath day, and keep it holy. The word Sabbath comes from the verb meaning "stop, rest." There have been attempts to derive the Hebrew Sabbath from other ancient Near Eastern practices based on linguistic similarities; the Akkadian *shapattu* marked the full moon at the middle of the month, but the similarities are not close enough to show a connection. The Sabbath is also sometimes compared to the Babylonian practice of considering every seventh day of the lunar cycle unlucky, but the Hebrew Sabbath is not based on the lunar cycle and is not considered unlucky.

The Sabbath developed from two factors: it is beneficial to have regular days of rest, and the number seven already had special significance in the ancient Near East. The benefits of having days of rest are obvious, but it would not always make sense that they be *fixed* days, or that they be the same days for everyone in the community. In particular, such a practice would have been quite impractical for those Israelites who came from an agricultural background. The practice requires some degree of urbanization, as well as a community cohesive enough to enforce it. If the Sabbath had premonarchic roots, it would have been in the Canaanite cities, although there is no evidence for that. More likely, it developed during the Israelite monarchy.

The number seven is used not only for the Sabbath, but has special significance in the Bible and in the rest of the ancient Near East. In the Ugaritic epics and in the Gilgamesh Epic from Mesopotamia things frequently happen seven times or after seven days or seven years. One possible explanation for seven being a special number is that in the ancient world astronomers were aware of five planets, plus the sun and the moon, making seven objects that moved about in their positions in the sky. Another is that the Babylonian number system, while not strictly base-60, used the number 60 very prominently, and seven is the first number that does not divide evenly into 60. For whatever reason, or combination of reasons, seven became a special number in the ancient Near East.

When the Sabbath was instituted during the Israelite monarchy, a cycle of seven days became the norm because it turned out to be a practical period of time and the number already had symbolic significance. There is some evidence of how the Sabbath was observed. Amos mentions it along with the new moon as a time when grain may not be sold (8:5). Hosea groups it with new moons and other festivals as a time of celebration (2:11). Ezekiel says failure to keep the Sabbath was one of the reasons God allowed Judah to fall (22:26; 23:38).

The Sabbath existed during the monarchy, but it was during the exile that it became the central religious observance, to be singled out and made part of the decalogue. The Sabbath was a religious practice that could continue despite the loss of the temple. It also helped unify the Jews and set them apart from the peoples around them. The Pentateuch thus made it the sign of the covenant and the one religious day that is commanded in the decalogue. That the Sabbath was not so cen-

tral or universally accepted before the Pentateuch gave it such prominence is shown by the fact that after the exile Nehemiah had to take
strict measures to re-establish it in Jerusalem (Neh 13:15-22).

Honor your father and your mother. Honoring one's parents is a
common theme in the wisdom tradition (Prov 15:5; 20:20; 30:17),
which along with worship and prophetic ethical teachings is one of the
three types of material in the decalogue. This command adds a reward
for following it, saying that those who do will lengthen their days in the
land God is giving them. Wisdom teachings frequently promise rewards
for those who act properly, but this particular reward also serves
another purpose, that of tying the command more closely to the Pentateuch's narrative. The command may have universal applicability, but it
is also part of a particular covenant God is making with these people on
their way to the promised land.

You shall not kill. Other parts of the Hebrew Scriptures assume that
killing is justified in some circumstances, so an absolute prohibition is
clearly not meant. The Hebrew word *ratsah* is not the most common
word for killing, but it can cover almost any kind of killing; in Deuteronomy 4:42 it is used for unintentional killing, and in Numbers 35:30 it is
used both for murder and for executing the murderer. It is the same
word used in the prophetic lists of sins (Hos 4:2; Jer 7:9); this and the
next three commands come from such lists used in prophetic circles.

You shall not commit adultery. Adultery is also from the prophetic
lists. The Hebrew word *naaph* refers specifically to sex between a man,
married or unmarried, and a woman married to another man. That is, it
was gender specific, and would not have covered sex between a married man and an unmarried woman. In the patriarchal biblical world,
adultery was a sin against another man's marriage.

You shall not steal. This command also uses the same word, *ganab*, as
the prophetic lists (Hos 4:2; Jer 7:9). Occasionally the word is used
specifically for kidnapping, but here it has its more general meaning,
covering any kind of theft.

You shall not bear false witness against your neighbor. The
prophetic lists cover similar types of deception—"lying" in Hosea 4:2,

and "swear falsely" in Jeremiah 7:9—but this command does not cover all lying, just false testimony that harms someone.

You shall not covet . . . Interpreters of these commands against coveting often puzzle over exactly what is meant. If it refers only to a form of desiring, then it would seem excessive to have commands against thoughts. But if it refers to a desiring that leads to certain actions, then it would seem to cover matters already covered by the commands against adultery and stealing. The apparent problem comes about because the adultery and stealing commands come from prophetic circles, while the coveting commands come from wisdom teachings on proper character (cf. Prov 6:25; 12:12; Job 20:20). Wisdom teachings and ethical teachings from prophets are not mutually exclusive, but frequently touch on the same subjects, even if from different perspectives.

Exodus 20:22–23:33. The collection of laws that follows the decalogue is often called the Covenant Code because, after the decalogue, it is at the head of the covenant God makes through Moses. It contains a variety of laws on worship, slavery, property, and personal injury. Since it seems to interrupt the flow of the story, between Moses receiving the ten commandments on Mt. Sinai and his carrying out the covenant ceremony in chapter 24, it existed as an independent collection, and has been inserted here by the author.

It is difficult to date laws precisely, but most of these assume a settled agricultural society, and if they have premonarchic roots they would have been from Canaanite agricultural communities, and not from an exodus group or other nomadic people who became part of the Israelites. The law on making altars of earth or stone (20:24-26), while presupposing a settled people, also presupposes that there will be several places of sacrifice and so predates the centralizing reform of the Deuteronomic movement and King Josiah (ca. 622 BCE). Thus, the Covenant Code is one of the oldest parts of the Pentateuch.

There is insufficient space here to discuss every individual law, but a few deserve comment. It is sometimes a problem for modern readers that the Bible accepts the existence of *slavery* (21:1-11). Slavery was an accepted institution throughout the ancient Near East, and while some biblical laws try to make it more humane, they also remind us that the Bible comes from a particular time and culture and passes on some of the shortcomings of its world. One can be true to the overall message of the Bible without accepting every one of its views in a literal way. (For a comparison of the Covenant Code's laws on slavery to other laws on slavery, see Appendix III.)

In addition to slavery, the Covenant Code includes several other **economic laws**, on not charging interest to Israelites (22:25), not requiring burdensome pledges for loans (22:26-27), and leaving the land fallow every seventh year and allowing the poor to gather whatever grows (23:10-11). The laws promote a just economic life, especially for people who are most vulnerable. (For a comparison with other economic laws in the Pentateuch, see Appendix II.)

Another case of laws that made sense in biblical times but might not be appropriate today are the ones on **capital punishment** (21:12-17; 22:18-20). The Pentateuch calls for the death penalty for a wide variety of offenses, as did most of the ancient world, and is reflecting the views of the time. In addition, ancient Israel did not have a prison system such as exists today, capable of keeping a large number of dangerous people away from society. In many cases, the death penalty was the only way to protect the community.

The list of **sabbatical and liturgical laws** (23:10-19) is generally considered an early list, but it also fits the needs of the exiles, whose identity would be strengthened by practices that set them apart from the peoples around them. An indication of the list's early date is the fact that the law in 23:19, "You shall not boil a kid in its mother's milk," is included among liturgical laws. There is evidence from Ugarit of a Canaanite ceremony involving boiling a kid in milk.[18] During the monarchy, as the Israelites forged a non-Canaanite identity, laws that distinguished their worship from past Canaanite practices became important. Here (and in Ex 34:26) the law is in the context of worship; in Deuteronomy 14:21 the same law occurs in the context of dietary rules, indicating a later date when the original purpose of the law had lost its force. Another indication of the early date of these laws is the calendar of festivals. The old Canaanite name Abib is used for the feast of Unleavened Bread (23:15), and the dates of First Fruits and Ingathering (Booths) are not yet fixed, but are determined by agricultural events (23:16). (For a comparison of this religious calendar with other ones in the Hebrew Scriptures, see Appendix I.)

Exodus 24. There is now a ceremonial ratification of the covenant, involving a public reading of it, the people's response, and a sacrifice.

This passage was shaped by covenant renewal ceremonies that were periodically carried out, but the use of multiple sources has led to some disunity in the text, such as why Moses does not obey immediately when he is summoned to the mountain, and who exactly accompanies Moses. But it is essential for the story that the people formally accept the covenant. The author is saying that it was by being in this covenant relationship with Yahweh that the nation became great in the past. If they want to regain that greatness after the exile they must once again accept a covenant with Yahweh.

The Cult (Exodus 25–31)

After the ratification of the covenant, Moses returns to the mountain for forty days, and during that time God instructs him on how the Israelites are to worship. They are to make a tabernacle or dwelling place for God to be present among them, and they are to place in the tabernacle an ark containing the tablets of the covenant and several other items for worship. The instructions go on to describe the vestments for priests, their ordination rites, and the sacrifices to be offered. The section concludes with God reiterating to Moses the importance of keeping the Sabbath.

Most scholars agree that these instructions come from the Priestly source, and represent an exilic view of idealized worship, rather than something that was actually done by a group in the desert. Although some attempt is made to describe the items as portable, they are far too large and too elaborate to have been constructed and used by this group who elsewhere in the story barely have food and water. The passage is about re-establishing a cult that will unify the nation after the exile. The Priestly author inserted it at this point in the narrative in order to put worship on the same level as the covenant.

Although the description of the tabernacle and other items as a whole is artificial, it is possible that the idea of a tent as a shrine has roots in the practices of nomadic ancestors of the Israelites. Portable shrines similar to tents are known among desert nomads, and if some of the ancestors of the Israelites were desert nomads they may have had tent-like shrines. However, it is likely that the majority of Israelites descended from indigenous Canaanites, so it is questionable whether authentic desert practices had a lasting role in Israelite religion during the monarchy. Any similarities that these instructions (or the tent of meeting in 33:7-11) have to actual desert religious practices may be better explained by the exilic authors' knowledge of contemporary desert peoples than by the preservation of ancient traditions among the Israelites.

These instructions reveal some of the Priestly understanding of holiness. The holy is something that is set apart, and is a reminder of how different God is from the created world. Human contact with God is possible through sacred space, personnel, times, actions, and objects, all of which are marked as different from the ordinary in some way. In these instructions, precious materials are used for the most sacred items, and in some cases there are explicit prohibitions against the materials here being used for anything other than sacred items. These instructions do not cover all aspects of holiness; more of the Priestly view can be seen in the laws in Leviticus and Numbers. It should also be noted that the Priestly view of encountering God is only one of the views represented in the Pentateuch. Other stories, especially from the Yahwist source, portray people encountering God through more ordinary activities.

Exodus 25. In preparation for making the items for the cult, Moses collects precious materials from the Israelites. A migrating group in the desert, of course, would not have such materials, but the story has already prepared for this by claiming that when the people left Egypt they were given gold, silver, and other materials by the Egyptians (Ex 12:35-36).

A key item in these instruction is the ***ark of the covenant,*** or ark of testimony (25:10-22). It is described as a wooden chest decorated with "pure gold," about four feet long and two feet wide, with rings on the sides, through which poles run for carrying the ark. It is regarded as a throne of Yahweh, and is also to contain the covenant they make with Yahweh. There are various traditions about an ark elsewhere in the Hebrew Scriptures. In Deuteronomy 10:1-5 it is a simple container for the tablets of the covenant, and, unlike in Exodus, Moses makes it before receiving the second set of tablets, and takes it with him up Mt. Sinai. The Deuteronomic History preserves several stories about an ark, usually as an item representing the presence of Yahweh, with no mention of tablets in it. It is carried in battle (cf. especially 1 Sam 4–7), and people go to it to inquire from Yahweh (Judg 20:27-28). After David makes Jerusalem his capital, he brings the ark there and puts it in a tent (2 Sam 6). When Solomon builds the temple he places the ark in the holy of holies, and the ark is said to contain the two tablets (1 Kgs 8). Historically there were probably several ark-like items used by Israelites, from portable objects to fixed objects in shrines. The fate of the ark of the covenant in the temple is unknown; presumably it was destroyed or taken by the Babylonians when they destroyed the temple in 587 BCE. The claim that Jeremiah hid it in a cave on Mt. Nebo is certainly not historical (2 Macc 2:4-8).

The lampstand and the table for the sacred bread are not as sacred as the ark, but will be in close proximity to it, so are also made with pure gold and other precious materials. The materials represent degrees of holiness. The items closest to the divine are covered with pure gold, while those outside the tabernacle, in the courtyard, will be made with bronze.

Exodus 26. The *tabernacle* is the tent in which Yahweh dwells. The description here is very detailed, but still puzzling, and assumes that the reader already knows much of what such a structure looked like. The basic shape is clear: It is a rectangular tent, 30 by 10 cubits (about 45 by 15 feet), with a screen in the middle separating the inner one-third—the holy of holies, where the ark will be—from the rest. Since the curtains of the tent are in contact with holy space, they are made of the most precious material—a blend of linen (Hebrew *shesh*) and three colors of yarn (Hebrew *shani*). Such material was difficult to make, and was thus reserved for sacred uses; elsewhere the use of blended fabrics for ordinary garments is prohibited (Lev 19:19; Dt 22:11).[19]

Exodus 27. The *altar for burnt offerings* will be outside the tabernacle in the courtyard. The courtyard is a roofless tent, 100 by 50 cubits, with the entrance at the east. The horns of the altar are the raised four corners, typical of altars in Israel and earlier in Canaan. The materials here are not as precious as those inside the tabernacle. The altar is covered in bronze, and the tent walls are made of only one fabric, except for the screen over the entrance, which is a blend of linen and yarn. Again, the grades of material represent different degrees of holy space.

Exodus 28. Next the *vestments* of the priests, the sons of Aaron, are described. These include an ephod (some kind of long decorated vest), a decorated breastplate that held the Urim and Thummim, and other items such as a robe and headdress. The Urim and Thummim are said to be used in making judgments, and were probably small items used for casting lots. These priestly vestments are made with a blend of linen and yarn and are decorated with gold—the same materials used for the tabernacle and its furnishings—and represent the fact that the priests have the degree of holiness necessary to enter the sacred space.

Exodus 29. The ***ordination*** ceremony involves a washing, clothing, and anointing of the priests, and several sacrifices. The washing, clothing, and anointing make the priests pure and set them apart from ordinary people; these actions are similar to the postexilic prophet Zechariah's description of the high priest Joshua being made worthy to serve (Zech 3–4). The term translated "ordain" literally means "fill the hand." Its use for installing priests predates the Priestly source; it is used in two stories in the Deuteronomic History (Judg 17:5, 12; 1 Kgs 13:33). Ordination does not refer to a ritual act, but metaphorically either to a priest being empowered to carry out his duties, or to a priest receiving a share of the offerings that are brought to his sanctuary.

The ordination instructions are followed by instructions on one of the regular duties of the priests, the daily offering at the altar. Instructions on other sacrifices will be given in Leviticus 1–7, but the daily one is mentioned here to make the point that what consecrates a priest is not so much a separate ritual as the regular carrying out of his sacred duties.

Exodus 30. The instructions now return to worship items and a temple tax. The ***altar of incense,*** unlike the bronze altar for burnt offerings in the courtyard, is inside the tabernacle, and is thus covered in gold because it is in more sacred space. It also will have horns at the four corners, and will be used for the twice-daily burning of incense and an atonement ritual once a year, although the description here is not the same as the Day of Atonement description in Leviticus 16. The bronze ***basin*** is just outside the tabernacle, and is used to purify the priests who will enter the sacred space. The oil and incense are blends of precious substances. Like the fabric used for the tabernacle curtains, they are not to be used for anything other than sacred purposes: "Whoever makes any like it to use as perfume shall be cut off from the people" (30:38).

The half-shekel tax to the temple is called a "ransom" (30:12) and an "atonement" (30:15), and is to be paid when a census is taken. The reason an atonement needed to be made at the time of a census originally had to do with the fact that the census would be taken for military service (cf. Num 1:2-3), and ritual purity needed to be followed by those in military service. The ransom payment would purify the army from past infractions. Over time it expanded into the idea that any census was a time when God might punish infractions. The connection of a census to the danger of provoking God's wrath is also seen in the story of King David taking a census of Israel and Judah (2 Sam 24).[20]

Exodus 31. The tabernacle instructions conclude with the naming of two people who will be in charge of its construction, Bezalel from the tribe of Judah and Oholiab from the tribe of Dan. During the monarchy one of the major temples besides the one in Jerusalem was located in Dan, so the tribes of Judah and Dan here represent two religious traditions being united by the tabernacle.

The command to keep the Sabbath is repeated to highlight its importance, and it will be mentioned again in 35:2-3, when the tabernacle instructions begin to be carried out. The minutiae of all the liturgical items must not distract from the one religious observance that the Pentateuch singles out as the sign of the covenant with Yahweh. The separation of the holy from the ordinary, so prominent in these instructions, is put into perspective by this reminder that the most important religious observance is one which requires no sacred space and no sacred personnel, but is observed in the same way by everyone everywhere.

The Golden Calf and Remaking the Covenant (Exodus 32–34)

While Moses is on the mountain, the people get tired of waiting for him and make a golden calf to worship, violating the worship commandments and breaking the covenant they have just made. Moses breaks the tablets of the commandments and destroys the calf, then has several dialogues with God, ending with God giving him two new tablets.

This story is clearly not something that happened to a group in the desert before the beginning of Israel. It is unlikely that such a group would have had the ability to make such a statue, and there are contradictions in the order of events between this and the other version in Deuteronomy 9:8–10:5. It is based on circumstances in the monarchy and on the needs of exilic Jews. Calves and bulls were used in Canaanite and Israelite worship, and one purpose of the story is to warn that this is a violation of the covenant. The other purpose is to show that after an apostasy God will not abandon the people. God will continue to be present by meeting with Moses and leading the Israelites through the wilderness, and God will rewrite the tablets Moses smashed. For the Jewish exiles in Babylon, the story assures them that God will find some way to be present and give them another chance at a covenant relationship.

Exodus 32. In Canaanite religion Baal was represented by a bull, and sometimes depicted standing on a bull. The bull imagery continued in the Israelite period; a bronze statue of a bull was discovered at an open-air shrine in Samaria near Iron Age I settlements.[21] The prophet Hosea criticized the northern kingdom for worshiping a calf (Hos 8:5; 10:5). According to the Deuteronomic History, Jeroboam, the first king of the northern kingdom, established two national shrines at Bethel and Dan, and set up golden calves in them (1 Kgs 12:25-33). This story in Exodus is probably influenced by the Jeroboam story; it uses the same acclamation, "These are your gods, O Israel, who brought you up out of the land of Egypt," which makes more sense if its original use was in 1 Kings, since it is in the plural.[22]

Moses' destruction of the calf, by burning it and then grinding it up and scattering it, does not seem like a possible way to destroy a gold statue. In fact, the same series of actions, even using the same (cognate) verbs, occurs in the Ugaritic story of Anat destroying Mot, the god of death.[23] Evidently it was a stereotypical Canaanite and Israelite way of describing the destruction of an enemy god.

Exodus 33. After the incident with the golden calf, the continuation of the covenant relationship is in doubt. But God pledges to fulfill the promises to Abraham, Isaac, and Jacob. God will continue to be with the Israelites, but only outside the camp, in a "tent of meeting" with Moses. "Tent of meeting" is used in two different ways in the Pentateuch. There are other passages where, as here, it is a simple tent where Moses and other specially selected people encounter Yahweh outside the camp (Num 11:16-30; 12:1-16). Elsewhere it is the more elaborate tabernacle that God had instructed Moses to build, associated with the ark of the covenant and other worship items and located at the center of the camp (Ex 27:21; 40:22-38; Num 2). The simple tent of meeting here is an early version of the tradition of how God would be present during the journey, probably from the Yahwist source, which the Priestly source transformed into a more elaborate item.[24]

Exodus 34. God formally re-establishes the covenant through Moses, and the author uses the setting to include another list of laws. The laws in 34:17-26 are from an early liturgical code, but the introduction is addressed to postexilic Jews, warning against covenants and intermarriage with the other people who live in the land. The liturgical laws are similar to those in the Book of the Covenant (cf. 23:10-19), and while they date from the monarchy, the emphasis on the Sabbath and religious festivals fits the needs of the exiles.

Moses makes two new tablets, but it is not clear whether God or Moses is to write on them; in 34:1 it is God, in 34:27 it is Moses, and 34:28 says "he wrote." Also, in 34:27 God seems to tell Moses to write the liturgical laws just given, but 34:28 specifies that what gets written on the tablets are the "ten words," i.e., the decalogue. The ambiguity is probably intentional. It allows the author to incorporate this other list of laws in a story that is about remaking the original covenant.

Implementing the Cult (Exodus 35–40)

The instructions God gave Moses in chapters 25–31 on building the tabernacle, ark, and other worship items are now carried out. Much of this section is an almost word-for-word repetition of the instructions, with a few changes in order. The one major omission is the ordination of priests, which was instructed in 29:1-37 but will not take place until Leviticus 8. The characteristics of the Priestly source are seen not only in the concern with the details of worship, but also in the precise dating: on the first day of the first month of the second year Moses sets up the tabernacle and tent of meeting (40:2, 17). Thus, three months passed from the time the Israelites left Egypt until they arrived at Mt.

Sinai (19:1), and now another nine months pass until they put up the tabernacle. Although this passage gives the impression that it was set up all in one day, later in the Priestly source it becomes clear that it was finished some time in the second month of the second year (Num 1:1; 7:1).

After the completion of the construction, "the cloud covered the tent of meeting, and the glory of the LORD filled the tabernacle" (40:34). The cloud and glory that had previously covered Mt. Sinai (24:15-18) have now moved to the portable shrine. This marks a transition in the journey, as God will now be present in a new way, and is another reminder to the Jews of the exile that as circumstances change God will find new ways to be with them.

The interspersing of the Priestly material here and in chapters 25–31 with the other parts of the narrative serves two purposes. It raises the level of this liturgical material to that of the covenant, broadening what the covenant is about. And it makes for a smoother transition to the material in Leviticus, which will include many more ritual laws. The character of the Pentateuch has shifted. The dramatic narrative has given way to laws, and now specifically to laws on worship. This part of the Pentateuch may be less interesting to read, but it is just as revealing of how Judaism saw its foundations.

CHAPTER SEVEN

Leviticus

Leviticus 1–7 — Sacrifices

Leviticus 8–10 — Ordination of Priests

Leviticus 11–15 — Purity

Leviticus 16 — The Day of Atonement

Leviticus 17–26 — The Holiness Code

Leviticus 27 — Supplement on Vows

L eviticus is mostly instructions on rituals and purity, with very little narrative. In its place in the Pentateuch it is part of the larger narrative, with God giving these instructions to Moses and Aaron while the Israelites are at Mt. Sinai. But the material certainly existed as independent collections of religious laws before being gathered together and inserted into the Pentateuch's story. These collections come from Priestly circles, but are not entirely uniform. In particular, chapters 17–26, called the Holiness Code, have a style and emphasis different from the rest of the book and probably came from a different group.

These laws assume an established worship system with a temple and plenty of animals available for sacrifice, and obviously did not originate with a group in the desert. The material in Leviticus is a combination of practices that were common during the monarchy, and exilic ideas of what should be done in the future. The Jews were under Persian rule after the exile and, not having an independent nation, worship became central to their identity. Leviticus takes worship practices that may have existed during the monarchy and elevates them to a new level of importance. It also emphasizes dietary and ritual purity laws that set the Jews apart from the peoples around them. In Leviticus, the same practices that strengthen the people's awareness of God also strengthen their sense of being a unique community.

Although much of the material existed in smaller collections before becoming part of this book, there is a logic to the way it is arranged in Leviticus. The instructions on sacrifice (1–7) are followed by the sacrifices at the ordination of the priests (8–9) and a story about illegitimate offerings (10). The instructions on purity and impurity (11–15) are followed by instructions on the Day of Atonement, to remove impurity (16). The Holiness Code (17–26) has its own arrangement, blending ritual and moral laws.

Characteristics of Laws in Leviticus

The basic purpose of the Priestly laws is to establish a uniform system of worship and purity in order to form a more cohesive Jewish community. The Holiness Code, as one strand within the Priestly tradition, expands this to other areas besides worship and purity, but with the same basic purpose of strengthening the community. The laws can be thought of both theologically and sociologically. Behind the sometimes bizarre rituals is a vision of who God is, how this community relates to God, and how this community lives in the world.

Central to laws in Leviticus is the concept of *holiness*. What is holy is something that is separate, other, and different from ordinary experience. God is holy, and one encounters God by entering a holy place, such as the tabernacle, which is kept separate from other places. There are also holy times—the Sabbath and annual festivals—which are different from other days and are marked by ritual acts in the presence of God. Objects used in worship have varying degrees of holiness, as do personnel involved in worship. Finally, the people as a whole are to be set apart from other peoples by their observance of these laws. "You shall be holy, for I, the LORD your God am holy" (Lev 19:2, etc.), is a line the Holiness Code uses to highlight the uniqueness of the chosen people.

Holiness is also dangerous, and there are strict penalties to ensure maintenance of the separation of the divine. Two of Aaron's sons are killed by the Lord for making an offering with the wrong fire (Lev 10:1-

3), and those who violate ritual and sexual laws are to be put to death or cut off from the community (Lev 20). The idea that the holy is dangerous is partly to discourage people from unofficial religious practices, but also is a reminder of the unpredictable power of God. Under these laws one does not approach God casually. The idea that the holy is dangerous is not unique to Judaism, but it fit well the Priestly theology developing during the exile: the practice of religion needed to be a conscious decision, not something automatically done because it was part of the dominant culture.

A related concept is that everything has its proper place in the **order** of the universe. The Priestly creation story (Gen 1:1–2:4) emphasizes that order, and it shows up in laws on what animals are proper for human consumption (Lev 11) and on not mixing unlike seeds, animals, or fabric (Lev 19:19). The orderly structure of the tabernacle and other worship items (Ex 25–30) reflects the orderly structure of the universe. The emphasis on order may have had early roots, but it became more important as a way of overcoming the sense of disorder after the fall of the kingdoms of Israel and Judah.

Another characteristic of the laws in Leviticus is that they are an **ideal**, rather than a minimum that everyone was expected to always follow. The law represents a vision of what the nation was to become, even though parts of the law would not have been practical for most people to keep. The laws on purity could have been kept closely by priests and a few others, but most people would have been in a state of impurity most of the time. The laws on offerings assume more prosperity than many of the people enjoyed. The Priestly laws are not unusual in their idealism. Law collections from the ancient Near East are often more like literary works than statutes that were strictly enforced. Torah is instruction, and these laws instruct the postexilic community on what kind of people to become.

Law and Narrative

One feature that does make the Priestly laws unusual is their integration into the extended narrative of the Pentateuch. Other ancient Near Eastern law collections sometimes had brief narrative introductions describing the promulgation of the laws,[1] but nothing like the Pentateuch's long story. Of course, the Priestly laws existed as smaller collections separate from the rest of the Pentateuch at an earlier date, but at some point it was decided that these laws would be best understood as part of a story, and not as independent collections.

The question of why law was combined with narrative is somewhat speculative, but a few factors were likely significant. First, it allowed all the law collections (the Covenant Code, Holiness Code, other Priestly material, Deuteronomic Code, and other smaller collections) to be put on the same level and all be connected to Moses. By the late monarchy, Moses had become a key figure in the stories of Israel's formation, and the Pentateuch uses him to unify the various legal and ritual traditions. Unifying law and narrative was a natural part of unifying several law collections around Moses.

Second, making the laws part of a narrative of the people's formation, before they were in the land, made those laws a more appropriate program for rebuilding the exilic community at the time that they were outside of the land. The story of promises, oppression, a new covenant, and a long wilderness journey is a metaphor for the hopes and struggles the people would experience in using these laws for a restored Israel. The fact that so much of the story is about the people failing to stay faithful is an acknowledgment that these laws are not easy to follow.

And third, combining laws and narrative was simply a cumulative process—once it began in a small way it was easier for subsequent editors to add more. The Deuteronomist may have been the first to begin the process by adding laws at the beginning of the Deuteronomic History (see chapter 9). The Yahwist included the Covenant Code in the Mt. Sinai story. The Deuteronomic laws were incorporated into the Pentateuch, and the Priestly writers continued the process with longer law collections. The end result is an unusual type of work, but because it developed slowly it did not seem unusual to its compilers.

Sacrifices (Leviticus 1–7)

The opening chapters of Leviticus give instructions for various types of sacrifice, including animals, grain offerings, well-being, purification, and guilt offerings. These types of sacrifices come up often in the Hebrew Scriptures, although usually not with the same precision of terminology as in Leviticus, and occur in settings ranging from one-time individual offerings to large annual festivals at the temple.

Sacrifice is a nearly universal religious activity, and some form of sacrifice must have existed in Israelite religion from the earliest days. The particulars of sacrifice in Israel go back to its Canaanite ancestors. The little information available on Canaanite sacrifices indicates that they practiced burnt offerings, sacrifices of communion with gods, and offerings of grain and incense, all of which continued in Israel. Some of the Israelites' ancestors may have come from nomadic backgrounds, but their practices had less impact on later sacrifices, except perhaps for the Passover and the dedication of firstborn male animals. The prophets Amos and Jeremiah say that when the Israelites were in the desert they did not offer sacrifices, suggesting further that the practices are mainly from a Canaanite background, and not from nomads or an exodus group (Jer 7:22; Am 5:25).

During the monarchy, sacrifices were offered at numerous places, until late attempts to centralize the cult. The rituals in Leviticus 1–7 require a large and reliable supply of animals, which would have been difficult to obtain at outlying local shrines. Although individual parts of these rituals go back to earlier times, the system set out here would have been more practical at a centralized cult backed by the authority of the state. During the monarchy the king was that authority, and state authority over the system continued when the second temple was built after the exile, with backing from the Persian empire.

The Hebrew Scriptures do not set out a systematic theology of sacrifice, but some of the understanding of it can be inferred from the descriptions of it. By putting these instructions in the narrative of God making a covenant with the Israelites, the Pentateuch is saying that their purpose is to maintain or re-establish a good relationship with Yahweh. Sacrifices are described in terms of a gift to Yahweh, with emphasis on the perfection of the animal or grain offered (1:3; 2:1; 3:1), and the need for it to be acceptable and pleasing to Yahweh (1:4; 3:5). They establish communion with God, especially when a sacrificial meal takes place, with part of it consumed by God in fire and part consumed by the priests or people (6:14-30 [6:7-23 in Hebrew]; 7:11-18). When the relationship has been broken by any violation, whether intentional or not, the sacrifices make atonement (4:1–6:7 [4:1–5:26 in Hebrew]). The idea of a sacrifice being a means to appease an angry God is not present, although it may have existed on a popular level. The sacrifices were meant to change people, not God. By symbolically giving something back to God, the offering reminded people that everything they had came from God in the first place.

This section describes five types of sacrifice. There is much overlap of the occasions on which each of these might be offered, suggesting that there were various traditions among different groups in different places, and the Priestly compilers have attempted to put them all together into one system.

Leviticus 1. The first of the five types of sacrifice is the ***whole burnt*** sacrifice (1:3-17), in which the entire animal was burned. It is called *olah* in Hebrew, from the verb meaning "go up," which refers either to the smoke of the sacrifice going up or the person going up to the altar to make the offering. This was the regular daily sacrifice at the temple, and also took place on festivals, such as Passover (Num 28), Booths (Num 29:12-16), and the Day of Atonement (Lev 16). In addition, individuals made whole burnt offerings after childbirth (Lev 12:6-8), after being cured of skin disease (Lev 14:19), and in fulfillment of vows (Lev 22:18). The frequency of this type of sacrifice shows that it expressed well the relationship between Yahweh and the people. However, that frequency could be a burden on the poor, so provisions are made for a lesser offering, of a dove or pigeon, for those who could not afford a larger animal (e.g., for childbirth, Lev 12:8, or skin disease, Lev 14:21-22).

Leviticus 2. In the ***grain offering,*** a small amount of the grain was burned with incense, and the rest was kept by the priests. The basic idea here is a gift, and the Hebrew word *minhah* is used outside of ritual contexts for any kind of gift, as well as required tribute. As part of the sacrificial system it is a gift to God, and functions as a tax for the upkeep of the cultic personnel. After the exile, the Persian empire provided financial support to establish the Jerusalem temple, especially under Darius (522–486 BCE), but that support ended under the next king, Xerxes (486–465), making a tax like this all the more necessary.[2]

The requirement that salt be included with all such offerings probably comes from the fact that salt helps preserve the grain. This would make the offering more practical for the priests to use, and would symbolize the desire to preserve the covenant with Yahweh.

Leviticus 3. The ***well-being*** or ***peace*** sacrifice (*zebah shelamim*) involved part of the animal being burned and part of it being eaten by those making the offering. It was a voluntary offering that could be made on a wide variety of occasions. The additional instructions on this sacrifice (Lev 7:11-26) divide the occasions into praise, vows, and freewill offerings, and elsewhere in the Hebrew Scriptures the occasions include asking for help in times of distress (Judg 20:26; 21:4; 1 Sam 13:9; 2 Sam 24:25) and Solomon's dedication of the temple (1 Kgs 8:64). Because some of the animal was given to God on the altar and some was consumed by the offerer, it represented a meal that united the worshiper with God.

Leviticus 4:1–5:13. Sacrifices of ***purification*** were done after becoming ritually impure for violations of the law. The term used for this type of sacrifice, *hatah*, comes from the common Hebrew word for sin, but here it is qualified as unintentional sin. A few of the cases are listed in 5:1-4, including accidentally touching something impure and making a rash oath. Other cases mentioned later are for skin diseases (Lev 14:19-20) and sexual discharges (Lev 15:13-15, 28-30).

Leviticus 5:14–6:7 (5:26 in Hebrew). The ***guilt*** offerings (*asham*) are for cases where, in addition to the sacrifice, the person must pay reparations for the violation. Such cases include misuse of sacred items and cheating an associate out of property. These are still qualified as inadvertent, and would refer to cases where people later realized what they had done, including saying something untrue under oath about it. These matters are considered more serious, because they involve profaning something sacred, or hurting another person, and so require the additional payment.

Ordination of Priests (Leviticus 8–10)

In Exodus 28–29 God had instructed Moses on the vestments and ordination of Aaron and his sons as priests, and now Moses carries out those instructions. This section describes the ordination rites, and not the function of priests, but it does give us an idea of what functions were thought most important. Coming right after the instructions on sacrifice (1–7) and right before the instructions on purity (11–15), it further emphasizes those two areas by having Moses cleanse Aaron and his sons at the beginning of the rites, and by including several sacrifices as part of the rites. Sacrifice and purity were key priestly concerns after the exile, but not always before the exile.

Priesthood is a specialized religious office, and is found more among settled agricultural and urban groups than among nomads.[3] Thus, the background of Israelite priesthood would have been Canaanite religion. Most likely, Zadok, one of David's official priests at the beginning of the monarchy, had been a Canaanite priest in Jerusalem; he was provided with an Israelite genealogy only in late texts (cf. 2 Sam 8:17; 1 Chron 24:3).[4] This, however, should not be seen as unusual, as most of the Israelite population had been Canaanite as well, and there was more continuity than discontinuity in religious practice.

Some studies suggest that the basic function of priests in the Hebrew Scriptures was to serve at a sanctuary.[5] Sacrifice, at least in the early periods, could be offered by others besides priests, but the priest was to do those things associated with a particular sanctuary: receive oracles from the god of the sanctuary, assist people who came to worship there, and offer sacrifice when it took place at the sanctuary. During the monarchy, sacrifice took on a more central role, especially with the centralization of the cult in Jerusalem. In exilic books we see a close identification of priests with sacrificial worship (Jer 33:18; Ezek 44:15-16) and an increased concern for the ritual purity of the priest (Ezek 44:25-27).

The general picture in the Hebrew Scriptures is that all priests were from the tribe of Levi, which did not have its own allotment of land. But there are differences in the details. Here, in the Priestly source, only the descendants of Aaron, a subset of the tribe of Levi, are legitimate priests; the rest of the Levites are a lower order who assist in some temple duties (Num 3:5-13; 8:5-26). In the Deuteronomist source, however, any male from the tribe of Levi may serve as a priest when he is at the central temple (Dt 18:1-8). A similar inclusion of all the tribe of Levi is seen in the fifth-century prophet Malachi, who refers to the institution of the priesthood as the "covenant of Levi" (Mal 2:4-9). Ezekiel has yet another view, saying the only legitimate priests are the descendants of Zadok, David's priest (Ezek 40:46; 43:18-19; 44:15-16). These differences show that there was no one single definition of official priesthood during Israelite history. The Persian-backed cult would have included an official priesthood, of course, but the various definitions of what made them legitimate are all artificial uses of genealogy and tribal identity.

Leviticus 8. The ordination rituals begin with Moses cleansing, clothing, and anointing Aaron and his sons and sacrificing a bull and two rams, after which Aaron and his sons remain in the tent of meeting for seven days. This description has several similarities to the prophet Zechariah's oracles on the priest Joshua. Writing shortly after the exile, Zechariah says that before Joshua will be worthy to serve as high priest his unclean clothes must be removed, he will put on a clean turban and priestly clothes, he will be given access to God's courts, and he will receive an engraved stone (Zech 3:1-9). Further, Joshua is represented by an olive tree next to a lamp, and is called an anointed one (Zech 4:1-14), in a manner similar to the anointing Aaron and his sons receive here. Both Zechariah and Leviticus show the postexilic concern for strong, ritually pure priestly leaders, using imagery usually used for royal leaders. Since the Jews no longer had their own king, both symbolically and practically the high priest took on roles formerly fulfilled by kings.

Leviticus 9. After spending seven days in the tent of meeting, Aaron and his sons carry out their first priestly function, offering sacrifices. Four of the five types of sacrifice listed in Lev 1–7 are offered, the exception being the guilt offering. The several different types of sacrifice here show the priests' control over the entire sacrificial system, countering any latent attempts to continue the practice of having sacrifices offered by unofficial priestly groups. The sacrifices conclude with Aaron blessing the people, another important priestly function, and with fire coming from the Lord to consume the burnt offering, a sign that God has approved the proceedings.

Leviticus 10. Two of Aaron's sons make an illegitimate offering, apparently because they used a different fire for their incense rather than the fire already at the altar, and the Lord puts them to death. The severity of the penalty makes it clear that priests must offer sacrifice as part of one single system. The independence of local shrines that existed during most of the monarchy will not be tolerated in the postexilic period.

The other points of proper priestly behavior brought up here include eliminating rituals that involved getting intoxicated (10:9), distinguishing between sacred and profane and clean and unclean (10:10-11), and eating sacrificial food (10:12-20), although the point of the dispute between Moses and Aaron's two remaining sons is unclear (10:16-20).

Purity (Leviticus 11–15)

The concept of ritual purity can be difficult to grasp because it is so different from modern religious ideas. Purity is not the same as morality, although the two are sometimes blurred because immoral behavior is metaphorically described as impure. In the system in Leviticus 11–15, eating certain foods, contact with certain animals, giving birth, having skin diseases, and various kinds of sexual activity made a person ritually impure. People became pure by a combination of ritually washing themselves, waiting a period of time, offering a sacrifice, or, in the case of skin diseases, being examined by a priest.

Becoming impure was perfectly natural and was not considered evil or shameful. Sex, menstruation, and childbirth were ordinary activities, and for people living on farms or in homes with dirt floors, occasional contact with dead or unclean animals would have been unavoidable. It was not possible to always be in a state of purity, but it was necessary to be pure to enter the sanctuary. In a state of purity, one was removed from the ordinary, and able to approach the divine.

The origin of this system is debated. Some parts, such as keeping a person with a contagious skin disease separate, were undoubtedly influenced by health concerns. Some parts developed as Israelite religion tried to separate itself from other Canaanite religion. Fertility rites and sacred prostitution had been part of Canaanite religion, so by separating sexual activity from the sacred realm this system abolishes Canaanite practices. During and after the exile the system served as a reminder of the people's holiness, and, in practical matters, to separate them from the peoples around them. The food laws and laws on contact with anything unclean meant that the easiest way to stay pure was to associate only with other Jews who were following the system. On the negative side, it could lead to divisions among Jews. The poor and the people who lived on the land would find the system burdensome and would most often be in a state of impurity, which the wealthy could use as an excuse to have nothing to do with them. The negative side is somewhat ameliorated by occasional provisions allowing the poor to substitute a less costly offering to complete the purification rite.

Leviticus 11. The discussion of clean and unclean animals treats them in four groups: land animals, fish, birds, and insects. Discussion of the first, land animals, begins with the general principle that to be clean for human consumption an animal must have divided hoofs and chew its cud. Thus, cattle and sheep would be acceptable and pigs would not, but the list is based on external appearances rather than scientific fact, so, for example, the hare is described as chewing its cud when in reality it does not. The general principle is probably a later justification for exclusions that had developed for a variety of practical reasons. The requirement that food from the sea had to have both fins and scales (thus excluding shellfish) may have been based on the idea that clean animals had to fit a proper order of creation, and fins and scales are proper to sea life.[6] With the birds no principle is given, but the excluded ones tend to be scavengers and meat eaters. The exclusion of most insects may have been because of their contact with dirt and decay.

The exclusion of pigs from the diet was one of the earliest practices of the Israelites. Iron Age I settlements in the highlands included almost no pig bones among their faunal remains, while Philistine and other low-land sites did include pig bones.[7] The reason for the exclusion may have been that pigs have a varied diet and root up things from the ground to eat, and sometimes eat meat, in contrast to the cleaner vegetarian diet of other livestock. It is also possible that the scarcity of pigs in the Iron Age I settlements had more to do with practical factors than a religious taboo. It would have been easier to raise hogs in the lowlands where there was more surplus grain; the isolation and subsistence living of the new Israelite settlements would have demanded more efficient use of resources. Pigs had been occasionally used in sacrifices in Egypt and Mesopotamia, and their exclusion in Judaism was also influenced by a desire to distinguish their religion from that of their neighbors.[8]

Leviticus 12. The impurity of a woman after giving birth is an example of a natural activity making a person impure. Here the concern is with the discharge of blood accompanying birth.[9] Purification occurs by waiting a period of time and making an offering. The woman makes the offering after waiting seven days, during which she is unclean, then an additional thirty-three days, for a total of forty days for a male child, and twice that for a female. The numbers seven and forty are used frequently in the Bible for processes that bring wholeness.

This is one of the cases where the poor can make a lesser offering, in recognition of the fact that the sacrificial system could be an economic burden. It is also significant that the woman presents the offering, showing that worship was not carried out exclusively by males.

The origins of these rules, like the origins of other parts of the system, are impossible to determine, but the importance of childbirth means that from the earliest times there would have been some rituals surrounding it. It may seem strange that something as joyful as a new child would be a cause of impurity, but there are both practical and symbolic aspects to these customs. The period of waiting and separation provided a time for the woman to regain her strength. And a birth represented both a blessing and a time of vulnerability and threat to the present order of the family. Those things that give life—food and reproduction—are surrounded by rituals of purity so that they will be a source of blessing and not a cause of disorder.

Leviticus 13–14. The laws on skin disease are among the strictest of the impurity laws, and the separation of the unclean person the most severe, requiring a person with an unclean skin disease to live apart from the community. In part the severity stems from revulsion to a very visible form of impurity, but the detailed rules also come from a desire to distinguish among afflictions that looked similar. This section gives rules for priests examining people and declaring them clean or unclean, the rituals for the purification of a person who had been unclean, and related laws on the growth of mildew or mold on walls and clothing. The reasons for these laws involved both hygiene and the symbolic lack of wholeness of the diseased person.

Contrary to what is found in many translations, the disease in question is not leprosy (Hansen's disease). Hansen's disease produces numbness, facial nodules, and ulceration of the extremities, none of which are described here. The word used here, *saraat*, covers a variety of temporary and long-term skin afflictions, probably including psoriasis, rashes, hives, boils, and fungal infections. Moreover, the same word is used for the mildew or mold on clothing and walls (13:47; 14:34), so it does not refer specifically to a medical condition.

The ritual for readmitting a person to the community after having such a skin disease is elaborate and combines at least two different rituals. The first ritual (14:2-9) involves symbolic acts using two birds, cedar, crimson yarn, and hyssop. The release of the living bird into the field is similar to the release of the goat on the Day of Atonement (16:20-22), and represents the impurity being carried away. Cedar is a wood that resists decay and represents the restored purity of the person. The color red of the yarn was thought to frighten away the demons that had brought on the corruption. This part of the ritual does not involve an urban temple, and preserves elements that were used in villages during the monarchy or even earlier. The second purification ritual, on the other hand, assumes a large temple with animal sacrifices, grain offerings, and anointing with oil (14:10-32). This ritual also provides for a lesser offering for the poor, one of the accommodations required after the centralization of worship in Jerusalem, when the kinds of sacrifices done at the large urban temple were too much of a burden for many members of the community. The fact that the process of readmission includes two different rituals for purification shows that the issue of skin disease and purity had a long history in Israel, and the compilers of the Priestly code could not ignore traditional practices.

Leviticus 15. Any sexual discharge—whether voluntary or involuntary, a normal occurrence or the result of a disease (e.g., gonorrhea), or from a male or a female—made a person unclean. Purity was achieved by waiting a period of time and bathing, and by making an offering in the case of a disease.

The main idea behind these rules was to separate sex from the cult, which is brought out in the summary statement: "Thus you shall keep the people of Israel separate from their uncleanness, so that they do not die in their uncleanness by defiling my tabernacle that is in their midst" (15:31). Earlier Canaanite practices involved sacred prostitution and fertility rites, and some of those practices continued during the Israelite monarchy. For example, small fertility figurines have been found at several sites from the eighth and seventh centuries, and were probably part of household piety.[10] These rules are designed to keep postexilic Judaism distinct from other traditions by keeping sexual motifs out of public worship. A secondary reason for considering sex as a cause of impurity was the symbolic loss of wholeness that comes from the loss of life-giving body fluids.

For the vast majority of the population it would not have been practical to follow these rules. Although later, by New Testament times, there were *mikvaot*, ritual bathing pools, at many Jewish homes, frequent bathing would not have been possible for most Jews earlier in the postexilic period. When these rules were promulgated, probably only priests and a few upper-class people followed them closely.

The Day of Atonement (Leviticus 16)

The Day of Atonement (Yom Kippur) eventually became the most holy day in Judaism, and the only day on which the high priest could enter the holy of holies in the temple. In the instructions here, Aaron is to sacrifice a bull as an offering for his own sins and a goat for the sins of the people, and sprinkle the blood of these animals on the mercy seat in the innermost part of the tabernacle. Then he is to lay his hands on the head of a living goat to transfer all of their sins to it, and the goat is to be sent into the wilderness, "for Azazel."

Once again, two different rituals have been combined in these instructions. One is a temple sacrifice, and the other a rural tradition of transferring evil to an animal and sending it away, similar to the bird carrying away the corruption of skin disease (Lev 14:49-53). Since both rituals were for atonement, the Priestly school combined them and fixed a date for the feast, the tenth day of the seventh month (late September or early October). But this fixed form came about quite late. There are no references before the exile to a Day of Atonement. The exilic prophet Ezekiel described a purification ritual similar to part of this: a bull is sacrificed and its blood put on the temple doorposts and corners of the altar, but the ritual takes place on a different date (Ezek 45:18-20). Somewhat later, the books of Ezra and Nehemiah still do not mention a Day of Atonement, although there is a one-time day of fasting and repentance on the twenty-fourth day of the seventh month (Neh 9:1-5). The Day of Atonement did not become fixed until well into the postexilic period.

The live goat sent away "for Azazel" (16:8, 10, 26) has been understood in various ways. Some early translations, including the Septuagint, took it to mean "goat of departure," leading to the idea of the escaping goat and the term "scapegoat." Some in the rabbinic tradition and others have taken it as a place name, the remote rocky place to which the goat is sent. But since it is in parallel with "for Yahweh," Azazel is most likely the personal name of a demon of the wilderness. Ancient Israel believed that demons, including a goat demon, inhabited desolate places (Is 13:21; 34:14). The apocryphal book *I Enoch*, written about 200-100 BCE, includes Azazel among the fallen angels who bring corruption to the earth (*I Enoch* 10:4-8; 13:1-2; 54:1-6). The ritual here is a way of sending the evil back to its source.[11]

The Holiness Code (Leviticus 17–26)

The next several chapters of Leviticus are different from what preceded them. Rather than dealing with just worship and purity, this section is also concerned with sexual morality, social justice, property laws, slavery, and other issues. There are also differences in the vocabulary and typical phrases used. In particular, there are frequent repetitions of the phrases "I am the LORD" (18:5, 6, 21; 19:12, 14; etc.), "I am the LORD your God" (18:2, 4, 30; 19:3, 4; etc.), and phrases similar to "You shall be holy, for I the LORD am holy" (19:2; 20:26; 21:8). The emphasis on holiness has given rise to the designation "Holiness Code."

The viewpoint of the Holiness Code is similar to that of the rest of the Priestly source, but it also has points in common with Deuteronomy, especially in its ethical laws and its curses for not staying faithful to the covenant (Lev 26; cf. Dt 28). It was probably written independently, with influence from the Priestly and Deuteronomic movements and others, and incorporated into Leviticus by the Priestly authors. However, it is doubtful that the Holiness Code was a single composition before becoming part of Leviticus. There is no overall logical arrangement of its diverse material, suggesting that it existed as several small collections of laws. Some scholars believe there was a Holiness school that contributed other parts of the Pentateuch besides Leviticus 17–26.[12] However, because of the similarity of the Holiness and other Priestly material, it is difficult to determine which passages those might be, so the discussion of the Holiness material will be limited to this part of Leviticus, which almost all scholars recognize as distinct from other Priestly material.

While some of the laws in the Holiness Code are early, there are indications that its composition was late. The frequent references to being brought up from Egypt and into the land of Canaan (18:3; 19:23, 34; etc.) suggest the late monarchy at the earliest, since that is when the exodus story became prominent, and the curses warning of an exile probably come from after the Babylonian conquest (26:14-45). Like other law collections in the Pentateuch, it went through a long process of composition and was included in the Pentateuch out of a desire to preserve multiple traditions.

Leviticus 17. The requirement that sacrifice take place only at the tent of meeting reflects the centralization of worship that took place late in the monarchy. This passage begins ambiguously, using the word "slaughter" (*shahat*), which can also be used for non-sacrificial killing of animals for food. But the rest of the passage uses technical sacrificial words and is clearly not insisting on the impractical requirement that every slaughter take place at one central location. The concern, though, is related to ordinary slaughter. The code seeks to ensure that family or village slaughter for meat does not take on overtones of offerings to minor deities or demons. The similar passage in Deuteronomy 12:15-27 explicitly allows ordinary slaughter to take place elsewhere.

Also related to ordinary slaughter is the sacredness of blood (17:10-16). The blood of the animal may never be eaten, since "the life of every creature is its blood" (17:14). This passage reveals something of the understanding of sacrifice in Israel. All life is from God, and sacrifice is a symbolic giving back of part of it to God. But because blood was seen as carrying life, it all belonged to God and could not be put to human use, whether it came from a sacrifice or an ordinary slaughter. The sacredness of blood illustrates an important aspect of Israelite cultic thinking, that those things that are most sacred cannot be used in profane ways.

Leviticus 18. This section of rules is arranged into two groups, one prohibiting sex with close relatives (18:6-18), and the other prohibiting sex and related activities that were associated with impurity and false worship (18:19-23). Some of the included laws may be quite old, but the introduction (18:1-5) and conclusion (18:24-30) reveal the exilic perspective of the arrangement.

The introduction states that the reason for following these rules is to stay distinct from Egypt and Canaan. The exilic desire to preserve Judaism by keeping it different from its neighbors is present throughout the Pentateuch, but some of the practices here were known specifically in Egypt or Canaan, as well as in Israel during the monarchy.

The prohibition against sex with close relatives was common in the ancient Near East. The law code of Hammurapi, for example, lists daughters, daughters-in-law, mothers, and foster mothers as people a man may not have sex with.[13] However, in Egypt royal marriages occurred between brother and sister, and in Ugaritic mythology Anat is both sister and wife of Baal, so one reason for these laws was to condemn ideas associated with Egypt and Canaan.[14] The main concern in Israel, though, was neither being different from other nations nor biological problems of such unions, but to maintain proper relationships within a clan under male leadership. Relationships that are most disruptive to order in the extended family are prohibited. Thus, the list of prohibited relationships includes people related by marriage but not by blood, and includes aunts except in the case of the wife of one's mother's brother, who would normally be in a different household.

The second group of laws begins by prohibiting sex with a woman who is menstruating, indicating that the concern has shifted to impurity (cf. Lev 15:19-24). The law against offering children to Molek, i.e., as human sacrifice, may seem out of place among sexual laws; it may have been included because it would often involve a newborn child and is thus close to sexuality. It also reveals a concern of this section, false worship. Occasional child sacrifice existed in Israel, probably until late in the monarchy (cf. Gen 22). Male homosexuality is included because it also was connected to worship in Canaan and Israel, in the form of cultic prostitution (2 Kgs 23:7). Sex with an animal may have been considered repulsive in its own right, but also had Canaanite religious connotations; in Ugaritic mythology, Baal has sex with a heifer.[15] These prohibitions are defining a Judaism that is distinct from its neighbors, and distinct from its own Canaanite past.

The conclusion of the section warns that these practices defile the land, and if people engage in them they will be expelled. The warning reveals that impurity rather than ethics is the major concern, and that the section was almost certainly written during the exile as an explanation for why they had been forced from the land.

Leviticus 19. Chapter 19 is perhaps most typical of the Holiness Code. It combines laws on worship, social justice, family and community relationships, and other topics, with no apparent logical arrangement. It introduces the laws with the phrase, "You shall be holy, for I, the Lord your God am holy," and it frequently repeats "I am the Lord." Many of the laws are well-known from elsewhere in the Pentateuch. Worship laws include observing the Sabbath (19:30) and not making images (19:4). Social justice laws include paying wages immediately (19:13) and not oppressing refugees (19:33-34). Family and community laws include revering one's parents (19:3) and respecting the elderly (19:32).

A few laws do require explanation. The Israelites are not to interbreed animals, plant two different kinds of seed in the same field, or wear garments made from two different kinds of cloth (19:19). The ideology of not mixing is related to the Priestly view of creation, in which everything is created in an ordered way according to its kind (Gen 1:1–2:4); this took on great importance during the exile, when Jews were urged to stay separate from foreigners. However, not mixing two different kinds of cloth brings up a problem. In the Priestly instructions on the tabernacle, the curtains next to the most sacred parts are to be made from a blend of wool and linen (Ex 26:1, 31; 36:8, 35), as are the vestments for the priests (Ex 28:5; 39:2). If blending fabrics is evil, why is it done, of all places, in cloth that is put to sacred use? Most likely, the law was originally not about this kind of cloth being evil, but about it being so precious that it should not be profaned by using it for everyday purposes. A blended fabric was more difficult and expensive to make, so reserving it for sacred uses was a way of expressing the otherness of the holy places and of the actions of the priests.[16] This is another example of an idea at the center of Israelite cultic thinking, that sacred items are not be put to everyday use. But by the time the Holiness Code was being compiled, the ideology of not mixing had become more important, and so the law on fabric was put into the context of other laws on not mixing different types of things.

The law against cutting the hair and beard in certain ways (19:27) is related to ritual practices. Hair was a symbol of vitality; it was not cut during the time a person was under a Nazirite vow (Num 6:1-21; Judg 13–16). Shaving one's head was also part of mourning rituals (Is 22:12; Jer 16:6). Evidently the type of trimming prohibited here was associated with rituals that were practiced at one time and later condemned. Gashing one's skin (19:28) was also part of mourning rites in Israel (Jer 16:6; 41:5) and earlier in Canaan—El gashes his skin at Baal's death.[17] Tattoos are condemned (19:28), probably because they were used to change one's appearance to confuse evil spirits. All of these rules go back to particular nonstandard rituals, which is suggested by the fact that the Holiness Code also includes similar laws specifically for priests (Lev 21:5). But they have an additional function, that of preserving the wholeness of the body.

Leviticus 20. The laws here repeat the laws of Leviticus 18, but now penalties are given. Although parts of the chapter read like a law code, its purpose is rhetorical rather than practical. Some of the penalties only God could impose, such as causing a person to be childless, and others are too extreme to have been practical. The concern is again purity and not morality. Thus, when a man has sex with his wife's mother, all three of them must be put to death, even though the wife has done nothing immoral (20:14), and in cases of bestiality both the person and the amoral animal must be put to death (20:15-16).

Leviticus 21. The laws on priests have mainly to do with death and marriage. There are separate laws for regular priests (21:1-9) and the chief priest (21:10-15), with slightly stricter rules for the chief priest, followed by restrictions on sacrifices by priests who are blind, lame, or have other blemishes (21:16-24).

Contact with a corpse made a person impure and required a ritual and a period of seven days to restore purity again (Num 19:11-13). Priests, however, are to avoid becoming impure by such contact in the first place, except with very close relatives, and for the chief priest even those exceptions are not allowed. In addition, the priests are not to engage in other mourning rites, such as shaving one's hair, making gashes on one's body, or tearing one's garments (in Lev 19:27-28 all Israelites were prohibited from doing similar things). The chief priest is even required to stay inside the sanctuary (21:12; presumably it means during the mourning and burial of someone). This separation from death may seem odd to people used to religious ministers' close involvement in death and funeral rites, but the purpose is to end past practices of consulting and worshiping the dead. Such rites were still practiced after the exile, and are also condemned in Third Isaiah (Is 65:4).

Priests are not to marry prostitutes or divorced women; a regular priest may marry a widow but the chief priest may not. A slightly different rule is given by Ezekiel, who says a priest may marry a widow only if she is the widow of another priest (Ezek 44:22), showing that these rules were still evolving during the exile.

Leviticus 22. The rules on offerings overlap the instructions in chapters 1–7, but also address some specifics not mentioned there. Priests who are in an unclean state may not touch sacred offerings; the priest's portion of a sacrifice may be eaten by members of his household but not by others; and more details are given on what animals are acceptable for sacrifice.

Much of the material is practical. The members of a priest's household allowed to eat the sacrifice include slaves, even though they do not have any priestly ancestry or function. Not included is a daughter married to a non-priest, since she would be living in a different household. The exclusion of animals during the first seven days of life has a practical side; it makes it easier to determine if the animal has any flaws. The exclusion of an animal and its mother is not explained, but may have been directed against certain fertility rites.

Leviticus 23. The Holiness Code's calendar of festivals is more complete than the earlier calendars, and is most similar to the Priestly calendar in Numbers 28–29 (cf. Appendix I: Festivals). It also shows signs of the calendar changing over time. Unlike the earlier lists in Exodus 23 and 34, this one gives precise dates, indicating that it is intended for an urban temple. The earlier agricultural bases for the festivals allowed for variable dates, depending on when the harvests actually took place. A comparison of the calendars also shows that the relationship among Unleavened Bread, First Fruits, and Weeks varied. The Holiness Code preserves a tradition of there being three distinct festivals, with Weeks coming fifty days after First Fruits. The celebration of Trumpets at the beginning of the seventh month is probably a remnant of a New Year's celebration from the earlier calendar, when the year began in the fall;

Nehemiah also describes a celebration on that day, with a reading of the law (Neh 8:1-12). The Day of Atonement, which is never mentioned before the exile, is included here and in Numbers, but not in the other calendars (cf. Lev 16). This is a postexilic, urban calendar, which nonetheless preserves some earlier traditions.

Leviticus 24:1-9. These instructions on the lamp and sacred bread complement the Priestly liturgical instructions (Ex 25:23-40; 27:20-21). Like the Priestly instructions, they assume a settled society with a steady supply of olive oil and grain, and do not come from a nomadic desert group. Beyond that, it is impossible to determine their origin.

Leviticus 24:10-23. This story of the person blaspheming "the name" is unusual in several respects, and there are indications that it is later than most of the Pentateuch. It is the only bit of narrative in the Holiness Code. It includes a rare use of the circumlocution "the name" for Yahweh, a practice that became more common late in the biblical period. It is the only place (besides a probable textual error in 2 Sam 17:25) where *yisraeli(t)* is used as the gentilic term for "Israelite," rather than the more common *bene yisrael*; this usage likewise became common later. And the fact that the person has an Israelite mother and Egyptian father is odd, since earlier in the Pentateuch the Israelites were said to be living completely separate from the Egyptians (Gen 46:34; Ex 8:22). Mixed marriages, however, were common after the exile, leading people like Ezra and Nehemiah to take steps to end them, and there were Jews living in Egypt at that time. Most likely, this story comes from well after the exile and addresses the problem of applying Jewish law to a mixed population. The solution, "You shall have one law for the alien and for the citizen: for I am the LORD your God" (24:22), gives a theological justification, although a uniform legal system was probably mandated by the Persian (or Hellenistic, if it is that late) rulers anyway.

Leviticus 25. The broad interest of the Holiness Code is seen in these economic laws, covering the Sabbatical year, the Jubilee year, and the redemption of land and slaves. Every seventh year is to be a year of rest for the land, during which no crops are to be grown. Every forty-ninth (or fiftieth) year is to be a Jubilee, in which all land that has been sold is returned to the family that originally owned it, and anyone who had been sold into slavery is freed. In addition, family members have the right to redeem—that is, buy back land or buy a slave's freedom—before the Jubilee year.

The evidence for the observance of a Sabbatical year for the land comes from after the exile, and is not strong. As part of Nehemiah's reforms in the fifth century, the people vow to observe the Sabbatical year in the future (Neh 10:31), and during the Maccabees' revolt in the second century people were said to be keeping it, despite the severe hunger it caused (1 Macc 6:48-54). Both books, however, tend to exaggerate the people's religious commitments. In a study of agricultural practices in ancient Israel, David Hopkins points out that to keep the land productive it would have been necessary to have fallow years much more frequently than once every seven years, and that because of the variability of climate and pest problems, a rigid system specifying which years had to be fallow would have been impossible.[18] Moreover, real agricultural societies do not put their entire land base out of use all at the same time. The seven-year cycle here should be seen as a symbolic ideal of superabundance, made possible by divine blessings.

The Jubilee year return of land is also idealistic. In agrarian villages during the monarchy and after the exile, land ownership was the basis of wealth and essential for a family's livelihood. Land belonged to the extended family, called the *beth ab* (house of the father). However, the king had the power to take land, either for his own use or to give as a reward to supporters, so there was always the possibility of a few wealthy people having large estates and others becoming landless. Prophetic texts condemn the building up of large estates (Is 5:8-9; Mic 2:1-2), and after the exile the problem of people becoming landless became worse. The Persian empire imposed increasingly high taxes, which would have forced some to sell their property. Nehemiah complained about the rich accumulating land and others losing theirs (Neh 5:1-13), and there were disputes over land ownership between returning exiles and people who had stayed in Judah and taken over their land. The idea that land should stay in the same family is present in several biblical texts, although in different forms (cf. Ruth 4:1-6; 1 Kgs 21:1-16; Jer 32:6-15). The system given here is an idealized view of a just and stable society, based on ancient ideas but prompted by the problems in the postexilic period. It urges widespread land possession, and emphasizes divine ownership of all the earth.

The rules on slavery are slightly different from the ones in Exodus 21:2-11 and Deuteronomy 15:12-18 (see Appendix III for a comparison). Here, no one is to become a slave of a fellow Israelite, but if necessary will become a "bound laborer," and will serve until the Jubilee year (25:39-40). In the other passages, one can become a slave of a fellow Israelite, and is freed in the seventh year. Again, the rule in Leviticus was probably not literally followed, but was an idealized picture of a just society, taking account of the fact that slavery was considered normal in biblical times.

Leviticus 26. The Holiness Code, and the rest of Leviticus, do not usually speak of the laws as part of a covenant, but this chapter refers eight times to a covenant with Yahweh. Blessings for keeping the laws and curses for not keeping them are the typical conclusion of covenants in the Bible (Dt 28) and elsewhere in the ancient Near East,[19] and this chapter brings the Holiness Code to an end. The specifics of the curses reveal that the chapter was written after the exile (26:27-39), and the historically inaccurate claim that the land was empty during the exile reflects the views of Jews in Babylon.

The references to Abraham, Isaac, and Jacob (26:42), and to the exodus (26:45), along with the summary statement that the laws were given to Moses at Mt. Sinai (26:46), mark this chapter as part of the late editorial stage of incorporating the Holiness Code into the Pentateuch.

Supplement on Vows (Leviticus 27)

The final chapter of Leviticus is not considered part of the Holiness Code, because it lacks the typical phrases used there and because chapter 26 already seems to be a conclusion to the Holiness Code. But it does assume knowledge of the Holiness Code's laws on the Jubilee year (Lev 25), and is probably a late expansion of the Priestly part of the Pentateuch.

The regulations here are on making a monetary payment in place of something pledged in a vow. Like blessings, vows, once spoken, cannot be taken back (Num 30:2; Dt 23:21-23; cf. Gen 27). These rules balance that absolute requirement with a concern for the practical difficulty of fulfilling a vow in some circumstances, not just for the person making the vow, but for the temple itself. Particularly under Persian rule, with its heavy taxation, the temple had a greater need for money than for more animals and property.

The occasion for making a vow is not discussed here, but biblical narratives of vows show that they were a way of asking God's help in time of need, such as in battle (Num 21:1-2; Judg 11:30-31), on a journey (Gen 28:20-22), or in barrenness (1 Sam 1:11). The practice of pledging a human being in a vow was not common; it occurs in two stories, that of Hannah pledging her child Samuel to the temple at Shiloh (1 Sam 1), and that of Jephthah inadvertently pledging his only daughter as a human sacrifice (Judg 11:30-40).

CHAPTER EIGHT

Numbers

Numbers 1–4 — Census and Organization

Numbers 5–6 — Expansions of Laws

Numbers 7–10 — Final Preparations and Departure

Numbers 11–32 — Incidents on the Journey

Numbers 33–36 — Concluding Instructions

The English title of the fourth book of the Pentateuch comes from the fact that there is a census of the people at the beginning of the book, and another one near the end for the next generation. The Hebrew title, taken from the first sentence, is *Bemidbar*, "In the Wilderness," and is more descriptive of the entire contents of the book, covering many events that take place during the journey through the wilderness.

Exodus 19–40 and all of Leviticus took place at Mt. Sinai. Numbers begins at Mt. Sinai with the census (1–4), then additional laws (5–6) and final preparations and departure (7–10). The middle part of the book is a combination of incidents during the journey and more laws (11–32). The book concludes with the Israelites encamped at Moab, east of the Jordan River, preparing to enter the promised land (33–36). The framework of the journey is artificial, and in any case the locations of many of the places mentioned are not known, so it is not possible to reconstruct a route that an exodus group took on their way to Canaan. Rather, the book is a collection of stories and laws that reflect the concerns of postexilic Judaism, and its relationships with the surrounding peoples during the monarchy and postexilic period. In addition to the metaphorical use of a journey, the framework allows Israel to be shaped into a people outside of the promised land, which fit the ideology of the Jews who were exiles in Babylon.

On the composition of Numbers, scholars generally believe that the Priestly source is responsible for the overall framework of the book and most of the legal and liturgical material, while most of the narrative parts come from the Yahwist or Yahwist and Elohist sources. In addition, there are a few poetic sections that may be older than the rest of the material, including the priestly blessing (6:22-27), the song of the ark (10:35-36), a quote from a lost work called the Book of the Wars of Yahweh (21:14-15), and four oracles of the prophet Balaam (23–24).

The Development of the Wilderness Tradition

The Hebrew word *midbar* is usually translated desert or wilderness. Wilderness is probably more accurate; *midbar* is uninhabited or sparsely inhabited territory, often with a connotation of desolation. Because many of the areas around Palestine are semi-arid, the traditional translation of desert is often used. The wilderness was considered a dangerous place, with wild beasts and shortages of water, but at the same time it could be a place of refuge from the wars, oppression, and decadence of the cities. As a place outside the control of kings and powerful cities, the wilderness was both a place of danger and a place of purity—which made it a perfect place to encounter God.

The tradition of a wilderness formation of Israel took shape in the monarchy and reached its full form in the exile, when it was given greater importance for shaping the future identity of a restored Judaism. A story of a journey is a story of transition, and Judaism was in transition. The period of national independence had ended with the coming of the Assyrian empire at the end of the eighth century, and finally with the Babylonian conquest in 587. The losses led to efforts to reshape a religious and national identity that would be purified of past mistakes. The journey through the wilderness is a figurative expression of the dangers involved in that transition and purification.

The roots of the wilderness tradition are early. Although most of the ancestors of the Israelites had come from Canaan, a few did migrate in from nearby areas, possibly including a small exodus group (see chapter 5). An early reference to a wilderness tradition is Hosea 13:4-6, which says the Lord knew the Israelites in the wilderness. There was also an admiration for the purity of groups from the wilderness, such as the Rechabites (Jer 35). The Deuteronomic movement developed a story about the wilderness journey (Dt 1–3), which became the basis for the full version of the Yahwist and Priestly writers.

Many of the places in the story cannot be identified, but of the ones that can, two are the center of much of the action: Kadesh in the Negev, and the Transjordanian plains just outside the border of the promised land. Kadesh (also called Kadesh-Barnea) first comes up in Numbers 13–14, in the story of the spies sent into Canaan and the unsuccessful invasion from the south. The Israelites arrive in Kadesh again in Numbers 20, where Miriam dies and is buried, a drought occurs and is ended by the waters of Meribah, and the Israelites send their request to Edom to pass through their land. The prominence of Kadesh is probably due to groups in southern Judah who had historical connections to the area.[1] Those connections, though, do not go back to the premonarchic period. Archaeological evidence shows no occupation at Kadesh in the Late Bronze Age or Iron Age I (i.e., in the immediate centuries before 1000 BCE). A large fortress was there from the tenth century to the end of the monarchy (although it was periodically attacked and abandoned), and the pottery indicates a close interaction between the fortress and the local seminomadic population.[2] Thus, some of the southern desert groups on the Edom-Judah border became part of Israel during the monarchy and preserved memories of the Kadesh region, and those memories were incorporated into the wilderness journey story.

Several incidents at the end of the story take place in Transjordan. The arrival in Moab is marked with a quote from the ancient Book of the Wars of Yahweh (Num 21:14-15), indicating that connections with that region were early. The prophet Balaam, who is unable to curse Israel (Num 22–24), shows up in a text from east of the Jordan from around 800 BCE,[3] indicating religious connections between Israel and Transjordan during the monarchy. The story of the settlement of Israelite tribes east of the Jordan (Num 32) mentions some of the same villages that the Moabite Stone says Israel and Moab fought over in the ninth century,[4] suggesting that the Transjordanian settlement tradition goes back at least to the first half of the monarchy. These Transjordanian stories are based on memories of groups that were part of Israel, but they have no intrinsic connection to a long wilderness journey. Rather, they were made part of the journey story in order to preserve the definition of the promised land as beginning at the Jordan River.

The development of the wilderness tradition involved combining historical memories, mostly from the monarchy, of groups that became part of Israel, especially groups in the Negev and Transjordan at the edges of Palestine. These memories were put into the form of a story connecting the exodus from Egypt with the taking possession of the promised land. The story became part of the foundational story of Judaism, a story of a people formed in the wilderness. During the exile, this story became useful as a metaphor for the danger and purification that Judaism was going through as it shaped its new identity.

Census and Organization (Numbers 1–4)

Through use of a combination of religious and military terminology, the organization of the people during their journey through the wilderness is described. This section, in typical Priestly style, uses precise numbers, repetition, and genealogies.

Much attention is given to the role of the Levites. As discussed in chapter 7, the general picture in the Bible is that priests were a subset of the tribe of Levi, and the rest of the Levites had a lesser role, but the sources disagree on the exact distinction. The Priestly view represents a late stage in the evolution of Israelite priesthood. By this time the priesthood of those claiming descent from Aaron is firmly established, and with official Persian backing there is no serious threat to its claim. Thus the Priestly source portrays the Levites here as a lesser clergy, but without any polemic against them, in contrast to the earlier Ezekiel, who portrays the Levites as lesser, but needs to justify it as a punishment for their unfaithfulness (Ezek 44:10-14). A further evolution is that the word "Levite" at one time referred to one type of minor clergy, but gradually became a general term for all those who had minor duties at the temple (cf. Ezra 2:40-58).

Numbers 1. Numbers begins with an exact date, the first day of the second month of the second year (after the Israelites left Egypt). The last time a date was mentioned in the Pentateuch was back in Exodus

40:17, when it was reported that Moses set up the tabernacle on the first day of the first month of the second year. No dates were given for the events in Leviticus. In fact, some events in Numbers will be told out of chronological order; see the comments on Numbers 7–10 below.

The numbers in the census are unrealistically high. The total of 603,550 males above the age of twenty was used earlier in Exodus 38:26, as if the census had already been done then. It roughly corresponds to the 600,000 men claimed in Exodus 12:37, and the author has distributed them in what seemed like a reasonable way among the twelve tribes. The order in which they are listed is based on their positions when they encamp around the tent of meeting, described in Numbers 2, except that here the three tribes on the south side are listed first, bringing it closer to the birth order of the twelve sons of Jacob. The tribe of Levi is left uncounted for the time being, since they will have religious rather than military duties, and will be treated later.

Numbers 2. Each time the Israelites stop to camp, they are to form a precise arrangement around the tent of meeting. The twelve tribes are divided into four regiments of three tribes each, with a regiment on each side of the tent. The regiments are determined by the birth mothers of the ancestors of the tribes, and by the traditional importance of the tribes. The east and south sides are listed first, and include the tribes descended from Jacob and Leah, plus Gad, descended from Jacob and Leah's maid Zilpah. The west regiment comes next, and is made up of the three tribes descended from Jacob and Rachel. Finally, there is the north regiment, made up of the remaining three tribes descended from Jacob and the maids Bilhah and Zilpah. Judah's position at the front reflects the prominence of Judah during the monarchy.

The Hebrew word used for regiment here, *degel*, is rare outside of Numbers. But it is attested, in its Aramaic equivalent, in several non-biblical texts from the Persian period, referring to military regiments, often with the families stationed along with the soldiers.[5] It is used here because the author wanted to describe the march through the wilderness in military terms that postexilic readers were familiar with.

Numbers 3. After listing the rest of the tribes, the author turns to the tribe of Levi. The census of the Levites includes all males above one

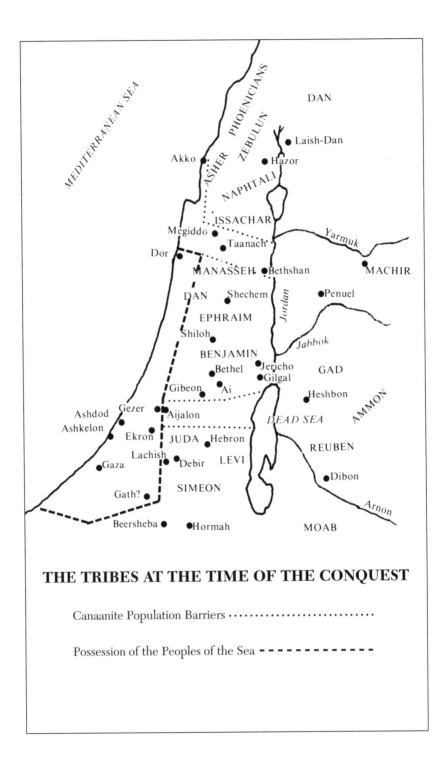

THE TRIBES AT THE TIME OF THE CONQUEST

Canaanite Population Barriers ·

Possession of the Peoples of the Sea – – – – – – – – – – – – –

month of age, since it is not for military duty, but to count the Levites as substitutes for all firstborn males being offered to God. By virtue of their work at the sanctuary they are an offering to God, substituting for everyone else. As with the other census, the numbers are artificial. The total of 22,000 Levites[6] would seem too high for the number of generations it represents, but the total of 22,273 males who are firstborn out of all Israelites is impossibly low, since the other census had 603,550 total Israelite males, without even including the ones under age twenty. The sources of the numbers are not known, but the author's concern is that the Levite males be fewer than the firstborn Israelite males, to have an excuse to present the law on redeeming firstborn males by paying five shekels rather than substitution by a Levite (3:46-51). That payment would have been an important source of temple income in the postexilic period.

Numbers 4. The exact duties of the priests and Levites at the tent of meeting are now described, with particular care that only the priests touch or even look at the most sacred items. The Levites are to carry the tent and its furnishings on the march through the wilderness, a duty that was seen as equivalent to the level of responsibility the Levites had after the exile. The actual duties of the postexilic Levites would have been similar to those described in the literature of that period, and included music, gatekeeping at the temple, caring for sacred items and food for sacrifice, teaching, and other ways of assisting the priests (1 Chron 9:17-23; 23).

A second census of the Levites (4:34-49) includes only males from age thirty to fifty, and is for the ones who will have duties at the tent of meeting. Other texts give different ages for when Levites begin their service (twenty-five in Num 8:24; twenty in 1 Chron 23:24; 2 Chron 31:17; Ezra 3:8), another indication of the multiple traditions about the duties of the Levites.

Expansions of Laws (Numbers 5–6)

With the census and instructions on duties completed, the Israelites are ready to prepare for their departure from Mt. Sinai. But the

Priestly source inserts a few more laws first. These are laws that could fit in almost any context, and are expansions or variations of laws found elsewhere.

Numbers 5:1-10. The requirement that people with skin disease be kept outside the camp repeats the law of Leviticus 13:46, but the other two groups who are put out go beyond other laws. On bodily discharges and contact with a corpse, other laws (Lev 15 and Num 19:11-22 respectively) required others to avoid contact with the impure person, but did not insist that the impure person be kept out of the camp.

The law on making restitution to a person one has harmed repeats Leviticus 6:1-7 (5:20-16 in Hebrew), and expands it to situations where the harmed person has died and left no heirs. In such cases, the monetary restitution goes to the priest who is offering the sacrifice to expiate the offense. The law illustrates the Priestly concern with income for priests and the temple.

Numbers 5:11-30. This unusual trial by ordeal covers cases where a husband suspects a wife of committing adultery, and is another case of the Priestly source dealing in this section with circumstances not completely covered in other laws. In Leviticus 20:10 the punishment for adultery was the death penalty. However, adultery is often suspected without being proven, so the law here provides a way to try such cases by having the woman drink a bitter potion; the consequences will reveal her guilt or innocence.

The text does not state whether the woman is pregnant, but the consequences of the ordeal suggest that she is. If she is guilty, she will have "bitter pain, and her womb shall discharge, her uterus drop" (5:27), a euphemism for a miscarriage. If she is innocent, she will remain pregnant (5:28; *nizreah zara*, lit. "be sown with seed"). Abortifacients were known in biblical times, and this type of trial is similar to other ancient practices.[7]

It is not known how often this trial by ordeal took place; the Priestly author may have simply described a custom he was aware of in order to make the law code more complete. The passage has been a difficulty for later interpreters. The Mishnah, written about 200 CE, devotes a tractate to it, and notes that the practice was discontinued because men were committing adultery without facing a corresponding

ordeal (*Sotah* 9:9). It is a text that is often ignored because of the problem of a biblical passage seeming to call for an abortion. It should be
noted, though, that in other cases of adultery, the death penalty for the
woman in Leviticus 20:10 would necessarily also involve the death of
her fetus if she were pregnant. While placing great value on human life,
the Hebrew Scriptures do not have the same understanding of unborn
children as some modern theologians do.

Numbers 6:1-21. The basic meaning of the word Nazirite is something that is "set apart," and it comes from the same root as the word
for vow.[8] There are three restrictions for a person who takes a Nazirite
vow: avoid wine and other products from grapes, avoid cutting one's
hair, and avoid impurity by contact with a corpse. At the end of the
period of the vow, one makes an offering at the sanctuary, cuts one's
hair and burns it with the sacrifice, and may drink wine again. Anyone
can make such a vow, and there are no restrictions on how long the
period of the vow will be. Nothing is said about the reason a person
would become a Nazirite, although in later times it became a common
way of expressing thanks to God.

These instructions are a Priestly codification of vows that existed
earlier in various forms. The prophet Amos complained that God had
made Nazirites, but the Israelites had made them drink wine (Am 2:11-
12). Amos groups Nazirites with prophets as people called by God to a
religious way of life, but gives no other details. Samson is called a
Nazirite; the only explicit restriction put on him is that his hair never be
cut, although his mother is told to avoid strong drink and unclean food
(Judg 13:4-5). Samson's hair is eventually cut off and he is captured by
the Philistines. That story portrays a Nazirite as a (rather fallible) holy
warrior, and sees the hair as the thing that makes him stronger than
everyone else. On other ways in which hair is ritually significant, see
Leviticus 19:27.

Numbers 6:22-27. The priests' blessing is one of the early poetic com-
positions included in this book. An almost identical blessing was found
on a silver talisman discovered in 1980 in a burial cave near Jerusalem.[9]
The talisman, along with a smaller one with part of the same blessing,
has been dated to the seventh or sixth century BCE, late in the monarchy. The existence of the talisman does not, of course, mean that the

Book of Numbers was written by the end of the monarchy, but that it is quoting an earlier known blessing.

Final Preparations and Departure (Numbers 7–10)

The final preparations for the departure from Mt. Sinai are quite elaborate. The leaders of the tribes present offerings for the journey and the dedication of the altar, some additional liturgical items are made, the Levites are consecrated, and the Passover is celebrated.

One odd feature that comes up in this section is that the Priestly account is not strictly chronological. In Numbers 9:1-5, the second Passover is celebrated on the fourteenth day of the first month of the second year. But back in Numbers 1:1 it was already the second month of the second year. The reason for presenting these events out of chronological order is probably to give the Passover a more prominent place in the order of narration, right before the departure from Sinai.

Numbers 7–8. For all its precision on dates, the Priestly source can sometimes be deliberately vague. These offerings begin "on the day when Moses had finished setting up the tabernacle." In Exodus 40:17, Moses began setting up the tabernacle on the first day of the first month of the second year. These offerings must come after the census of Numbers 1–4, since the leaders of the tribes and the division of duties among the Levites are known, so the date is sometime early in the second month of the second year. But the Priestly author is vague about the exact date, so that it will not be so obvious that some events are told out of order.

Each tribe presents an equal offering, representing the exilic ideal that the restored Israel will be a place of equality for all tribes—not unlike the idealistic land division among the tribes in Ezekiel 48. The generosity of the gifts is far beyond what would have been possible for a group in the desert, and is aimed at the people returning from exile, inspiring them to support the temple.

The preparations for departure also include two liturgical matters, making the lampstands and purifying the Levites for service. The Levites are not anointed, as the sons of Aaron were, nor do they wear priestly vestments (cf. Lev 8–9). Their cleansing and shaving is modeled after the rituals done when completing a Nazirite vow (Num 6) or when being purified after a skin disease (Lev 13–14). The age for beginning Levitical service is here said to be twenty-five, which differs from the age of thirty given in Numbers 4, another indication that the use of the term "Levite" evolved from multiple minor clergy groups with different practices.

Numbers 9. Although narrated as if coming after the events of Num 1–8, the second Passover is actually dated earlier. It is presented here to more closely associate it with the departure from Sinai. The description of the cloud and fire reiterates the end of Exodus. The author also uses this opportunity to expand the laws on keeping the Passover, with the provision that anyone who is unclean from touching a corpse, or who is away on a journey, can celebrate the Passover a month later.

Numbers 10:1-28. The trumpets, the last items made before the departure, serve both military and liturgical purposes. As such, they characterize the Priestly depiction of the desert journey, which is both a military march and a religious gathering.

The Israelites depart from Mt. Sinai and head toward the wilderness of Paran, in the northern Sinai Peninsula. They march in the order given in Numbers 2, except that there the Levites were all in the center and here some are positioned after the first regiment and some in the center. The reason seems to be so that the Kohathites, carrying the holiest items, will arrive later than the other Levites, who will then have had time to set up the tent before the holy items arrive.

Numbers 10:29-36. After all the preceding Priestly material, there is finally narrative from another source, the Yahwist. Unlike the Priestly account with the ark in the center, here the ark goes ahead to find a place for the Israelites to camp. This is similar to other biblical stories in which the ark is an item with power to lead people in battle (1 Sam 4–7). The song of the ark (10:35-36) is also based on the ark's function of empowering the people in battle, and is quoted here from an old battle song.

This passage depicts a close relationship with the Midianites, even suggesting that they will have a share in the promised land. Since the Israelites came from mixed backgrounds, it is likely that some had ancestors related to Midianite groups. Here Moses' father-in-law is called Hobab, although elsewhere he is called Reuel (Ex 2:18) or Jethro (Ex 3:1; 18:1). The inconsistency probably comes from various groups in Israel claiming a connection to Moses.

Incidents on the Journey (Numbers 11–32)

The journey though the wilderness, with occasional regulations on worship and other matters, takes up the next several chapters. There are repeated obstacles along the journey, from other peoples encountered by the Israelites and from their own lack of trust in Yahweh and Moses.

A recurring theme in this section is the people's murmuring against Yahweh and their leaders. The theme is given attention in the Pentateuch because of the reluctance of many of the exilic Jews to return to Judah, which the author is acknowledging by including so many obstacles. Similar murmuring occurred in Exodus 15–18, during the journey from Egypt to Mt. Sinai. But the difference is that the earlier complaints were more justified by the circumstances, and Yahweh responded by patiently providing for the people's needs. Here, the complaints are less justified, and Yahweh's response usually includes punishing the people. Now that Yahweh has established a covenant with the Israelites, more is expected of them, and rebellion will not be tolerated.

The other obstacle is the several battles they fight with people along the way. In these, the Israelites become progressively more successful. They are defeated in their attempt to enter the land of Canaan from the south, so they must detour around to the east. Their journey is made even longer when the Edomites refuse to allow them to pass through their land. But then they are successful in several battles, and finally some of the tribes take possession of land east of the Jordan. Through these battles they become a nation that cannot be defeated, and are prepared to conquer the promised land.

Numbers 11. Two seemingly unrelated stories have been woven together, one about the people complaining about the food, Moses in turn complaining about the people to God, and God responding with both food and a plague to punish them, and the other about a prophetic spirit coming upon seventy elders Moses has chosen to assist him. The result is a complex picture of the failings of the people and God finding other ways to guide them through prophecy. Late in the monarchy and during the exile, the prophets of Israel gained increasing respect as the institutional leaders failed to preserve the nation. This story reminds the exilic Jews that God will come up with ways to get around their failings.

Both parts of the story are similar to incidents that occurred before the Israelites reached Mt. Sinai. In Exodus 16, the people complained and God sent manna, and in Exodus 18 Moses delegated judging authority to others because of the burden on him. In this case the complaint about food is not as justified, since they already have the manna, so God takes a less tolerant attitude.

Unlike in the Priestly account, here the tent of meeting is outside the camp, indicating that the Pentateuch has preserved multiple traditions of portable desert shrines (cf. Ex 33).

Numbers 12. This is one of several stories of opposition to Moses' leadership. Cush is the area south of Egypt, and the wife referred to would be someone other than Zipporah, his Midianite wife. The complaint of Aaron and Miriam seems to be based on Moses' marrying a foreign woman. The author uses the story, though, to emphasize Moses' uniqueness as a prophet. It follows up on the previous story, where several people received a prophetic spirit, by saying that nonetheless no prophet will come who knows the Lord as intimately as Moses did.

Numbers 13–14. This story explains why the Israelites had to wander forty years in the wilderness instead of entering the promised land immediately. Of the twelve spies sent into Canaan, only Caleb and Joshua bring back encouraging reports about the Israelites' ability to conquer the land, and the people complain against their leaders and want to go back to Egypt. After hearing they will be punished, the Israelites try to invade the land, but without the Lord's backing, and are defeated by the Amalekites and Canaanites.

The event is told with some unevenness, and is probably a Yahwist story to which the Priestly author has added some elements, such as broadening the spies' mission to include all of Canaan and not just the area around Hebron, and giving Joshua as well as Caleb a positive role. Also, the spies are sent from the wilderness of Paran (13:3) and return to "the wilderness of Paran, at Kadesh" (13:26), although the wilderness of Paran is normally not considered to extend that far north. Elsewhere it is stated that the Israelites did not arrive in Kadesh until much later, around the fortieth year of the journey (Num 20:1,14-29; 33:36). Most likely the Yahwist itinerary had the Israelites arriving in Kadesh early in the journey, and the Priestly one had them arriving later in order to have them spend more time close to Mt. Sinai.[10]

Caleb is mentioned several times in the Pentateuch and in Joshua and Judges. Elsewhere he is called a Kenizzite (Num 32:12; Jos 14:6, 14), and in the conquest and settlement stories he and his clan settle in Hebron (Josh 14:6-15; 15:13-19). Little is known about the Kenizzites, but they are listed as one of the groups in Canaan before the Israelites lived there (Gen 15:19), and may have been related to the Edomites (Gen 36:11, 15, 42). Many scholars believe that the stories about Caleb are meant to account for one of the groups that joined with the Israelites in their formative days.[11] It is even suggested that the Calebites were the source of the traditions about Abraham, who is also associated with Hebron,[12] and that King David was a Calebite.[13] While it is likely that such a group was part of the mixed ancestors of the Israelites, it is impossible to know their history with certainty, or when they became part of the nation. If the group was from Kadesh, then archaeological evidence indicates that it was around the beginning of the monarchy when they first became associated with Judah (see Development of the Wilderness Tradition, above).

Numbers 15. The Priestly source inserts some additional cultic laws here. Grain and wine offerings are to be added to animal sacrifices (cf. Lev 1–3) and further instructions on sin offerings are given (cf. Lev 4–5).

On violating the Sabbath, Exodus 31:14-15 already called for the death penalty. This incident is similar to one in Leviticus 24:10-23, in which a man caught blaspheming is temporarily held in custody until the decision is made to stone him. Imprisonment as a punishment in itself is not part of the Pentateuch's legal system, and would not have been practical through much of the Israelites' history, which is why the death penalty is used for any violation considered serious.

The blue cord on the corner of garments illustrates the Priestly concern with the symbolism of garments, similar to the instructions on the tabernacle fabrics and priests' vestments (Ex 26, 28).

Numbers 16–17. This is another composite of two stories, a revolt led by Korah, and one led by Dathan and Abiram of the tribe of Reuben. The Dathan and Abiram revolt is referred to in Deuteronomy 11:6 and Psalm 106:16-17 without any connection to Korah. The Reubenite revolt is probably related to other negative passages about Reuben, to explain why the tribe is not the most prominent despite the fact that Reuben was the eldest of the sons of Jacob (Gen 35:22; 49:3-4).

The Korah story stems from rivalry among priestly factions before the priesthood of Aaron became the only officially accepted one. There is other evidence of a Korahite cultic group. Several psalms are entitled "Of the Korahites" (Pss 42; 44–49; 84; 85; 87). In 1 Chronicles 9:17-19, Korahites are prominent gatekeepers at the temple. There is archaeological evidence of the Korahites in the south, an inscription with the name "sons of Korah" at a temple at Arad.[14] Korah is also listed as an Edomite clan (Gen 36:14, 16, 18), an example of the blurring of Edomite and Israelite identities in the south. This story is a polemic against them, but it is careful not to include the family of Korah, and Numbers 26:11 will add that the sons of Korah were not killed in the punishment, to account for the fact that the Korahites still existed during the monarchy.

The budding of Aaron's staff is a folkloric element to show divine selection. It is inserted here to reaffirm the primacy of Aaron and the tribe of Levi after the revolts, although it probably existed as an independent story of God choosing Aaron and the Levites.

Numbers 18. This summary of the priests' and Levites' duties is inserted right after their authority has been reaffirmed. For the most part, it is a restatement of regulations listed earlier. The payment of five shekels to redeem firstborn humans is stated as the norm here (18:15-16), whereas earlier it was presented as something allowed only to make up for there being more firstborn Israelites than total Levites, who were considered substitutes for firstborn males (3:40-51). The payment for all firstborn called for here was more likely the usual practice, as it provided revenue for the temple. The policy of giving all the tithes to the Levites (18:21-24) differs from that of Deuteronomy 26:12-13, which says that tithes are to be shared among the Levites, aliens, orphans, and widows. The Deuteronomic Code comes from late in the monarchy, and uses "Levites" to refer to priests recently dispossessed when worship was centralized in Jerusalem; it is sympathetic to them and groups them with other disadvantaged people. Here, they are minor but well-established clergy at the temple, and for the Priestly code temple revenue is a priority. One new piece of legislation here is that the Levites are to give a tithe of everything they receive to the priests (18:25-29). It is not known how that was put into practice; it may be stated here as a way of emphasizing the Levites' subordination to the priests.

Numbers 19. Impurity caused by contact with a corpse is mentioned frequently in the Pentateuch, but this is the only place where a complete ritual for purification is given. The seriousness of this type of impurity is brought out by the careful descriptions of what kinds of contact cause it and the details of the purification ritual, including the preparation of the cleansing water, with the strange, and probably quite old, ritual with the red cow. The ritual is most similar to the purification from skin disease, in that it involves an animal, cedar, hyssop, and crimson yarn (cf. Lev 14:1-7, 49-53). The red color of the cow and yarn was thought to frighten away demons, and cedar represents purity because it resists decay. One reason the impurity of a corpse is stressed so much is to make sure no past practices of consulting and worshiping the dead are connected with the temple (cf. Lev 21, which sets strict limits on priests' involvement in mourning rituals).

Numbers 20. The events at Kadesh and Mt. Hor are about the first generation coming to an end. Because of the earlier lack of trust after the spies' report, the whole generation, except Caleb and Joshua, was condemned to die in the wilderness (Num 13–14). Now the same punishment is given specifically to Moses and Aaron. To make it clear that things will not be easy for this generation, they are forced to detour around Edom, and Aaron dies, fulfilling part of the threatened punishment.

The story of the people complaining about no water (20:1-13), used to explain why Moses and Aaron will not enter the promised land, leaves much unclear. Moses and Aaron are punished for their lack of trust, and will not enter the promised land, but there is no obvious offense mentioned in the story. The story existed in at least two different forms; in Exodus 17:1-7 there is a similar account, although set next to Mt. Sinai (Horeb) rather than Kadesh, and there are brief mentions of the incident in several places (Dt 6:16; 32:51; Pss 81:8; 95:8; 106:32-33), some-times naming the place Meribah, sometimes Massah, and sometimes both. In part, the story is an etiology of a name—"Meribah" means quarrel—but beyond that there is no adequate explanation for it.

The Israelites encounter another obstacle, as Edom refuses to let them pass through its territory. The story depicts Edom as a powerful country in possession of the Negev as far west as Kadesh. During the monarchy the border between Judah and Edom shifted, with Edom at times in control of that much territory. Edom is especially remembered as evil for helping the Babylonians destroy Judah in 587 BCE, and that may be part of the reason it is portrayed negatively here. The story is not consistent with Deuteronomy 2:28-29, which claims that the Israelites did pass through Edom; it probably originated with southern Judean groups who had more contact with Edom.

The death of Aaron signals that God will indeed carry out the pun-ishment. On the positive side, it leads to an orderly succession of the position of chief priest, to Aaron's son Eleazar. The location, Mt. Hor, is unknown; since it is at the border of Edom, somewhere south or south-west of the Dead Sea is meant.

Numbers 21:1-3. The story of the defeat of a southern Canaanite king contradicts the mainstream tradition of the invasion from the south being unsuccessful (Num 13–14). It also claims to be the reason for the name "Hormah" (destruction), but that name had already been used when they were defeated by the Canaanites (Num 14:45), and later there is a different story that claims to be the reason for the name (Judg 1:17). This is an isolated tradition that circulated among some southern Judean groups. Despite its problems, it is included here after the death of Aaron to mark a turning point in the journey. Now that the first gen-eration is dying, the Israelites will be successful in their battles, and will be prepared to conquer the promised land.

Numbers 21:4-9. The Israelites continue their journey toward the Gulf of Aqaba (which is what "Sea of Reeds" refers to here), and com-plain again about the food and lack of water. God punishes them by sending fiery serpents that bite and kill many of them. When they beg for forgiveness, God has Moses make a bronze serpent on a pole, and anyone who looks at it is healed.

Serpents have been much used in religious iconography. Protective snake figurines were used in Egypt and Mesopotamia, several bronze snakes have been discovered in Late Bronze Age Canaanite sites, and a gold-plated bronze snake was found at a shrine at Timna, just north of the Gulf of Aqaba.[15] In Canaan, snakes were associated with fertility, while the healing symbolism of snakes is best known from the Greek god Asclepius.

According to the Deuteronomic History, Hezekiah carried out a religious reform and removed items used for false worship, including a bronze serpent said to have been made by Moses (2 Kgs 18:4). The serpent Hezekiah destroyed was probably a carryover from Canaanite practices. While not directly criticizing Moses, that story does connect him with false worship. This story in Numbers is a later attempt to show that Moses had no guilt in the original making of the serpent.

Numbers 21:10-35. A series of incidents in Transjordan brings the Israelites farther north, and begins the conquest of the land some of the tribes will possess. The author pieces together older traditions of Israelite encounters east of the Jordan, although the specific people and most of the places mentioned are unknown.

The Book of the Wars of Yahweh (21:14-15) is a lost work. The quote from it is probably authentic, since the language is archaic. Such collections of battle stories preserved traditions of early Israel, but the fact that it is used here only to locate an encampment shows how selective the author was in making use of early traditions. Most likely, the book was used so selectively, and not itself preserved, because much of it did not fit the national story of origins that the Pentateuch presents. In the song about Heshbon (21:27-30) the author uses part of the prophet Jeremiah's oracle against Moab (Jer 48:45-46), another example of using a source in a selective way.

The kings Sihon and Og are mentioned in several other places of the Hebrew Scriptures (Dt 2:24–3:11; Judg 11:19-22). A tradition preserved in the Psalms makes their defeat a more prominent part of the conquest of the promised land (Pss 135:11-12; 136:18-21). The Pentateuch downplays their importance because of its own ambivalence on whether territory east of the Jordan should be considered part of the promised land. On one level, it clearly is not part of the promised land, since the first generation has not completely died out while the

Israelites are taking possession of this land, and it is the crossing of the Jordan that marks the entry into the land. But with these stories and others, such as that of Jacob encountering God at Peniel (Gen 32:22-32), the Pentateuch also acknowledges ties to the land east of the Jordan. The actual settlement of this land by some of the tribes will be reported in Numbers 32, again with concern about whether it is really part of the land God wanted them to have. This way of treating Transjordan probably comes from the situation after the exile, when some Jews had ties to that land, but the ties were not as strong as those to the land west of the Jordan.

Numbers 22–24. In the story of Balaam the Israelites themselves have no role; only foreign opponents do. Because it is loosely connected to its context, it is probably based on independent stories. Balaam is mentioned several other times in the Bible, usually more negatively than this story would warrant (Dt 23:3-6; Num 31:16; 2 Pet 2:15-16; Rev 2:14), so there must have existed other stories about him that have been lost.

In 1967 an inscription was found in Deir Alla, in Jordan, around the very place where these events in Numbers are set, which preserves another story about Balaam. It is dated to around 800 BCE, in the middle of the Israelite monarchy. The inscription is fragmentary, and not all of it can be read, but it tells of a prophet, Balaam son of Beor, who receives a disturbing oracle in the night from the god El. The gods, called "Shaddayin," have met, one goddess is about to block the sun from the earth, and various other disruptions are taking place on earth. Balaam reports the oracle to people, and there is some kind of response, but at that point the text is unclear and has been read in different ways.[16]

The similarities between the biblical Balaam story and the Deir Alla text are remarkable. Besides the name of the prophet and the location being the same, both use the less common divine names, El and Shaddai/Shaddayin, and in both cases the prophet receives his oracles during the night. The Deir Alla text is probably part of a larger circle of traditions about this Balaam, coming from a group of people whose religion was close to the official Israelite religion. The stories may even go back to a historical person Balaam, although if so it would have been a prophet who lived during the monarchy and not as early as the setting of the story in Numbers.

Because of its unusual features, the composition of Numbers 22–24 is difficult to determine. The four oracles of Balaam are likely older poetic blessings (with some later additions), around which the Yahwist has built a narrative. The Yahwist uses it at this point to add to the picture of the Israelites' success as they prepare to enter the promised land. Military efforts could not stop them, and now attempts to curse them are equally unsuccessful.

The incident of the talking ass, though, does not completely fit (22:23-34). God had just told Balaam to go to King Balak to prophesy, but then becomes angry at him for doing so and blocks the road. Balaam seems to be alone, rather than with the large Moabite delegation that was supposedly accompanying him. Balaam's character seems different, too, more in line with the negative traditions about him. It is also a peculiar story in that it is a rare case of a talking animal in the Bible. This is probably an independent story, which has been inserted here because the ass is a figure for Balaam himself. Balaam is an unexpected character speaking the truth, going against the wishes of the one who thinks he is his superior, King Balak.[17]

Numbers 25. The theme of sex with foreign women leading to false worship is common in the Bible (e.g., 1 Kgs 11:1-8 on Solomon; 1 Kgs 16:31-33 on Ahab). This story is made up of two separate incidents, one involving Moabite women and one involving a Midianite woman. The story glorifies Phineas, grandson of Aaron, in order to praise leaders who take strict measures to keep the community intact. A similar attitude is seen in the efforts to prevent mixed marriages after the exile (Ezra 9:1-4; 10:10-11; Neh 13:23-27). A different version of the story is preserved in Psalm 106:28-31, in which the people offer sacrifices to the dead, and Phineas intercedes for the plague to stop, rather than killing anyone. False worship at Baal Peor is also mentioned in Hosea 9:10, so the core of the story is based on an old tradition.

Numbers 26–27. The plague killed off the last of the first generation, and now preparations to enter the promised land begin, starting with a new census to determine how to allot the land. Most of the numbers are similar to those of the first census. The biggest difference is that Simeon is drastically reduced, from 59,300 to 22,200; Simeon will be absorbed into the tribe of Judah and cease to exist as an independent tribe (cf. Jos 19:9).

Another type of preparation has to do with laws on land ownership (27:1-11). As with most legal material in Numbers, this expands on other laws. Inheritance was normally through sons, and this expansion addresses cases in which a man dies with no sons. Daughters are given the first right of inheritance, and if there are no daughters, the inheritance passes to the next closest relative. This law will be further expanded in Numbers 36:1-12, with restrictions to make sure that the marriage of a daughter does not cause the land to pass to a different tribe.

Leadership is also an important part of the preparation, and Joshua is commissioned to replace Moses when he dies. The commissioning subordinates Joshua to Eleazar, the chief priest. The Urim, which Eleazar is to use in making known the Lord's will to Joshua, has been mentioned along with the Thummim as part of the chief priest's vestments (Ex 28:30), although nowhere is there a clear explanation of what these items are. Apparently they were devices used for some manner of casting lots, and small enough to be carried inside the priest's vestments.

Numbers 28–29. The material here can be compared to that found in other liturgical calendars (see Appendix I: Festivals). This is not really a separate calendar, but detailed instructions on what offerings to use, based on instructions in Exodus 29:38-42 and Numbers 15. It uses the calendar of Leviticus 23, but also includes daily and monthly offerings. Like Leviticus 23, this includes more feasts than the shorter calendars that list the three major festivals (Ex 23:14-17; 34:18-26; Dt 16:1-17), and it uses fixed dates rather than dates based on agricultural events, indicating that it comes from an urban temple setting. It differs from Leviticus 23 in treating First Fruits and Weeks as a single festival, which was probably the normal practice.

Numbers 30. In theory, a vow could not be taken back once it had been spoken. But for practical reasons, exceptions were made; Leviticus 27 allowed the substitution of monetary payments for people or objects that had been pledged in a vow. The rules here allow a father to nullify the vow of a daughter living in his house, and a husband to nullify the vow of his wife. The rules assume a patriarchal society in which women had little independence.

Numbers 31. The story of the war against Midian is problematic in several ways. Elsewhere Midian is portrayed as a friend—Moses lived there for a time, and his Midianite father-in-law aided the Israelites and joined with them on the journey (Ex 18; Num 10:29-32). This war follows two negative incidents involving Midian, their joining Moab in asking Balaam to curse Israel, and a Midianite woman marrying an Israelite man at the time Israelites were having sex with Moabite women. Both seem artificially attached to stories about Moab, and were probably added only to justify this war. Here, Balaam seems to be living among the Midianites and is blamed for the apostasy at Baal Peor, although in that story itself he was never mentioned (Num 25). This story claims that every Midianite except for virgin girls was killed, yet in a later story Midian not only still exists, but is strong enough to rule over Israel for a time (Judg 6–8). Clearly this story had an origin different from that of the others.

The victory over Midian is described in idealistic terms. No Israelites are killed, the enemy is completely wiped out, and a huge amount of booty is taken. The booty is divided equitably, with generous amounts given to the Levites and tabernacle. This is the first war of the new generation, and the author describes it in this idealistic way to show that now that the old and faithless generation is gone, the Israelites are more perfectly prepared to take the promised land.

Numbers 32. Gad, Reuben, and part of Manasseh settle in lands east of the Jordan, even though it is not strictly a part of the promised land. The story accounts for this by saying that Moses allowed it after Gad and Reuben agreed to also cross the Jordan and help the other tribes conquer the land of Canaan.

There is good historical evidence that Israel at times controlled land in Transjordan. On an inscription discovered in Jordan known as the Moabite Stone, King Mesha of Moab claims he has defeated Israel, after Israel had ruled parts of his land since the time of Omri.[18] Omri reigned in Israel ca. 876-869 BCE and was one of its most powerful kings, although the Deuteronomic History says little about him except for noting his religious sins (1 Kgs 16:21-28). It does, however, later report that Moab rebelled against a king of Israel, Jehoram (ca. 849–842), and that Israel was not able to hold onto its land in Moab (2 Kgs 3:4-27), supporting what the Moabite Stone says. Several of the places listed in Numbers 32 as Israelite settlements are listed in the Moabite Stone as places King Mesha took back from Israel; these places include Ataroth, Kiriathaim, Nebo, and Baal-meon.

The descendants of Machir, said to be part of the tribe of Manasseh, also settle part of Transjordan, even though they were not part of the story earlier (32:39-42). In the ancient poem in Judg 5:14, Machir is listed as equivalent to the full tribes, and was probably at one time a significant group that later diminished. It is another example of the scheme of twelve tribes evolving from a more complex situation of several small groups in Israel's past.

Concluding Instructions (Numbers 33–36)

The journey through the wilderness is complete, and there will be no more battles in Transjordan. The final part of Numbers gives an itinerary for the entire journey and instructions for use of the land in Canaan after they conquer it. It reads very much like a conclusion to the Pentateuch, except that the death of Moses does not yet take place, which is why many scholars believe Deuteronomy was written separately and incorporated into the rest of the Pentateuch at a late editorial stage.

Numbers 33. Although in the form of a complete itinerary, this list of names is not helpful in reconstructing a route through the wilderness, since most of the places are unknown. Several of the places, in fact, are mentioned in none of the stories of incidents that have taken place along the way. The itinerary is set almost entirely before the arrival in Kadesh (33:36), which fits the Priestly view that most of the forty-year journey was spent in the Sinai (cf. Num 13–14).

The instructions on making a complete conquest of Canaan and destroying all of the religious places are written from an exilic perspective. The conclusion, that if they do not do these things, then "I will do to you what I thought to do to them," shows that it is meant as an explanation for why God allowed the exile to occur.

Numbers 34. The boundaries of the land are described as if they will be fixed, although in reality during the monarchy the amount of land under Israelite control frequently changed, and after the exile the Persian province of Judah was far smaller than what is described here. It is similar to the description in Ezekiel 47:13-20 of the ideal boundaries of the restored postexilic Israel. The southern boundary includes territory in the Negev that Judah and Edom fought over. The western boundary is the Mediterranean Sea, as if the Philistines did not exist. The northern boundary is difficult to determine, since the places mentioned are not known, but it must be some distance north of the Sea of Galilee, since the eastern boundary begins above it; Ezekiel puts the northern boundary along the border of Damascus. The eastern boundary is the Jordan River, in line with the view that Transjordan is not part of the promised land.

The leaders responsible for apportioning the land are Eleazar and Joshua, the religious and military leaders. The tribal leaders assisting them are people who have not been mentioned before, except for Caleb, who, along with Joshua, is the only survivor from the first generation (cf. Num 13–14).

Numbers 35. The cities for the Levites and cities of refuge are presented in an orderly, idealistic way that probably does not correspond to an exact historical situation. Cities where clergy had special status would simply have been cities where shrines were located. The area allowed for pasture, a perfect square, would not have made sense in most of the terrain in Palestine.

The idea of having cities of refuge originates with the practice of using sanctuaries as places of refuge. A person accused of murder could go to a sanctuary and hold onto a horn of the altar and, at least temporarily, not be taken away and punished (cf. Ex 21:12-14; 1 Kgs 1:50-53; 2:28-34). The value of the practice was in putting a limit on rash judgment, especially in cases of accidental killing. The rules here are a more developed system, with guidelines on when a person may use a place of refuge, dating from after the centralization of worship in Jerusalem. Since there are supposed to be no other altars in the land, they have been transformed into cities of refuge.

Even in accidental killings, the victim's family is considered to have the right to avenge the blood of the one killed. However, that right ends when the high priest dies, and the killer can then leave the city of refuge. Why that should be the case is not explained. It may go back to an ancient practice of granting a general amnesty at the death of a king, or to a developing idea that the high priest's death was an atonement for all unavenged deaths. The atonement idea is supported by the text's concern that the land becomes defiled by a killer whose victim has not been avenged (35:33-34). The office of high priest did not exist until after the exile, another indication of the late date of these rules.

Numbers 36. The Book of Numbers ends with one more example of expanding on laws that were given earlier. In Numbers 27:1-11, it was stated that daughters could inherit land if a man died with no sons. Now, to make sure that land does not pass to a different tribe through marriage, a requirement is added that the woman must marry within her tribe.

Deuteronomy

The final book of the Pentateuch is in the form of Moses' farewell speech before he dies. The Israelites have reached the border of the promised land, and are encamped in Moab, east of the Jordan River. In his speech, Moses summarizes the journey through the wilderness, presents the laws that the Israelites are to follow, and, in homiletic fashion, encourages them to be faithful to the laws. The book ends with the death and burial of Moses.

There are several reasons to believe that Deuteronomy had an origin separate from that of the other parts of the Pentateuch. The book seems almost unnecessary if the rest of the Pentateuch already existed, since in Numbers the Israelites had already reached the end of their journey and were prepared to enter Canaan. Deuteronomy repeats much of the material already given, and in some cases has different versions of laws that are found elsewhere in the Pentateuch. Deuteronomy also has its own unique style of writing and typical phrases.

According to the documentary hypothesis, most of Deuteronomy constitutes the Deuteronomist source, one of the four major sources that made up the Pentateuch. However, unlike the other sources, with the Deuteronomist there is more specific evidence of its historical development. There are also similarities between Deuteronomy and other parts of the Hebrew Scriptures, leading to theories that there was a movement, the "Deuteronomic movement," that produced or at least contributed to other writings besides this book.

The Deuteronomic Movement

According to 2 Kings 22–23, King Josiah discovered a book in the temple and, after consulting a prophet, carried out a religious reform based on the book. His reform included centralizing worship in Jerusalem, eliminating worship of other gods, and destroying unorthodox forms of worship, such as the high places, sacred pillars, temple prostitution, and divination. All the elements of his reform are things Deuteronomy calls for, so it is believed that the book discovered in the temple was an early version of Deuteronomy. The Deuteronomic movement was the group of people responsible for this book, and the people behind Josiah's reform.

There are a number of disputed questions, though, about Deuteronomy and Josiah's reform. We do not know how historically reliable 2 Kings 22–23 is. If an early version of Deuteronomy was connected to a religious reform, we do not know if the book actually existed previously or was written only as part of the reform, with the story about "finding" the book in the temple invented to give it greater authority. (The parallel account in 2 Chron 34 has the discovery of the book take place six years after the reform began.)

Another issue is the connection between the Deuteronomic movement and other biblical literature. Scholars have noted similarities between Deuteronomy and the six historical books Joshua, Judges, 1 and 2 Samuel, and 1 and 2 Kings. These books emphasize the role of prophets, condemn worship of other gods, praise the centralization of worship in Jerusalem, and explain that the exile occurred because Israel did not stay faithful to its covenant with Yahweh, all important themes in Deuteronomy. Moreover, these books speak of the "book of the law of Moses" in a way that clearly refers to Deuteronomy (Josh 8:30-32; 2 Kgs 14:6). For these reasons, these historical books are often called the Deuteronomic History, and are thought to have been written by the same religious movement that produced Deuteronomy. Many scholars believe that Deuteronomy actually makes more sense as an introduction to the Deuteronomic History than as a conclusion to the Pentateuch, and may have served that purpose before being incorporated into the Pentateuch.

It is also possible that this Deuteronomic movement had a role in compiling or editing some of the prophetic books. The themes of social justice, worshiping only one god, and staying faithful to the covenant are found in several prophetic books of the late monarchy. Some of the vocabulary and phrasing in these books is also similar to that of Deuteronomy (e.g., Jer 7; 11:1-17). And the way the careers of several prophets are dated, according to the reign of the king, is similar to what is done in the Deuteronomic History (Jer 1:1-3; Hos 1:1; Am 1:1; Mic 1:1).

It has also been noted that other parts of the Pentateuch besides Deuteronomy seem to have Deuteronomic characteristics. For example, the call of Moses in Ex 3–4 is similar to the calls of heroes in the Deuteronomic History (Judg 6:11-18) and prophets in books that show Deuteronomic influence (Jer 1:4-10). A Deuteronomic editing of other sources of the Pentateuch is possible, *if* any of the other sources were written earlier than Deuteronomy, the Yahwist being the most likely candidate. However, it is more likely that most of the material in the Yahwist and Priestly sources was written after Deuteronomy. Deuteronomic characteristics in other parts of the Pentateuch are more likely the result of the other sources being influenced by Deuteronomy and the Deuteronomic History.

This Deuteronomic movement was prolific—writing, contributing to, and influencing many parts of the Hebrew Scriptures—and scholars have naturally wondered just who the people were who were part of this movement. Because of the connections to prophecy and the positive depictions of prophets in the history, it is sometime suggested that the movement originated as a prophetic reform group. The eighth-century prophet Hosea, in the northern kingdom Israel, spoke out on social justice and warned about the downfall of the nation as a punishment for not staying faithful to Yahweh, issues that became important for the Deuteronomic movement. The late eighth-century Judean prophets Isaiah and Micah emphasized similar issues, and, further, are said to have influenced King Hezekiah (Is 36–38; Jer 26:16-19). According to the Deuteronomic History, Hezekiah carried out a religious reform, eliminating the high places, sacred pillars, and other unorthodox forms of worship. The reform was short lived, however, because Assyria invaded and he was forced to become a vassal to them. The reform ideas did not die, but may have stayed underground, until Assyrian power declined during the reign of Josiah, when they were brought out in a more extensive reform, accompanied by the early version of Deuteronomy and supported by prophets.

A weakness of the prophetic explanation is that there are major parts of Deuteronomy, especially on cultic and military matters, which would be unlikely to have come from prophets. An alternative explanation, made popular by Gerhard von Rad, is that the Deuteronomic movement began among Levites of the northern kingdom.[1] Such people would have been teachers of religious traditions and, after the fall of Israel in 722, some would have come down to Judah, preserved their traditional laws, and influenced others who felt a religious reform was needed. Deuteronomy gives a greater role to Levites than other parts of the Pentateuch do, allowing them to minister at the temple in Jerusalem (Dt 18:1-8) and giving them a leading role in reaffirming the covenant (Dt 27:9-26). A difficulty with this explanation is that the term "Levite" was evolving, and Deuteronomy does not seem to use it in the same sense that the Priestly writings do.

Yet another explanation, from Moshe Weinfeld, among others, is that the Deuteronomic movement originated among wisdom teachers.[2] One of the characteristics of wisdom literature is its concern with the proper behavior of kings and other leaders. The Deuteronomic History certainly has such a concern, and, compared to the rest of the Pentateuch, Deuteronomy also does (Dt 16:18–17:20). Many teachings in Deuteronomy are in proverbial form, typical of wisdom (e.g., "You must not accept bribes, for a bribe blinds the eyes of the wise and subverts the cause of those who are in the right"—Dt 16:19), and there are frequent references to rewards for following the law, also characteristic of wisdom (Dt 7:12-16; 8:1; etc.). However, wisdom is normally not as concerned with cultic and nationalistic matters as Deuteronomy is.

Because of the shortcomings of trying to identify the Deuteronomic movement too closely with any one type of religious movement, a better explanation is that it was a distinct group that brought together prophetic, cultic, and wisdom teachings. This movement began around the time of King Hezekiah, and was supported by him. It is significant that Hezekiah is associated with the three types of teachings in Deuteronomy: he has a positive relationship with the prophets Isaiah and Micah, unlike most kings; he carries out a cultic reform; and his name is attached to wisdom literature—the title in Proverbs 25:1 says its sayings were put together by "the officials of King Hezekiah." After its introductory material, Deuteronomy begins its teachings with the decalogue, which also brings together prophetic, cultic, and wisdom teachings.

The Deuteronomic movement began when Israel and Judah were resisting Assyrian rule, and one result of that is that the laws in Deuteronomy are presented as part of a treaty, an alternative to the type of vassal treaty Assyria would impose on the states in its empire. Deuteronomy calls itself a "covenant," and the Hebrew word *berith* is also used for international treaties and other formalized relationships. The organization of Deuteronomy is similar to Assyrian vassal treaties, whose parts included promises of loyalty, stipulations to be followed, blessings and curses, and provisions for public reading and deposit of the covenant. The people in the Deuteronomic movement would have been familiar with the Assyrian vassal treaties, but because they opposed Assyrian rule they wrote Deuteronomy as an alternative loyalty agreement with Yahweh.[3]

This Deuteronomic movement produced its law code in the form of a covenant, as well as a history of the nation, and possibly edited some prophetic books. It was only later, after the exile, that its law code was added to the Pentateuch. When that happened some modifications were made, most notably moving the death of Moses from the end of Numbers to the end of Deuteronomy. The editors did not feel compelled, however, to harmonize everything in Deuteronomy with the rest of the Pentateuch, so there are discrepancies in several of the laws. The editing of the Pentateuch was about preserving multiple traditions that fit the same basic story of Israel's foundations, and not about producing a completely uniform document.

Introductory Material (Deuteronomy 1:1–4:43)

The opening chapters of Deuteronomy consist of a general introduction to the book (1:1-5), the story of the Israelites' journey through the wilderness (1:6–3:29), and a homiletic section looking ahead to future events, including the exile and return (4:1-43). The first and third of these are clearly additions made when Deuteronomy was incorporated into the Pentateuch, but the composition of the story of the journey is less certain. In the past, the journey story was usually treated as an abbreviated version of earlier stories in Exodus and Numbers, but it has become clearer in recent times that the majority of the material in those books is later than previously thought, raising the possibility that the version here is earlier. There are differences in several details, and the exploration of them below adds weight to the view that Deuteronomy 1:6–3:29 is earlier than the corresponding accounts in Exodus and Numbers.

Deuteronomy 1:1-5. The introduction gives the purpose of the book—to explain the law—and the place and date of these speeches of Moses, which connect it to the previous narrative in Numbers. The places Tophel, Laban, and Di-zahab are mentioned nowhere else in the Bible, and the geographic description is somewhat vague, but the mention of Horeb (the name Deuteronomy uses for Sinai), Paran, Kadesh, and Moab connect the book to major parts of the wilderness journey that was narrated in Numbers. The date, in the fortieth year, on the first day of the eleventh month, is typical of the Priestly style of dating, indicating that this introduction was added by Priestly writers after this book was made part of the Pentateuch.

Deuteronomy 1:6–3:29. This version of the journey through the wilderness covers the same part of the story as Numbers 10–32, but does not include several incidents included there, and does not intersperse the narrative with legislation. It also differs in a few key points.

Moses' delegation of authority to other people (Dt 1:9-18) is here told in a direct manner and is not interwoven with other themes. It is based on the law in Deuteronomy 16:18-20, on appointing just judges. The parallel story in Exodus 18 has moved the setting to before the covenant at Mt. Sinai, and has the delegation come at the advice of Jethro, Moses' Midianite father-in-law. Connecting it to the Israelites' relationship with the Midianites is secondary, and it is more likely that the version here is more original.

In the story of the spies entering Canaan from the south (Dt 1:19-45), this version describes the area the spies go to as more limited (cf. Num 13:21-29), gives a positive role only to Caleb rather than to both

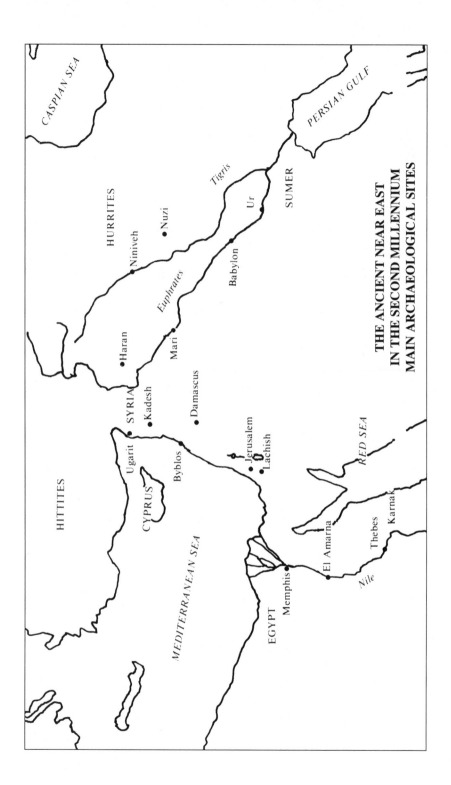

THE ANCIENT NEAR EAST
IN THE SECOND MILLENNIUM
MAIN ARCHAEOLOGICAL SITES

Caleb and Joshua (Num 14:6-10), and uses the incident to explain why Moses will not enter the promised land, instead of using the later incident of the waters of Meribah (Num 20:1-13). Depending on when one dates the Yahwist, these differences could be explained either as Deuteronomy following an earlier Yahwist version of the story before it was expanded by the Priestly writers, or as the Yahwist following an earlier Deuteronomist version. Based on this passage alone, both are equally plausible, but with the overall evidence that the Deuteronomist was earlier, the latter is more likely.

Here, the journey passes through Edom, from whom the Israelites buy food and drink (Dt 2:4-8, 28-29). This directly contradicts the Yahwist version of the journey, in which the Israelites are forced to detour around Edom (Num 20:14-21). On literary grounds, Van Seters argues that Deuteronomy is the earlier of the two versions;[4] in addition, the more negative depiction of Edom in Numbers 20:14-21 would be more likely after the Babylonian conquest, when Edom was condemned for attacking Judah.

This version of the journey does not mention several incidents that are in Numbers, including the jealousy of Aaron and Miriam (12), the revolt of Korah (16), the waters of Meribah (20:1-13), the bronze serpent (21:4-9), the oracles of Balaam (22–24), and the false worship in Moab (25). Since there is no obvious reason to eliminate these, it is more likely that Numbers represents a later expanded version of the journey than that Deuteronomy is a later abbreviated version.

Deuteronomy's story of the wilderness journey was probably composed at the time the law code in Deuteronomy was made into an introduction to the Deuteronomic History. Later, the Yahwist and Priestly writers developed a much more expanded journey story, adding other themes and legal material, and in a few cases contradicting Deuteronomy. When Deuteronomy was incorporated into the Pentateuch, the differences between the short version in Deuteronomy and the long version in Numbers were allowed to stand.

Deuteronomy 4:1-43. The style now switches to homiletic, to introduce the laws that are to follow and to persuade the nation to stay faithful to those laws. Part of the motivation to follow the law is gratitude for what God has done for the Israelites in the past—bringing them out of Egypt and making them into a people. Another part is to secure a good future—if they stay faithful, things will go well for them in the land, and if they do not, they will be defeated and scattered. The perspective is postexilic, and the warning about being scattered is in reality an explanation for why they were exiled. But the tone is confident; it is much like Second Isaiah, trying to persuade the people that they can have a new beginning in the land.

Covenant Exhortations (Deuteronomy 4:44–11:32)

The laws of Deuteronomy begin with the decalogue and other exhortations to worship only one God and to stay faithful to the covenant. More specific laws do not begin until chapter 12; for now the concern is the broader issue of Israel's relationship with its God. This section is one of the most theologically reflective parts of the Pentateuch, and most revealing of the theology of the Deuteronomic movement as it was taking shape late in the monarchy and during the exile. Much of the theology here originated late in the monarchy, drawing from the teachings of cultic reform, prophetic ethics, and wisdom, but the perspective of the finished form is exilic, preparing for a renewed Israel.

At the center of that theology is the command to worship only Yahweh. This is brought out most explicitly in the first commandment (5:6-7) and in the Shema (the Hebrew word for "hear"): "Hear, O Israel: the LORD is our God, the LORD alone" (6:4). The Yahweh-only movement was developing late in the monarchy, and can be seen in the teachings of prophets and the reform movements of Hezekiah and Josiah. It would not win out, though, until after the exile.

Israel's relationship with Yahweh is called a covenant, and the making of the covenant is described in chapters 9–11. Israel is privileged to be in this relationship; there is an emphasis on Israel being chosen from among all the nations (7:7). But the covenant also demands obedience. Israel will be punished if it fails to stay faithful, and, like other covenants, there are blessings and curses attached (11:26-30). The Deuteronomic movement used this covenant theology both as an explanation for the downfall of Israel and Judah, and as a program for their future after the exile. It is addressed to people on the verge of making a decision about the future, and the book repeatedly states that "today" they are presented with this choice (5:1; 8:1; 11:8).

Also important to the Deuteronomic movement is the gift of a land that is exceedingly bountiful (7). The former inhabitants are driven out by Yahweh, and the Israelites are to have nothing to do with them. For the Jews of the exile, the message is that it is not enough to hold on to a few traditions while living in a foreign land. They must return to the land God gave them. And when they return, they are to stay separate from the other inhabitants of the land and not allow themselves to be assimilated and disappear as a people. The warning that the other inhabitants are more numerous (7:7, 17) accurately reflects the situation of the small Jewish community.

Deuteronomy 4:44-49. The introduction to this part of the book is similar to Deuteronomy 1:1-5, which introduced the entire book. This is an earlier introduction for the core part of the book, before it was made part of the Pentateuch. Like 1:1-5, it gives a brief historical setting. The Israelites are on the east side of the Jordan River, ready to occupy the land Yahweh promised them, and they have just defeated two of the kings there, a sign that Yahweh will be fighting on their behalf.

Deuteronomy 5:1–6:3. The first part of the law is the decalogue. In Deuteronomy, the ten commandments are introduced with a setting at Mt. Horeb, and followed by a description of Moses' meeting with God. The commandments are stated in a manner almost identical to that of Exodus 20. There are a few minor differences in wording, and the order of things not to be coveted is different. But the major difference is the motive for keeping the Sabbath. In Exodus, the Sabbath was to be a day of rest as a reminder that God rested on the seventh day of creation. Here, there is more emphasis on slaves taking part in the day of rest, and the Sabbath is a reminder of God bringing the Israelites out of slavery in Egypt and giving them rest.

It is almost certain that the original place of the decalogue was here in Deuteronomy, and the version in Exodus is a later adaptation. The Exodus version of the Sabbath command assumes knowledge of the Priestly story of creation (Gen 1:1–2:4), which had not been written when Deuteronomy was first put together; even if the Priestly creation story is based on an earlier tradition, there is no evidence that it was known before the exile. Instead, Deuteronomy uses the exodus story, which was becoming well-known late in the monarchy.

Another reason for believing the Deuteronomic version of the decalogue is original is that it fits so well into the overall teaching of Deuteronomy. As discussed above, the Deuteronomic movement brought together ideas of cultic reform, prophetic ethics, and wisdom. These three types of teachings are also found in the decalogue, with commandments from the cult (worship only Yahweh, use no images, do not misuse the name, keep the Sabbath), from prophetic ethical lists (do not murder, steal, commit adultery, or bear false witness; cf. Jer 7:9; Hos 4:2), and from the wisdom tradition (honor your father and mother, do not covet). Deuteronomy puts these ten commandments at the beginning of its law collection because they are a concise statement of what is most important in the movement's teachings.

For additional discussion of individual commandments, see chapter 6.

Deuteronomy 6:4-25. In a manner typical of this part of the book, the author encourages the people to stay in a close relationship with Yahweh. This begins with the Shema, the classic declaration of Jewish faith. The Shema has been translated in various ways. The NRSV's "Hear, O Israel: The LORD is our God, the LORD alone" interprets it as saying that Yahweh is the only God for Israel, a restatement of the first commandment. Another possible translation is, "Hear, O Israel: The LORD is our God, the LORD is one." In this interpretation, the Shema is meant to counter multiple versions of who Yahweh is. Diverse Yahwehs could have developed when there were several different shrines where Yahweh was worshiped, as can be seen in inscriptions such as the ones at Kuntillet Ajrud, which ask for blessings from "Yahweh of Samaria" and "Yahweh of Teman." Both interpretations are consistent with the Deuteronomic movement's program of worshiping only Yahweh and centralizing the cult; perhaps the Shema is meant to express both ideas.

The close relationship with Yahweh is expanded with a reminder of the land that Yahweh is giving them (6:10-11), a warning not to follow other gods who are worshiped in the land (6:13-15), and instructions to teach each new generation about Yahweh bringing them out of Egypt (6:20-23). They are to have confidence that Yahweh acts in concrete historical events, and respond with loyalty to Yahweh alone.

Deuteronomy 7–8. The homiletic exhortation continues with guidance on how the Israelites are to live when they come into the land.

The Shema

The Shema is Deuteronomy 6:4-9, plus Deuteronomy 11:13-21 and Numbers 15:37-41, which express similar ideas.

> Hear, O Israel: The LORD is our God, the LORD alone. You shall love the LORD your God with all your heart, and with all your soul, and with all your might. Keep these words that I am commanding you today in your heart. Recite them to your children and talk about them when you are at home and when you are away, when you lie down and when you rise. Bind them as a sign on your hand, fix them as an emblem on your forehead, and write them on the doorposts of your house and on your gates. (Dt 6:4-9)

The Shema became an important prayer in Jewish worship. The instructions to "Bind them as a sign on your hand..." developed into the phylacteries worn on the forehead and arm and the mezuzah put on the doorpost, containing small scrolls of the text. The Mishnah says the Shema is to be recited twice daily, in the morning and in the evening (M. Berakot 1–3), as well as at synagogue gatherings (M. Megillah 3:4, 5-6). It also warns against the frequent recitation of it becoming mechanical.

> R. Simeon said: Be heedful in the reciting of the Shema and in the Tefillah [the Eighteen Benedictions]; and when thou prayest make not thy prayer a fixed form, but a plea for mercies and supplications before God, for it is written, For he is gracious and full of compassion, slow to anger and plenteous in mercy, and repenteth him of the evil; and be not wicked in thine own sight. (M. Abot 2:13; from Herbert Danby, *The Mishnah* [New York: Oxford University Press, 1933] 449)

The New Testament also gives the Shema great importance. As an observant Jew, Jesus would have recited it regularly, and in the gospels he singles it out as the greatest commandment.

> One of the scribes came near and heard them disputing with one another, and seeing that [Jesus] answered them well, he asked him, "Which commandment is the first of all?" Jesus answered, "The first is, 'Hear, O Israel: the LORD our God, the LORD is one; you shall love the LORD your God with all your heart, and with all your soul, and with all your mind, and with all your strength.'" (Mk 12:28-30; cf. Mt 22:34-38; Lk 10:25-28)

God will drive out the other peoples who are there, and the Israelites must stay separate from them, making no covenants and not intermarrying, and they are to destroy their altars and other religious items. They can know that they will be successful by remembering what God has already done for them. And if they stay faithful to the covenant, they will enjoy abundant blessings in the land.

The list of nations God will drive out is similar to other such lists, although the exact same seven nations are found only in Joshua 3:10; 24:11. These names are alternate names for the land of Canaan, or names of smaller groups remembered as living in Canaan. The Hittites had been a powerful empire to the north (in modern Turkey) in pre-Israelite times. The empire had diminished, but the name was still used, in the form Hatti, by the Assyrians when they ruled that region; when the Assyrian empire expanded into Syria and Palestine in the eighth century, the name was used for them as well. The biblical use of Hittite for a group of people in Canaan probably comes from the Assyrian use of Hatti for the land, and not from any pre-Israelite group who lived there. The term Amorite was used for people in Mesopotamia in the early second millennium, and a kingdom in western Syria in the mid-second millennium. The Pentateuch sometimes uses it as a name for all of Canaan (Gen 15:13-16), and sometimes for a kingdom in Transjordan (Num 21:21-31). The names Girgashite, Perizzite, Hivite, and Jebusite probably referred to smaller groups about whom little is known, except that the Jebusites are associated with Jerusalem. Thus, this list and similar ones use names that at one time referred to all of Canaan or small groups in Canaan, but were only vaguely remembered and were therefore suitable for a list of "ancient" inhabitants of Canaan. The name Canaanite itself, of course, by this time simply meant people in the land who did not follow Israelite religion.

There are other indications that the passage is a rhetorical ideal and does not correspond to any historical situation. The command that the Israelites not intermarry with the inhabitants was not the Deuteronomic law; Deuteronomy 21:10-14 gives guidelines to follow when marrying foreigners. Iron and copper (8:9) were not mined west of the Jordan. The descriptions are meant as a promise about the future, addressed to the audience of the book.

Deuteronomy 9–11. This homiletic part of Deuteronomy concludes with the story of how the covenant was made at Mt. Horeb, and a summary of what the covenant means for the Israelites. The covenant will lead to blessings for the nation if the Israelites follow its basic precepts of loving the Lord and treating people with justice, but the covenant was not originally made because of any merit on the part of the Israelites. In fact, they have been repeatedly unworthy. The sermon is balancing two ideas for the exilic audience: that the fall of the nation was justified because of their unfaithfulness, and that they still have another chance for a blessed life in the land.

The story of the making of the covenant emphasizes the failures of the Israelites. Several incidents are alluded to briefly—at Taberah, Massah, Kibroth Hattaavah, and Kadesh—but the one described at length is the making of an image of a calf. Van Seters has shown that this version of the calf story is older than the one in Exodus 32.[5] Calves had long been used in Canaanite and Israelite worship. A polemic against their use can be seen in the early prophetic roots of the Deuteronomic movement (Hos 8:5; 10:5), and the movement developed that polemic further with stories such as this one and the one in the Deuteronomic History about King Jeroboam making two golden calves (1 Kgs 12:26-32). The story in Exodus 32 is based on this one in Deuteronomy 9, and borrows additional elements from 1 Kings 12, such as the statement, "These are your gods, O Israel, who brought you up out of the land of Egypt," the fact that the calf is made of gold, and the offering of sacrifices and making it a feast day, none of which are in Deuteronomy 9.

Despite the Israelites' unfaithfulness, the covenant is made. Moses carves a second pair of tablets on which Yahweh writes the decalogue (10:1-5). This part of the story is slightly different from the one in Exodus. Moses makes the ark before going up the mountain the second time, and the ark is a simple container for the tablets rather than an elaborate throne for the divinity (cf. Ex 25:10-22). As we have seen, there were multiple traditions of ark-like items used in Israelite worship.

Once the covenant is made, the sermon summarizes its core:

So now, O Israel, what does the LORD your God require of you? Only to fear the LORD your God, to walk in all his ways, to love him, to serve the LORD your God with all your heart and with all your soul, and to keep the commandments of the LORD your God and his decrees that I am commanding you today, for your own well-being. (10:12-14)

The covenant also demands that they act justly for the widow, orphan, and stranger (or alien), "for you were strangers in the land of Egypt" (10:18-19). One of the key points of the Deuteronomic theology is to connect the injustice the Israelites experienced in the past with the demand that they form a different kind of people.

The Israelites will receive abundant blessings if they follow this covenant, and curses if they do not (11:8-17, 26-32). The rhetorical flourishes depart from a literal description of the land. The blessings are greatly exaggerated, as if the land were more fertile than Egypt. The geography of the people's entry into the land is somewhat vague, as if the Arabah, the Jordan valley, and the central highlands were all one place. But it is a persuasive conclusion to this part of Deuteronomy: despite the past, there is an opportunity for a glorious future.

The Law Code (Deuteronomy 12–26)

The Deuteronomic law code is the oldest part of the book, and is close to the book used in King Josiah's reform. It is not, however, the oldest collection of laws in the Pentateuch, but is an expansion and updating of the earlier Covenant Code (Ex 20:21–23:19). Deuteronomy repeats many of the laws of the Covenant Code, but also adds many more and changes some, most notably by centralizing worship (Dt 12; cf. Ex 20:24). Deuteronomy 12–26 contains specific laws, unlike the general exhortations of chapters 5–11. Still, the homiletic style continues, with laws frequently followed by explanations and motives to follow the laws (e.g., 12:25: "Do not eat [the blood], so that all may go well with you and your children after you, because you do what is right in the sight of the LORD"). Thus the theology of the Deuteronomic movement can be seen both in which laws are emphasized and in the explanations attached to them.

Many of the themes of the law code are the same ones emphasized in Josiah's reform: worshiping only one God, centralizing the cult, the role of prophets and other leaders. But other important themes in these laws, such as social justice and community conduct, were not reported as part of Josiah's reform. While we cannot be sure of how historically accurate the description of Josiah's reform is (2 Kgs 22–23), it seems that it was not as broad in its concerns as the Deuteronomic movement was.

The arrangement of the laws does not follow any logical order. If it was based on the order of laws in the decalogue, it has been expanded and revised to the point where that is no longer recognizable. The code begins with sections on two of its important issues, worship (12:1–16:17) and the role of leaders (16:18–18:22). The rest is an assortment of laws on all aspects of Israelite life, including cities of refuge, warfare, marriage, the poor and marginalized, debt, building codes, dress, agriculture, and workers' rights. The collection certainly grew over time, and reflects concerns of several different social settings—rural and urban, rich and poor, clergy and laity.

Deuteronomy 12. The law begins with proper worship, especially centralizing it in one place. Centralizing the cult had both a practical and a symbolic significance. It was practical, because it was the easiest way to ensure that the prohibitions against images and other gods, and laws on sacrifice, were followed. Symbolically, it reinforced the notion that Yahweh is one and that there is no other god for Israel. In Deuteronomy, worship is to be centralized at "the place that the LORD your God will choose." Jerusalem is never named, even though it is surely meant, in part because it would be anachronistic at this point in the story, and in part because the Deuteronomic movement considered previous places, before the temple was built, to have also been legitimate places of worship. The Deuteronomic History has worship take place at Shechem (Jos 8:30-31) and Shiloh (1 Sam 1–3), and the prophet Jeremiah, who has much in common with the movement, refers to Shiloh as the place "where I made my name dwell at first" (Jer 7:12).

Centralizing worship has certain consequences with which the law deals. One is that priests of the local shrines lose their work and income. Deuteronomy instructs people to give the Levites (which in Deuteronomy means all priests, but here specifically the ones from outside Jerusalem) a share of freewill offerings, and advises, "Take care that you do not neglect the Levites as long as you live in your land" (12:18-19). Another consequence is that ordinary slaughter of animals for food can no longer be considered quasi-sacrificial. Undoubtedly there were traditions of surrounding slaughter at homes and villages with rituals. It would be impossible to require everyone to slaughter their livestock at Jerusalem, so Deuteronomy allows ordinary slaughter to take place anywhere, as long as it is not done as a sacrifice (12:20-25).

One other specific practice condemned is offering children in fire (12:31). This practice occurred occasionally during the monarchy, but is condemned in writings from the end of the monarchy and later (Jer 7:31; 19:5; Lev 18:21).

Deuteronomy 13. While most of the Pentateuch maintains a fiction that Israel started out worshiping only Yahweh and all temptation to worship other gods came from the foreigners around them, here we see the true nature of the situation. This chapter portrays the struggle between Yahwism and worship of other gods as something happening within Israel itself. The ones who are worshiping other gods are people who are usually the most trusted: prophets, even ones whose prophecies have come true (13:1-5), family members and close friends (13:6-11), and whole Israelite towns (13:12-18). The Yahweh-only movement began as a minority in Israel, and their efforts to change the nation would have produced the kinds of conflicts described here. The call for the death penalty for anyone who disagrees is a rhetorical overstatement, but it does reveal the Deuteronomic movement's insistence on never compromising on the first commandment.

Deuteronomy 14. This chapter contains three types of laws—on mourning rites, clean and unclean food, and tithes. All three illustrate changes taking place in Israelite religion late in the monarchy, namely, separating Israelite practices from past Canaanite practices and making accommodations for the cult being centralized in Jerusalem.

The prohibitions against lacerations and shaving the forelocks (14:1-2) are aimed at mourning rituals that had become associated with worshiping dead ancestors. The Deuteronomic movement wanted to end all such unofficial religious practices.

The rules on clean and unclean food are almost identical to the ones in Leviticus 11. Here there is a list of clean mammals (14:4-5), which is not found in Leviticus 11, but Deuteronomy lacks any mention of reptiles and swarming things (cf. Lev 11:29-43). The similarity in wording suggests that either Leviticus is based on Deuteronomy 14, or both are taken from similar lists that circulated among priests. Strict rules on food have to do with separating Israelites from the peoples around them, but the system here is not as extensive as the later purity system in the Priestly writings. This code does show one development from the earlier Covenant Code, in the law on not boiling a kid in its mother's milk. The Covenant Code included that law among worship laws (Ex 23:19), while here it is among dietary laws (Dt 14:21). The worship context was earlier, because the law was originally meant to end a Canaanite ritual, but by the time of the Deuteronomic Code the original purpose had lost its force, so the law was put in what seemed like a more logical context of dietary laws.

The instructions on tithing (14:22-29) apparently refer to the feasts of Weeks and Booths (Dt 16:9-15). This is not a tithe to be paid to the temple, but a tithe that is used in the celebration itself, as a communal meal in God's presence. The provision for bringing silver instead of transporting the produce a long distance to the temple was a necessary allowance if people were to be persuaded to centralize their worship. It also indicates the beginning of a transformation from an exchange economy to a money economy. The oldest coins from Palestine are from the sixth century BCE, but before coins were used, set amounts of precious metals had begun to replace direct exchange of commodities and labor.[6]

The rules on keeping the tithe within each town every third year also reveals a sensitivity toward the effect centralization had on local communities. The requirement that food be shared with Levites, aliens, orphans, and widows is an example of the Deuteronomic movement's concern for social justice.

Deuteronomy 15:1-18. This chapter and chapters 23–24 cover several economic issues, including slaves, debt, interest, property ownership, and a fallow year for agricultural land. Three pentateuchal law codes—the Covenant Code, the Holiness Code, and the Deuteronomic Code—provide various and sometimes contradictory rules on these issues (see Appendix II: Economic Laws, and Appendix III: Laws on Slavery). All of the codes are idealistic on some points, and there is no hard evidence that they were followed literally in the biblical period. But they do reveal a concern for social justice and a confidence that God would make the people prosperous despite occasional poverty.

The Deuteronomic Code is the only one of the codes that has a provision for releasing people from debts in the seventh year. On a practical level this is the issue that would have affected poor farmers the most, as one bad year would be enough to force them to borrow seed for the next year. The goal of the Deuteronomic movement can be seen in two apparently contradictory statements. Deuteronomy 15:4 states, "There will, however, be no one in need among you," but Deuteronomy 15:11 says, "There will never cease to be some in need on the earth" (the verse quoted by Jesus in Mt 26:11; Mk 14:7; Jn 12:8). This is not simply a case of the former being idealistic and the latter realistic. Rather, the Deuteronomists recognized that because of the precarious economy there would always be people who would *become* poor and be in debt, but there should be a system in place so that no one is *permanently* in that condition.

Deuteronomy 15:19-23. The law on sacrificing firstborn male livestock is stated several times in the Pentateuch, including in the earlier Covenant Code (Ex 22:29-30). The Deuteronomic Code calls for it to take place at one central location, and says that any blemished animals unfit for sacrifice are to be eaten as ordinary food without any sacrificial rites ("as you would a gazelle or a deer"). It is unlikely this law was followed literally; if farmers had to come to Jerusalem as often as the Deuteronomic Code insists, they would have had little time for anything else.

Deuteronomy 16:1-17. Like the other law codes in the Pentateuch, the Deuteronomic Code has its liturgical calendar (see Appendix I: Festivals, for a side-by-side comparison). The calendar here is similar to the earlier one in the Covenant Code (Ex 23:14-17) in listing only the three major festivals of Passover/Unleavened Bread, Weeks, and Booths; in basing it on agricultural events rather than on fixed dates; and in using the older Canaanite month name, Abib. However, this calendar innovates by insisting that these celebrations take place at one central location, and in expanding the participants to include all family members, Levites, slaves, aliens, orphans, and widows, another example of the Deuteronomic movement's concern for marginalized people. The compilers of the code did not mind that preserving older regulations and adding new practices sometimes led to discrepancies; the requirement in 16:16 that the males appear before the Lord three times a year is taken from the Covenant Code (Ex 23:17) even though it differs from the new requirement that both males and females participate.

Deuteronomy 16:18–18:20. For the Deuteronomic movement to succeed, it needed leaders who would implement its policies and who were accepted as legitimate by the people. To that end, the code discusses the roles of judges, kings, priests, and prophets, and repeats some laws on false worship, since that was an issue with which all types of leaders dealt.

The appointment of **judges** (16:18-20) is somewhat vague, saying nothing about who does the appointing or how the functions of these judges are different from the traditional practice of elders making judgments at the city gates. In fact, this is not meant as some kind of constitutional law on a judicial system, but advice to judges on not letting anything corrupt their decisions. It is similar to the advice found in wisdom literature on not taking bribes and showing no partiality (Prov 17:23; 18:5) and is an example of the Deuteronomic movement drawing on wisdom teachings. The requirement of more than one witness for death penalty cases (17:6) and the sending of difficult cases to a chief judge and priests in Jerusalem (17:8-13) are further attempts to make judgments more just, although we have no concrete information on what kind of high court there was in Jerusalem.

The advice on **kings** (17:14-20) is the only place in the Pentateuch where that office is discussed, which is itself a remarkable fact, and one of the reasons to believe that most of the Pentateuch is from after the exile, when Judah did not have its own king. The Deuteronomic Code, from late in the monarchy, assumes there will be a king, but wants several restrictions. The king cannot be a foreigner, an understandable concern, since the Deuteronomic movement came about during the period of Assyrian hegemony, when the kings did not have complete independence. The king is not to acquire too many horses, especially through an alliance with Egypt, nor acquire too many wives or too much wealth. Similar concerns are expressed in the Deuteronomic History, in Samuel's warnings about a monarchy (1 Sam 8) and in the discussion of Solomon's excesses (1 Kgs 10:14–11:8). Late in the monarchy, alliances with Egypt were a tempting way to resist Assyrian, and later Babylonian, rule, but the Deuteronomic movement considered such a policy doomed to failure. King Josiah, influenced by the movement, evidently agreed, and ended up being killed in a battle against Egypt (2 Kgs 23:28-30).

The Deuteronomic policy on **priests** is different from that of the Priestly writings. Here, all the Levites are priests, and may serve at the temple in Jerusalem; there is no distinction between the descendants of Aaron and other Levites. However, the Deuteronomists were particularly concerned about the Levites outside Jerusalem. Since the local worship places were to be shut down in Josiah's reform, these priests would have no work, and in some cases no income. Thus, the Deuteronomic Code makes a special point of insisting that they be allowed to serve in Jerusalem and receive a share of the offerings there. This insistence seems to have been in vain. According to the Deuteronomic History, when Josiah shut down the local worship places, the local priests did not serve in Jerusalem, but stayed with their relatives in their towns (2 Kgs 23:9). This would be another case of Josiah's reform not doing everything the Deuteronomic movement wanted. Nonetheless, they supported him, because they realized they would not get another king as sympathetic to their views.

Besides priests, the other religious leaders endorsed by the Deuteronomic movement are **prophets**. In general, the Deuteronomic Code condemns unofficial religious activities, such as consulting mediums, because they would compete with the official centralized cult in Jerusalem (18:9-14). But it makes an exception for prophets. Prophets had no official standing, but the Deuteronomic movement was influenced by several of them, and wanted the rest of the nation to listen to them, at least to the ones who agreed with the Deuteronomic point of view (18:15-22). The main criterion for judging a true prophet is whether he or she speaks in the name of Yahweh or of some other god. The additional criterion, if the prophecy comes true, is, of course, useless for judging prophets at the time they are speaking. Rather, it is meant as a justification for accepting the authority of certain past prophets.

Deuteronomy 19. An important concern of the Deuteronomic movement was the integrity of the justice system. This concern was already expressed in the advice given to judges (16:18-20), and now it is expressed in some specific legislation. Having cities of refuge, respecting property, requiring multiple witnesses in criminal cases, and keeping punishment proportionate to the crime were ways to make sure injustice did not occur because of emotion or misuse of power.

Most of the specific policies here are repeated elsewhere in the Hebrew Scriptures. The place of refuge for someone who accidentally kills someone else is in the earlier Covenant Code, where the person must go to an altar for refuge (Ex 21:12-14). The Deuteronomic Code, and the later Priestly legislation (Num 35:9-29), change it from an altar to one of several cities throughout the land, since with worship centralized in Jerusalem the one legitimate altar would be too far away for many people. Respecting boundary markers (19:14) is a concern in prophetic ethical teachings (Hos 5:10) and wisdom literature (Prov 22:28), both of which influenced the Deuteronomic movement. On multiple witnesses, other legislation applied the requirement only to cases involving the death penalty (Num 35:30; Dt 17:6); the law here broadens it to all crimes, to protect the rights of the accused. And the *lex taliones* (19:21—"life for life, eye for eye, tooth for tooth, hand for hand, foot for foot") is in both the Covenant Code (Ex 21:23-25) and the Holiness Code (Lev 24:19-20). It serves the dual purposes of insisting that the guilty pay for their crimes and limiting the punishment to something proportionate to the crime.

Deuteronomy 20:1–21:14. Wars were religious affairs in biblical times, so priests were involved, there were rules on how to conduct battles, and it was believed that Yahweh was fighting on behalf of the nation. This section on warfare is not so much legislation as instruction on the ideal holy war. As Assyrian domination declined in the seventh century, Judah had more opportunity to fight its own battles, and the Deuteronomic movement provided guidelines on how to do that.

Many of these policies make warfare more humane. Men who have built a new house but have not yet dedicated it, planted a new vineyard but not yet enjoyed its fruit, or become engaged but not yet married, are exempt from service. The exemption for fearful people was probably, in practice, not a real exemption, but a way to encourage people to show no fear. The protection of fruit-bearing trees was in part utilitarian, but also shows more respect for creation than modern armies do; making war a religious act put some limits on what could be done. The treatment of female captives called for here is also more humane than what has been practiced through most of history, including in modern times.

Still, the holy war policies can seem shocking, in demanding that all males in defeated towns be killed, and that all living things in defeated towns within Canaan be killed. This latter policy comes up in the Deuteronomic History in the stories of the conquest of Canaan (Jos 6:15-21; 7). The reasoning behind the complete destruction is that any trace of the worship of other gods pollutes the land and must be eliminated. It is doubtful if such a practice was ever followed literally, especially since the majority of early Israelites had been Canaanites. But it is another illustration of the Deuteronomists' unwillingness to allow any exceptions to the first commandment.

The law on finding a body in the open country (21:1-9) is unrelated to war, and is an example of the Deuteronomic Code not putting its laws into a logical arrangement. The ritual for expiating the guilt for the death is similar to the ritual of sending out the goat on the Day of Atonement (Lev 16).

Deuteronomy 21:15–22:30. The various laws here illustrate the broad concerns of the Deuteronomic movement, combining old laws and Deuteronomic innovations designed to protect the rights of vulnerable people. These miscellaneous laws touch on almost all aspects of life. A firstborn son is protected from being disinherited (21:15-17). The land is not to be defiled by leaving the corpse of an executed criminal hanging out overnight (21:22-23). The proper order of creation is to be respected, by not allowing cross dressing (22:5) or mixing unlike seeds, animals, or fabric (22:9-11; cf. Lev 19:19). A sustainable ecosystem is to be maintained, by not taking a mother bird along with its young (22:6-7). Building codes must be followed to keep houses safe (22:8). The laws on marriage and adultery strike a balance between upholding the purity of marriage and protecting the rights of those falsely accused of adultery (22:13-30). A theme running through these laws is respect for people and all life created by God.

Deuteronomy 23:1-8. Membership in the assembly, that is, the determination of which males could take full part in worship, was another important issue for the Deuteronomic movement. The goal was to create a uniform religious system out of the diverse practices that existed, so it was necessary to define who was part of the system. One criterion was wholeness: anyone with mutilated sex organs, or born of an illicit union, was not qualified.

A second criterion put restrictions on foreigners. No Ammonite of Moabite, to the tenth generation, could be admitted, but Edomites and

Egyptians could be admitted at the third generation. Ancient Israel did not have an ethnic consciousness such as exists today. The nations of Israel and Judah came from people of diverse backgrounds, and during the monarchy the territory under their control continually changed. This passage assumes there would be intermarriage with the peoples around them, either with captives taken in battle or among people living next to each other in times of peace. After the exile there were attempts to end that intermarriage (Ezra 10:10-17; Neh 13:1-3), when it became more necessary to preserve a Jewish identity distinct from that of other people. The law here is the beginning of a movement in that direction.

Elsewhere in the Pentateuch, Edom is also portrayed as closer to Israel than Ammon and Moab are, despite the frequent animosity. Why Egypt should be given a more favorable status is less clear, since the Pentateuch is usually negative on any interaction with Egypt.

Deuteronomy 23:9–25:19. These additional laws again show the wide range of concerns of the Deuteronomic movement; the concerns include military matters, the cult, marriage, and purity. But the biggest concern of these laws is social justice in economic matters, especially for people who are most vulnerable: slaves, poor people, wage earners, aliens, widows, and orphans. (See Appendix II: Economic Laws, for a comparison with the Covenant and Holiness codes.)

The law on letting escaped *slaves* live freely in Israel (23:15-16) probably refers to slaves from other lands who have come to Israel, since elsewhere the Deuteronomic Code accepts slavery as part of the economic system (15:12-18). Nonetheless, it goes beyond other ancient law codes, such as the laws of Hammurapi, which require people to return fugitive slaves.[7] The laws against charging *interest* to an Israelite (23:19-20) and prohibiting burdensome *pledges* for loans (24:6, 10-13, 17) protect borrowers from losing their livelihood and getting into worse debt. The requirement that *wages* be paid immediately (24:14-15) shows that there were a significant number of people who had no land and were forced to hire themselves out, perhaps an indication of a worsening economic situation to which the Deuteronomic movement was responding.[8] The law that *gleanings* be left in the fields for poor people to gather (24:19-22) is another humanitarian law, but also reveals that the economic system was not working for everyone. The Deuteronomic program attempted both to prevent people from becoming poor and to guarantee some minimal security for people when they did become poor. It did not immediately achieve its goals; Josiah's reform focused on cultic matters rather than on social justice, and in any case came to an end when Josiah died in 609. But its ideas were picked up after the exile, and can be seen in Nehemiah's attempts to end poverty, interest, and burdensome pledges (Neh 5:1-13).

The law on **levirate marriage** (25:5-10; so-called because of the Latin word *levir*, "husband's brother") is designed to continue a family's name when a man dies with no children, and to protect widows. It shows up in the story of Judah and Tamar (Gen 38) and in the Book of Ruth, which assumes it extended beyond brothers to other male relatives.

Several of the laws involve **purity**: the military camp (23:9-14), cultic prostitution (23:17-18), the reason for prohibiting remarriage to a divorced wife who subsequently was divorced or left widowed by another man (24:1-4), and skin disease (24:8-9). The rules of purity are not as developed in the Deuteronomic Code as they are in the later Priestly writings, but we do see the beginning of their importance in these rules.

Deuteronomy 26. The Deuteronomic Code concludes with liturgical laws, on the offering of first fruits and the payment of tithes every third year. Both of these have been mentioned before (18:4 and 14:28-29, respectively), but here the emphasis is on connecting these liturgical acts with remembering past events—the stories of the patriarchs and the exodus—and shaping the present community—by sharing the tithes in a meal with Levites, aliens, orphans, and widows.

The Deuteronomic movement was becoming strong at the same time the patriarchal and exodus stories were becoming more widely known, and it is likely the movement was instrumental in making these stories part of the national stories of origin. Gerhard von Rad believed that the liturgical summary in 26:5-9 came from an early version of the story of origins, going back at least to the beginning of the monarchy, and noted that since it does not mention the events at Mt. Sinai, the exodus and Sinai traditions must have been originally independent.[9] While most scholars today doubt that the summary in Deuteronomy 26:5-9 is as old as von Rad believed, it does seem that the exodus and Sinai traditions both developed slowly, and independently, and became connected late in the monarchy. The Deuteronomic movement wanted a uniform national religion, and part of that involved selecting which stories about the past, among the many that existed, were to be accepted by all and recited in liturgical celebrations.

Besides selecting stories about the past, the movement wanted to shape the community for the future. Sharing the tithes and eating a meal with Levites who would be dispossessed from local shrines, and with aliens, widows, and orphans, would help build a community in which no one was left out. As part of the same ceremony, the people were to profess that they had followed the commandments and avoided certain sins (26:13-15). Worship of the dead was given particular attention, probably because the sacred meal was similar to feasts that were part of mourning rites (cf. Jer 16:5-9).

Preparations for Ratifying the Covenant (Deuteronomy 27–30)

After the law code, Deuteronomy describes liturgical acts connected with ratifying the covenant. These include instructions for the acceptance ceremony after the Israelites enter the promised land (27–28) and homiletic encouragements from Moses to accept and follow the covenant, in the form of a separate covenant while they are still in Moab (29–30).

The international vassal treaty form that the Deuteronomic covenant is based on typically had provisions for a public reading and deposit of the covenant, and blessings and curses for those who followed or did not follow its laws. These are found here, with instructions on setting up stones with the words of the covenant written on them (27:2-8), and lengthy blessings and curses (27:15–28:68). Another part of the international treaties was calling on the gods to be witnesses; since Israel's covenant is with the one God, this would not be possible here, but there is a trace of it in Moses calling on heaven and earth to be witnesses of the separate covenant in Moab (30:19).

The use of the covenant form comes from the Deuteronomic movement's desire to present an alternative to the nation's vassal relationship with Assyria. Thus the core of the material here dates from the time leading up to Josiah's reform and his efforts to break free from Assyrian rule. However, the material was later expanded, with the curses made to more specifically refer to the Babylonian exile (especially in 28:32-68; 29:20-29).

Deuteronomy 27. Ebal and Gerazim are the two mountains next to biblical Shechem (modern Nablus), in central Samaria. Their height and central location make them an appropriate place for a covenant acceptance ceremony for the entire nation. The instructions here will be followed in Josh 8:30-35; however, a later edition of the Deuteronomic History expanded the Shechem ceremony to include a recitation of the Pentateuch's history of the chosen people, so actually includes two ceremonies at Shechem (the second in Josh 24). The instruction to offer sacrifices here does not contradict the Deuteronomic centralization of worship in Jerusalem; Deuteronomy 12 refers to the proper place for sacrifice as "the place that the LORD your God will choose," allowing other places to be chosen before the temple was built in Jerusalem.

The separation of the tribes into two groups and the declaration of curses by the Levites (27:11-26) are presented as part of the same ceremony, although they are probably an exilic addition (in Josh 8 the people are simply divided in half with no separation by tribe, and the list of curses is not in either version of the Shechem ceremony in Joshua). The tribes on Mt. Gerazim for the blessing are the southern and central tribes, and the ones on Mt. Ebal for the curse are the Transjordanian and northern tribes. The scheme is artificial, and represents an exilic viewpoint of which tribes would have been most firmly a part of Israel and Judah. The specific crimes that bring a curse are taken from the Deuteronomic and Holiness Codes, and come from a time when the different legal traditions were being brought together in the Pentateuch. They are included at this point to associate them with the covenant curses that follow in chapter 28.

Deuteronomy 28. The formal section of blessings and curses is a regular part of international treaties. The blessings here are agricultural abundance, military success, and general prosperity. The curses are for their opposites, plus disease and social breakdown.

The most striking feature of this section is that the curses are so much longer than the blessings. In fact, this was the normal practice, as Assyrian vassal treaties also put more emphasis on curses.[10] From the beginning, the Deuteronomic movement probably emphasized the curses more, both to explain why the kingdom of Israel fell and to warn Judah that the same could happen to it. When Judah itself fell, the curses were expanded and made to describe more specifically the destruction and exile. There are several parallels between these expanded curses and the Book of Jeremiah, another exilic explanation for the fall of Judah (e.g., Dt 28:49-52 and Jer 5:15-17; Dt 28:53-57 and Jer 19:9).

The last part of the warnings (28:58-68) comes from a late stage of composition that considers Deuteronomy a finished book and alludes to the larger pentateuchal story of the promise to Abraham (28:62) and the time in Egypt (28:60, 68, although it is unclear why ships are mentioned). As terrible as the other curses are, this is perhaps the worst part of the warning, because it says Yahweh will undo everything that has been done for Israel in the Pentateuch. Indeed, it must have seemed that way to the Jews in exile. This book acknowledges the complete loss, but ultimately with a positive purpose—to offer a new chance to accept the covenant.

Deuteronomy 29–30. Following the instructions on ratifying the covenant after entering the land is a speech from Moses which, on the surface, is calling on the Israelites to make a covenant where they are at the moment, in Moab. This is presented as a separate covenant, "in addition to the covenant that he had made with them at Horeb" (29:1 [28:69 in Hebrew]). The idea of a separate covenant is strange, since the rest of Deuteronomy and the Pentateuch assume only the one at Horeb. In fact, this new covenant is a way of addressing the postexilic community, encouraging them to take advantage of a second chance with Yahweh.

The treaty structure is followed in this covenant as well, although more briefly than in the previous parts of Deuteronomy.[11] The covenant begins with a superscription (29:1) and historical prologue summarizing the exodus and wilderness stories, up to the settlement of the Transjordanian tribes (29:2-9). The parties of the covenant are Yahweh and the Israelites, described in the broadest way possible—leaders, women and children, aliens, the lowest servants, and even those not present (29:10-15). The inclusivity is meant to persuade postexilic Jews that the covenant is open to all, regardless of past events. The stipulations of the covenant are simple: worship only Yahweh and make no images (29:16-19). The curses for not following the covenant refer specifically to the exile (29:20-29), and the blessings refer specifically to a return to the land (30:1-10).

This second chance at a covenant concludes with one of the most eloquent and optimistic passages in the Pentateuch. Moses encourages the people, assuring them that this commandment is not too difficult for them, that "the word is very near to you; it is in your mouth and in your heart for you to observe" (30:14). The people have a choice between life and death; the covenant is not primarily a list of laws imposed by God, but a freely chosen relationship with a loving God. It is also significant that although Moses is offering this covenant to the Israelites in Moab, the story reports no response from the people. The book is not reporting past history here, but is persuading future generations that they have a choice about their relationship with Yahweh.

Final Events in the Life of Moses (Deuteronomy 31–34)

With the covenant presented, the Israelites have everything they need to be a people, so all that remains in the story is to bring the life of Moses to an end and look ahead to the future. Before he dies, Moses passes on the leadership to Joshua, ensures that the laws will be preserved and remembered, and sings two songs preparing the nation for the future.

The material in this last section is no longer strictly Deuteronomic, but blends it with other material that helps incorporate this book into the Pentateuch. Much of the story of the death of Moses is from the Yahwist, and originally came at the end of the Book of Numbers. The Priestly writers also expanded parts of the story, and the two songs were composed independently before becoming part of this book.

Deuteronomy 31–32. The commissioning of Joshua, the preservation of the law, and the first of the two songs are blended into one narrative. Joshua's commissioning is told in two versions. In one, it is done by Moses and is part of a general commissioning of the people to enter the land (31:1-8). This is part of the Deuteronomic narrative, but has been edited with Priestly material, such as reporting that Moses' age is one hundred and twenty, in line with the Priestly chronology. (The Priestly source had its own version of Joshua's commissioning in Num 27:12-23.) In the other version of the commissioning, it is done by Yahweh and takes place at the tent of meeting (31:14-15, 23). This tent of meeting is not mentioned elsewhere in Deuteronomy, but is the same tent used in other Yahwist stories (Ex 33:7-11; in Num 11:16-17 it is used for a similar commissioning). The second commissioning may seem unnecessary, but for the Yahwist the tent of meeting is where God spoke to Moses, so this is a way of saying God will continue to guide the Israelites under the leadership of Joshua.

Moses also prepares for the future by writing down the laws and giving them to the priests and elders to place next to the ark of the covenant and to read every seventh year at the feast of Booths (31:9-13, 24-29). This is another Deuteronomic narrative that has been edited with Priestly details, such as the role of the Levites in carrying the ark. The custom of reading the law every seventh year is not mentioned elsewhere.

The preparations also include a warning about future apostasy, so God instructs Moses to write down a song to be used to keep the nation faithful (31:16-22). The description of the apostasy, using imagery of prostitution, is similar to prophetic condemnations of worshiping other gods, and illustrates the influence of prophets on the Deuteronomic movement. The song itself (32:1-43) is more complex, with elements of prophecy and wisdom and older conceptions of the relationship of Yahweh to other gods. The view that the most high God Elyon divided the earth among his sons, and one of them, Yahweh, received the Israelites (32:8-9) is certainly pre-Deuteronomic.[12] The use of the name Jeshurun for Israel (32:15) is rare; the only other places it is used are Deuteronomy 33:5, 26 and Isaiah 44:2. The poetic image of God as a rock is used frequently in the Psalms. The content of the song—God bringing a charge against Israel for failing to stay faithful—is typical of prophetic books. And the song uses language that is characteristic of wisdom literature (32:7, 28-29). The origin of the song is impossible to trace, but it was used at this point in the narrative because its overall message was appropriate for the final preparations to enter the land.

Deuteronomy 33. Moses' blessing of the tribes is embedded in a poem about Yahweh as a divine warrior marching from the south. It is possible that the two parts were composed separately, with the blessings inserted into the older divine warrior poem, although they must have been put together before the whole was added here. It is not as well integrated into the narrative of Deuteronomy as the song in chap-

Yahweh: A Divine Warrior from the South

A few early poetic passages preserve a tradition of Yahweh as a divine warrior marching from a southern territory, similar to the poem in Deuteronomy 33. The tradition of Yahweh coming from the south is also preserved in the inscription from Kuntillet Ajrud, which asks for blessings from "Yahweh of Teman," and in the biblical passages which speak of a close connection between the Israelites and Edom and Midian.

Deuteronomy 33:2
The LORD came from Sinai
and dawned from Seir upon us;
he shone forth from Mount Paran.
With him were myriads of holy ones.

Judges 5:4-5
LORD, when you went out from Seir,
when you marched from the region of Edom,
the earth trembled and the heavens poured,
the clouds indeed poured water.
The mountains quaked before the LORD, the one of Sinai,
before the LORD, the God of Israel.

Habakkuk 3:3
God came from Teman,
the holy one from Mount Paran.
His glory covered the heavens,
and the earth was full of his praise.

ter 32 is, indicating that it was added to the book at a very late stage in its composition. On some points it departs from the Deuteronomic program, such as praising sacrifice outside of Jerusalem (33:19).

Whatever the origin of Deuteronomy 33, it is among the earliest biblical literature; the language and content suggest that at least parts of it come from early in the monarchy or before.[13] Rather than trying to distinguish Israelite from Canaanite religion, it makes heavy use of Ugaritic imagery for Yahweh.[14] Like Baal, Yahweh is a divine warrior who comes from a mountain (33:2), is accompanied by minor divinities (33:2-3), and rides his chariot through the clouds (33:26-27). Like El, Yahweh is among the "ancient gods" (33:27). The blessing on Joseph (33:13-17) makes use of Canaanite fertility imagery.

The tradition of a divine warrior coming from the south is preserved in other early poetry (Judg 5:4-5; Hab 3:3; Ps 68:7-8, 17), and an inscription from Kuntillet Ajrud, in the Negev, associates Yahweh with the region south of the Dead Sea.[15] This alternate tradition of Yahweh's home is largely ignored in the Bible, because it could compete with the Jerusalem-centered official cult, but it does reveal the diversity of Israelite religion earlier in the monarchy. The Pentateuch creates a single national epic while still preserving other traditions about Yahweh.

On the specific blessings for each tribe, the poem can be compared to Genesis 49, Jacob's blessing of his sons. Like that poem, this one is based on some historical memories of groups that became part of Israel and some vague descriptions showing that some of those groups were being forgotten. Simeon is not mentioned at all, and must have been absorbed by Judah by the time this was composed. Reuben is in danger of disappearing, but Gad, the other Transjordanian tribe, is expanding. Judah is portrayed as somewhat weak, while Joseph is the most powerful; that view would make sense at some point in the monarchy when the northern kingdom was dominant over the south. The priesthood of the Levites is assumed, although the reference to them going against their own parents and children does not correspond to any story the Pentateuch has preserved (the golden calf incident in Ex 32 comes closest, but there it is the other tribes that the Levites punish). Contrary to later orthodoxy, another priesthood is also accepted, as Zebulun and Issachar lead the offering of sacrifices at a mountain in their territory, probably Mt. Tabor; the prophet Hosea later condemned worship at Mt. Tabor (Hos 5:1). The other tribes are mentioned too briefly to provide any historical setting.

Deuteronomy 34. The death of Moses outside of the promised land has been anticipated several times in the story (Num 27:12-23; Dt 1:37; 3:23-29; 32:48-52) and is now finally reported. His death is also a chance to reiterate some of the themes of the Pentateuch: the gift of a land, as Moses looks out over its vastness; Yahweh's continued guidance of the Israelites, through the person Joshua; and the unique role of Moses, who knew the Lord face to face. The burial of Moses in an unknown place, like the vagueness of the location of Mt. Sinai, is typical of the Pentateuch in that it leaves this story in an unreachable past. The purpose of the story is not to make people worship relics of the past, but to provide a foundation for the future of Israel.

Before Deuteronomy became part of the Pentateuch, the story simply continued in the Book of Joshua. But with the formation of the Pentateuch, the death of Moses had to be told with a greater sense of completion. For the Pentateuch it is important that the story end outside the promised land and that the Israelites have everything they need to be a people before they are in the land. The book is addressed to exiles and stresses that they do not need to give up their identity as a nation just because they are outside the land. At the same time, the goal is to return to the land. And so it ends on the border. The land is within their reach, and, like the law, "It is not too hard for you, nor is it too far away" (Dt 30:11). After long delays, the land and the covenant are very near.

Appendix 1: Festivals

Ezek 45:18-25	Ex 23:14-17	Ex 34:18-26	Lev 23	Num 28–29	Dt 16:1-17
New Year 1st day, 1st month					
Atonement 7th day, 1st month					
Passover/Unleavened 14th day, 1st month	Unleavened month of Abib	Passover/Unleavened month of Abib	Passover/Unleavened 14th day, 1st month	Passover/Unleavened 14th day, 1st month	Passover/Unleavened month of Abib
	First Fruits	Weeks/First Fruits	First Fruits harvest	First Fruits/Weeks harvest	Weeks 7 weeks from first grain
			Weeks 50 days after First Fruits		
			Trumpets 1st day, 7th month	Trumpets 1st day, 7th month	
			Atonement 10th day, 7th month	Atonement 10th day, 7th month	
"the festival" 15th day, 7th month	Ingathering end of year	Ingathering turn of year	Booths 15th day, 7th month	"a festival" 15th day, 7th month	Booths end of harvest

Appendix II
Economic Laws

	Covenant Code	Holiness Code	Deuteronomic Code
Debts			Remitted 7th year Dt 15:1-11
Interest	None for Israelites Ex 22:25	None for Israelites Lev 25:35-37	None for Israelites Dt 23:19-20
Family Property		Returned 50th year Lev 25:13-17	
Fallow Land	7th year Ex 23:10-11	7th year Lev 25:1-7	
Pledge Burdens	Cloak Ex 22:26-27		Millstone, House, Cloak Dt 24:6,10-13
Wages		Pay immediately Lev 19:13	Pay immediately Dt 24:14-15
Gleanings		Leave for poor Lev 19:9-10	Leave for poor Dt 24:19-21

Appendix III
Laws on Slavery

The Pentateuch accepts the institution of slavery, but there was an evolution of the specific laws on it. The earliest law code, the Covenant Code, makes it most difficult for slaves to be freed, especially female slaves. The Deuteronomic Code treats male and female slaves equally, and makes provisions for their welfare when they are released. The Holiness Code says that only foreigners may be held as slaves; impoverished Israelites may be forced to hire themselves out as bound laborers, but are to be treated less harshly than slaves. (Italicized lines highlight similarities and differences.)

Covenant Code. When you buy a male Hebrew slave, *he shall serve six years, but in the seventh year he shall go out a free person, without debt*. If he comes in single, he shall go out single; if he comes in married, then his wife shall go out with him. If his master gives him a wife and she bears him sons or daughters, *the wife and her children shall be her master's and he shall go out alone*. But if the slave declares, "I love my master, my wife, and my children; I will not go out a free person," then his master shall bring him before God. *He shall be brought to the door or the doorpost; and his master shall pierce his ear with an awl; and he shall serve him for life*.

When a man sells his daughter as a slave, she shall not go out as the male slaves do. If she does not please her master, who designated her for himself, then he shall let her be redeemed; he shall have no right to sell her to a foreign people, since he has dealt unfairly with her. If he designates her for his son, he shall deal with her as with a daughter. If he takes another wife to himself, he shall not diminish the food, clothing, or marital rights of the first wife. And if he does not do these three things for her, she shall go out without debt, without payment of money. (Ex 21:2-11)

Deuteronomic Code. If a member of your community, *whether a Hebrew man or a Hebrew woman, is sold to you and works for you six years, in the seventh year you shall set that person free*. And when you send a male slave out from you a free person, you shall not send him out empty-handed. Provide liberally out of your flock, your threshing floor, and your wine press, thus giving to him some of the bounty with which the LORD your God has blessed you. Remember that you were a slave in the land of Egypt, and the

LORD your God redeemed you; for this reason I lay this command upon you today. But if he says to you, "I will not go out from you," because he loves you and your household, since he is well off with you, then *you shall take an awl and thrust it through his earlobe into the door, and he shall be your slave forever. You shall do the same with regard to your female slave.* (Dt 15:12-17)

Slaves who have escaped to you from their owners shall not be given back to them. They shall reside with you, in your midst, in any place they choose in any one of your towns, wherever they please; you shall not oppress them. (Dt 23:15-16; presumably this refers to slaves from another country; see the Hittite laws below)

Holiness Code. If any who are dependent on you become so impoverished that they sell themselves to you, *you shall not make them serve as slaves. They shall remain with you as hired or bound laborers. They shall serve with you until the year of the jubilee.* Then they and their children with them shall be free from your authority; they shall go back to their own family and return to their ancestral property. For they are my servants, whom I brought out of the land of Egypt; they shall not be sold as slaves are sold. You shall not rule over them with harshness, but shall fear your God. *As for the male and female slaves whom you may have, it is from the nations around you that you may acquire male and female slaves.* You may also acquire them from among the aliens residing with you, and from their families that are with you, who have been born in your land; and they may be your property. You may keep them as a possession for your children after you, for them to inherit as property. These you may treat as slaves, but as for your fellow Israelites, no one shall rule over the other with harshness. (Lev 25:39-46)

(Lev 25:47-55 covers cases of Israelites selling themselves to aliens in the land, with the same requirements that they be released in the jubilee year and not be treated with harshness.)

It should be noted that these laws represent an attempt to improve the condition of slaves, and do not represent actual practice. We know from Nehemiah 5:1-13 that after the exile impoverished Jews continued to sell their children as slaves, both to wealthier Jews and to foreigners.

These laws can also be compared to other law codes from the ancient Near East. The laws of **Hammurapi** are similar in some details, such as requiring the mutilating of an ear to mark a slave whose status might be doubted.

> If a male slave has said to his master, "You are not my master," his master shall prove him to be his slave and cut off his ear. (#282; ANET 177)

In the Covenant and Deuteronomic codes, the length of service for a debt slave was six years, while in the Holiness Code, bound laborers were to be released every fiftieth year. Hammurapi's laws provide for a much shorter three-year period of service.

> If an obligation came due against a nobleman and he sold the services of his wife, his son, or his daughter, or he has been bound over to service, they shall work in the house of their purchaser or obligee for three years, with their freedom reestablished in the fourth year. (#117; ANET 170)

Note, however, that this limit applies only to nobles, and not to common people.

In general, other law codes from the ancient Near East give more attention to the capture and return of escaped slaves, while the Pentateuch is more concerned about the conditions under which a slave can be released. One example from Hammurapi's laws:

> If a nobleman has helped either a male slave of the state or a female slave of the state or a male slave of a private citizen or a female slave of a private citizen to escape through the city gate, he shall be put to death. (#15; ANET 166)

Another code, the **Laws of Ur-Nammu**, provides an incentive for people to capture and return slaves who have escaped to another territory.

> If a slavewoman or a male slave fled from the master's house and crossed beyond the territory of the city, and another man brought her/him back, the owner of the slave shall pay to the one who brought him back two shekels of silver. (#14; ANET 524)

Hittite Laws provided various rewards, depending on the distance from which the slave was brought back.

> If a slave runs away and anyone brings him back—if he seizes him in the vicinity, he shall give him shoes; if on this side of the river, he shall give him two shekels of silver; if on the other side of the river, he shall give him three shekels of silver.
>
> If a slave runs away and goes to the country of Luwiya, he shall give to him who brings him back six shekels of silver. If a slave runs away and goes to an enemy country, whoever brings him nevertheless back, shall receive him (the slave) himself. (#22-23; ANET 190)

Note that the last case assumes a practice similar to that of Deuteronomy 23:15-16, in which a slave who escapes to another country is not normally returned.

NOTES

Chapter One: The Pentateuch and History

1. 3rd ed. (Philadelphia: Westminster Press, 1981) 103.

2. *Genesis (Old Testament Library)*, rev. ed. (Philadelphia: Westminster Press, 1972) 40–41.

3. See especially the Amarna letters; several can be found in James Pritchard, *Ancient Near Eastern Texts Relating to the Old Testament*, 3rd ed. (Princeton: Princeton University Press, 1960) 483–90 (abbreviated ANET); a complete collection is William Moran, ed., *The Amarna Letters* (Baltimore and London: Johns Hopkins University Press, 1992).

4. For recent theories see John McDermott, *What Are They Saying About the Formation of Israel?* (Mahwah, N.J.: Paulist Press, 1998).

5. Amihai Mazar, *Archaeology of the Land of the Bible, 10,000–586 B.C.E.* (New York: Doubleday, 1990) 375–90.

6. Baruch Halpern, "The Stela from Dan: Epigraphic and Historical Considerations," *Bulletin of the American Schools of Oriental Research* 296 (November 1994) 63–80.

7. ANET 284, 288.

Chapter Two: How the Pentateuch Was Written

1. *A History of Pentateuchal Traditions* (Englewood Cliffs, N.J.: Prentice-Hall, 1972).

2. *The Old Testament: An Introduction* (Philadelphia: Fortress Press, 1986).

3. Menahem Haran, *Temples and Temple Service in Ancient Israel: An Inquiry into Biblical Cult Phenomena and the Historical Setting of the Priestly School* (Winona Lake, Ind.: Eisenbrauns, 1985) 5–12, 140–48.

4. *In Search of History: Historiography in the Ancient World and the Origins of Biblical History* (New Haven: Yale University Press, 1983).

5. *The Making of the Pentateuch: A Methodological Study* (Sheffield: JSOT Press, 1987) 232–41.

6. *The Legends of Genesis* (New York: Schocken, 1964).

7. *Genesis: A Commentary* (Philadelphia: Westminster Press, 1972) 13–18.

8. *The Art of Biblical Narrative* (New York: Basic Books, 1981).

Chapter Three: Genesis 1–11

1. Van Seters speaks of "historicization of myth" and "mythologization of history," both of which occurred in Israel and its neighbors; see *Prologue to History: The Yahwist as Historian in Genesis* (Louisville: Westminster/John Knox Press, 1992) 25–28.

2. ANET 60–61.

3. Ibid., 67.

4. Ibid., 68.

5. For some examples, see Susan Niditch, *Folklore and the Hebrew Bible* (Minneapolis: Fortress Press, 1993) 35–47. For an example from the ancient Near East, see the Sumerian story of Enki and Ninhursag in ANET 37–41.

6. *The Pentateuch: An Introduction to the First Five Books of the Bible* (New York: Doubleday, 1992) 64–65.

7. G. Archer, *Encyclopedia of Bible Difficulties* (Grand Rapids: Zondervan, 1982) 77.

8. ANET 265.

9. G. von Rad, *Genesis: A Commentary,* rev. ed. (Philadelphia: Westminster Press, 1972) 69–70.

10. Niditch, 43. For examples from Greek literature, see R. Hendel, "Of Demigods and the Deluge: Toward an Interpretation of Gen 6:1-4," *JBL* 106 (1987) 13–26.

11. D. Redford, *Egypt, Canaan, and Israel in Ancient Times* (Princeton: Princeton University Press, 1992) 400–8.

12. ANET 375–376. Redford, 169.

13. "Second Isaiah" refers to that part of Isaiah (chapters 40–55) written at the end of the exile. Sources outside the Bible show that Cyrus also claimed the Babylonian god Marduk had chosen him to rule.

Chapter Four: Genesis 12–50

1. Summaries of these arguments can be found in John Bright, *A History of Israel*, 3rd ed. (Philadelphia: Westminster, 1981) 67–103; William Dever, "Palestine in the Second Millennium BCE: The Archaeological Picture," in John Hayes and J. Maxwell Miller, *Israelite and Judaean History* (London and Philadelphia: Trinity Press International, 1977) 70–120; and Kenneth Kitchen,

"The Patriarchal Age: Myth or History?" in *Biblical Archaeology Review* 21:2 (March/April 1995) 48–57, 88–95.

2. P. K. McCarter, "The Patriarchal Age," in *Ancient Israel: A Short History from Abraham to the Roman Destruction of the Temple*, ed. H. Shanks (Washington: Biblical Archaeology Society, 1988) 21–25; "The Historical Abraham," in *Interpretation* 42:4 (1988) 341–52.

3. On these arguments, see Thomas Thompson, *The Historicity of the Patriarchal Narratives* (Berlin/New York: Walter de Gruyter, 1974) and J. Van Seters, *Abraham in History and Tradition* (New Haven: Yale University Press, 1975). For a point-by-point rebuttal of Kitchen's recent arguments, see R. Hendel, "Finding Historical Memories in the Patriarchal Narratives," in *Biblical Archaeology Review* 21:4 (July/August 1995) 52–59, 70–72.

4. J. Van Seters, *The Pentateuch: A Social-Science Commentary* (Sheffield: Sheffield Academic Press, 1999) 135–39, and *Abraham in History and Tradition*, 13–87.

5. See especially "The Moabite Stone," ANET 320–321; and Jo Ann Hackett, *The Balaam Text from Deir Alla* (Chico, Calif.: Scholars Press, 1980).

6. "Abram the Hebrew," in *Bulletin of the American Schools of Oriental Research* 163 (1961) 36–54.

7. *Abraham in History and Tradition*, 304–8.

8. ANET 172, 173.

9. ANET 326.

10. Mark S. Smith, *The Early History of God: Yahweh and the Other Deities in Ancient Israel* (New York: Harper & Row, 1990) 132–38; Susan Niditch, *Ancient Israelite Religion* (New York: Oxford University Press, 1997) 114–18.

11. *The Art of Biblical Narrative* (New York: Basic Books, 1981) 47–62.

12. G. Ahlström, *The History of Ancient Palestine* (Minneapolis: Fortress Press, 1993) 163.

13. See Trude and Moshe Dothan, *People of the Sea: The Search for the Philistines* (New York: Macmillan, 1992) 215–18.

14. See Ahlström, 278–79; Judg 1:32; ANET 475–479.

15. Mazar, *Archaeology of the Land of the Bible*, 182; Edward Campbell, "Shechem," in *The New Encyclopedia of Archaeological Excavations in the Holy Land*, ed. Ephraim Stern (New York: Simon and Schuster, 1993) 1345–54.

16. ANET 485–486.

17. ANET 259.

18. Crystal-M. Bennett, "Excavations at Buseirah (Biblical Bozrah)," in *Midian, Moab, and Edom: The History and Archaeology of Late Bronze and Iron Age Jordan and North-West Arabia*, ed. J. Sawyer and D. Clines (Sheffield: JSOT Press, 1983) 9–17.

19. For more detailed suggestions on how these groups are related, see Lars Axelsson, *The Lord Rose Up from Seir: Studies in the History and Traditions of the Negev and Southern Judah* (Stockholm: Almquist & Wiksell International, 1987) 66–73.

20. See, for example, N. Gottwald, *The Tribes of Yahweh: A Sociology of the Religion of Liberated Israel, 1250–1050 BCE* (Maryknoll: Orbis Books, 1979) 430–34.

21. *Israel in Egypt: The Evidence for the Authenticity of the Exodus Tradition* (New York: Oxford University Press, 1996) 83–98.

22. Thomas Thompson, *The Mythic Past: Biblical Archaeology and the Myth of Israel* (New York: Basic Books, 1999) 138–49.

23. *Egypt, Canaan, and Israel in Ancient Times* (Princeton: Princeton University Press, 1992) 422–29. See also his earlier *A Study of the Biblical Story of Joseph* (Leiden, Netherlands: E. J. Brill, 1970).

24. *Genesis: A Commentary* (Philadelphia: Westminster Press, 1972) 433–39.

25. "The Joseph and Moses Narratives," in *Israelite and Judaean History*, ed. J. Hayes and J. M. Miller (Philadelphia: Trinity Press International, 1977) 179–80.

26. *The Art of Biblical Narrative* (New York: Basic Books, 1981) 3–12.

27. ANET 23–25. The oldest manuscript is from around 1220 BCE, but the story probably existed long before that.

28. ANET 212–214; these are from the reign of Thutmose III in the 15th century.

29. ANET 31–32.

30. ANET 259.

31. ANET 320–321.

32. Ibid.

33. Smith, *The Early History of God*, 15–19.

34. *Aqhat;* in ANET 149–155, and Simon Parker, ed., *Ugaritic Narrative Poetry* (Atlanta: SBL/Scholars Press, 1997) 49–80.

Chapter Five: Exodus 1:1–13:16

1. ANET 376–378.

2. ANET 262–263; James Pritchard, ed., *The Ancient Near East in Pictures Relating to the Old Testament*, 2nd ed. (Princeton: Princeton University Press, 1969) 350.

3. ANET 260–262.

4. On this argument, see Kenneth Kitchen, "Egyptians and Hebrews,

from Ra`amses to Jericho," in *The Origin of Early Israel—Current Debate: Biblical, Historical and Archaeological Perspectives* (Ben-Gurion University of the Negev Press, 1998) 86.

5. On this argument, see John Bright, *A History of Israel,* 3rd ed. (Philadelphia: Westminster Press, 1981) 123.

6. ANET 259.

7. James Hoffmeier, *Israel in Egypt: The Evidence for the Authenticity of the Exodus Tradition* (New York: Oxford, 1996) 116–21; Kitchen, "Egyptians and Hebrews," 69–79.

8. Hoffmeier, *Israel in Egypt,* 138–40.

9. Ibid., 140.

10. Kitchen, "Egyptians and Hebrews," 67.

11. Hoffmeier, *Israel in Egypt,* 117.

12. Kitchen, "Egyptians and Hebrews," 87.

13. ANET 119.

14. F. M. Cross and D. N. Freedman, *Studies in Ancient Yahwistic Poetry* (Missoula: Scholars Press, 1975) 45–65.

15. It is even possible that the Persian empire, ruling the Jews after the exile, promoted this anti-Egyptian story, since it fit their needs of discouraging Jews from joining Egypt in opposing Persian rule. The Persians frequently became involved in local religions, and a similar phenomenon is seen in Second Isaiah, which is influenced by Persian propaganda about Cyrus (cf. Is 45:1-3). This is not to say, of course, that the Persians had a direct role in creating the story, just that they had an interest in promoting it.

16. *The Life of Moses: The Yahwist as Historian in Exodus-Numbers* (Louisville: Westminster/John Knox Press, 1994) 35–63.

17. For example, compare William Propp, *Exodus 1–18* (New York: Doubleday, 1998) 180–97, and Brevard Childs, *The Book of Exodus* (Philadelphia: Westminster Press, 1974) 52–53.

18. F. M. Cross, *Canaanite Myth and Hebrew Epic: Essays in the History of the Religion of Israel* (Cambridge: Harvard University Press, 1973) 60–75; D. N. Freedman, et al., *Theological Dictionary of the Old Testament,* vol. V (Grand Rapids: Eerdmans, 1986) 513–14.

19. R. Giveon, *Les bédouins Shosou des documents égyptiens* (Leiden: E. J. Brill, 1971) 27–28, 74–76, 236, 241; see the discussion in L. Axelsson, *The Lord Rose Up from Seir,* 59–61.

20. ANET 320; cf. Freedman, 502.

21. Yohanan Aharoni, *The Archaeology of the Land of Israel* (Philadelphia: Westminster Press, 1982) 229.

22. *Israel in Egypt,* 146–49.

23. *Exodus 1–18,* 286–321.

24. *Introduction to the Pentateuch* (Grand Rapids: Eerdmans, 1995) 72–75.

25. Hoffmeier, *Israel in Egypt*, 148–49.

26. Hackett, *The Balaam Text from Deir Alla*.

27. For various explanations, see Joseph Blenkinsopp, *The Pentateuch: An Introduction to the First Five Books of the Bible* (New York: Doubleday, 1992) 155; Brevard Childs, *The Book of Exodus* (Philadelphia: Westminster Press, 1974) 175–77.

28. *The Life of Moses*, 114–19.

29. ANET 491.

30. For the various possibilities, see Childs, *The Book of Exodus*, 184–95; Propp, *Exodus 1–18*, 373–80; Blenkinsopp, *The Pentateuch*, 155–57.

31. ANET 320.

32. Roland de Vaux, *Ancient Israel: Its Life and Institutions* (London: Darton, Longman & Todd, 1973) 183–86; Propp, *Exodus 1–18*, 384–87.

Chapter Six: Exodus 13:17–40:38

1. Kitchen, "Egyptians and Hebrews," 73–77; Hoffmeier, *Israel in Egypt*, 179–81.

2. A. Alt, "The Origins of Israelite Law," in *Essays on Old Testament History and Religion* (Garden City. N.Y.: Doubleday, 1968) 79–132.

3. ANET 175–176.

4. G. Mendenhall, "Law and Covenant in Israel and the Ancient Near East," *Biblical Archaeologist* 17 (1954) 26–46; for examples of such treaties, see ANET 201–206, 531–541.

5. G. von Rad, "The Form-Critical Problem of the Hexateuch," in *The Problem of the Hexateuch and Other Essays* (Philadelphia: Fortress Press, 1984) 1–78; *Deuteronomy* (Philadelphia: Westminster Press, 1966) 156–59.

6. G. Mendenhall, "Law and Covenant in Israel and the Ancient Near East."

7. Van Seters, *The Life of Moses*, 128–34; Childs, *The Book of Exodus*, 218–21.

8. Hoffmeier, *Israel in Egypt*, 169–70.

9. Ibid., 170–71.

10. Propp, *Exodus 1–18*, 490–91; Hoffmeier, *Israel in Egypt*, 190–91.

11. W. F. Albright, *Yahweh and the Gods of Canaan: An Historical Analysis of Two Conflicting Faiths* (Garden City, N.Y.: Doubleday, 1968) 1–46; Cross and Freedman, *Studies in Ancient Yahwistic Poetry*, 45–65.

12. Blenkinsopp, *The Pentateuch*, 157–60.

13. Propp, *Exodus 1–18*, 563–68.

14. Redford, *Egypt, Canaan, and Israel in Ancient Times*, 312–15; Gösta Ahlström, *The History of Ancient Palestine* (Minneapolis: Fortress, 1993) 554–56.

15. Childs, *The Book of Exodus*, 223; Van Seters, *The Life of Moses*, 139–49.

16. Axelsson, *The Lord Rose Up from Seir*, 125–27.

17. Ahlström, *The History of Ancient Palestine*, 897–98.

18. Childs, *The Book of Exodus*, 485–86.

19. Haran, *Temples and Temple Service in Ancient Israel*, 160.

20. For explanations of why a census might anger God, see P. Kyle McCarter, *II Samuel: A New Translation with Introduction and Commentary* (Garden City, N.Y.: Doubleday, 1984) 512–14.

21. Mazar, *Archaeology of the Land of the Bible*, 350–52.

22. Van Seters argues that 1 Kgs 12 is a completely fabricated story, and that Ex 32 is based on 1 Kgs 12 and Dt 9:8-21, which mention the calf incident more briefly (*The Life of Moses*, 295–310). 1 Kgs 12 may be largely fiction, but since bulls or calves were used in Israel, it is possible there is some historical basis to it.

23. ANET 140; Simon Parker, ed., *Ugaritic Narrative Poetry* (Atlanta: SBL /Scholars Press, 1997) 156, 160.

24. Van Seters, *The Pentateuch: A Social-Science Commentary*, 172–74; Childs, *The Book of Exodus*, 589–93.

Chapter Seven: Leviticus

1. For some examples, see ANET 159, 164, 523.

2. Jon Berquist, *Judaism in Persia's Shadow: A Social and Historical Approach* (Minneapolis: Fortress Press, 1995) 92–93.

3. Paula McNutt, *Reconstructing the Society of Ancient Israel* (Louisville: Westminster/John Knox Press, 1999) 177–79.

4. 1 Chron 24:3 makes him a grandson of Aaron, which does not fit well with the biblical chronology that has some five hundred years between the exodus and the beginning of the monarchy; cf. p. 24 above.

5. Aelred Cody, *A History of Old Testament Priesthood* (Rome: Pontifical Biblical Institute, 1969). McNutt, *Reconstructing the Society of Ancient Israel*, 178.

6. Mary Douglas, *Purity and Danger: An Analysis of the Concepts of Pollution and Taboo* (London: Routledge & Kegan Paul, 1966) 55.

7. Israel Finkelstein, "Ethnicity and Origin of the Iron I Settlers in the Highlands of Canaan: Can the Real Israel Stand Up?" *Biblical Archaeologist* 59:4 (1996) 206.

8. G. J. Botterweck, *"chazir,"* *Theological Dictionary of the Old Testament*, vol. IV (Grand Rapids: Eerdmans, 1980) 291–300.

9. Mary Douglas, *Purity and Danger*, 51.

10. Mazar, *Archaeology of the Land of the Bible*, 501–2.

11. For more on Azazel, see B. Janowski, "Azazel," in *Dictionary of Deities and Demons in the Bible*, 2nd ed., ed. K. van der Toorn, et al. (Leiden: Brill/Grand Rapids: Eerdmans, 1999) 128–31.

12. I. Knohl, *The Sanctuary of Silence* (Minneapolis: Fortress Press, 1995).

13. ANET 172–173.

14. Mary Douglas, "Justice as the Cornerstone: An Interpretation of Leviticus 18–20," *Interpretation* 53:4 (1999) 345–46.

15. Simon Parker, ed., *Ugaritic Narrative Poetry* (Atlanta: SBL/Scholars Press, 1997) 148.

16. Haran, *Temples and Temple Service in Ancient Israel*, 158–74.

17. *Ugaritic Narrative Poetry*, 149–50.

18. *The Highlands of Canaan: Agricultural Life in the Early Iron Age* (Sheffield: JSOT Press, 1985) 192–202.

19. ANET 201–206, 531–541.

Chapter Eight: Numbers

1. Axelsson, *The Lord Rose Up from Seir*, 113–18.

2. Mazar, *Archaeology of the Land of the Bible*, 329–30, 446.

3. Hackett, *The Balaam Text from Deir Alla*.

4. ANET 320–321.

5. Baruch Levine, *Numbers 1–20* (New York: Doubleday, 1993) 146–48.

6. The apparent mistake in arithmetic, in which the three Levite groups add up to 22,300 but 3:39 claims 22,000, could be the result of a textual error. A Hebrew scribe may have skipped a letter in 3:28, changing the word *shelosh* (three) to *shesh* (six), making the number of Kohathites 8,600 instead of 8,300.

7. Levine, *Numbers 1–20*, 200–12.

8. G. Mayer, *"nzr,"* in *Theological Dictionary of the Old Testament*, vol. IX, ed. G. Botterweck, et al. (Grand Rapids: Eerdmans, 1998) 306–11.

9. Mazar, *Archaeology of the Land of the Bible*, 516–17, 524–25.

10. Levine, *Numbers 1–20*, 56–57.

11. Axelsson, *The Lord Rose Up from Seir*, 79–80, 136–37. J. Maxwell Miller, "The Israelite Occupation of Canaan," in *Israelite and Judean History*, ed. J. Hayes and J. M. Miller (Philadelphia: Trinity Press International, 1977) 222–24.

12. Axelsson, *The Lord Rose Up from Seir*, 87–91.

13. Ahlström, *The History of Ancient Palestine*, 455–56.

14. Aharoni, *The Archaeology of the Land of Israel*, 229.

15. R. S. Hendel, "Nehushtan," in *Dictionary of Deities and Demons in the Bible*, second ed., ed. K. van der Toorn, et al. (Leiden: Brill/Grand Rapids: Eerdmans, 1999) 615–16.

16. For two different readings, see Hackett, *The Balaam Text from Deir Alla*, 29–30, and Meindert Dijkstra, "Is Balaam Also among the Prophets?" *Journal of Biblical Literature* 114:1 (1995) 43–64.

17. Cf. Michael Barré, "The Portrait of Balaam in Numbers 22–24," *Interpretation* 51:3 (1997) 254–66.

18 ANET 320–321.

Chapter Nine: Deuteronomy

1. *Deuteronomy* (Philadelphia: Westminster Press, 1966) 23–27.

2. *Deuteronomy and the Deuteronomic School* (Oxford: Clarendon Press, 1972; Winona Lake, Ind.: Eisenbrauns, 1992) 260–319.

3. Cf. John Van Seters, *The Pentateuch: A Social-Science Commentary* (Sheffield: Sheffield Academic Press, 1999) 99–101.

4. *The Life of Moses: The Yahwist as Historian in Exodus–Numbers* (Louisville: Westminster/John Knox Press, 1994) 386–93.

5. *The Life of Moses*, 301–10. .

6. Paula McNutt, *Reconstructing the Society of Ancient Israel* (Louisville: Westminster/John Knox Press, 1999) 156–58.

7. ANET 166–167.

8. Rainer Albertz, *A History of Israelite Religion in the Old Testament Period, Volume I: From the Beginnings to the End of the Monarchy* (Louisville: Westminster/John Knox Press, 1994) 219.

9. *Deuteronomy*, 158–59.

10. ANET 534–541.

11. Dennis McCarthy, *Treaty and Covenant*, 2nd ed. (Rome: Pontifical Biblical Institute, 1978) 199–205.

12. The original reading "sons of God" is supported by the Septuagint and a fragment from Qumran. The traditional Hebrew reading, "sons of Israel," is a later change made to eliminate any suggestion of multiple gods.

13. F. M. Cross, *Canaanite Myth and Hebrew Epic: Essays in the History of the Religion of Israel* (Cambridge: Harvard University Press, 1973) 100–3; Axelsson, *The Lord Rose Up from Seir*, 48–50.

14. Smith, *The Early History of God*, 21–22, 49–55.

15. Ze'ev Meshel, "Kuntillet Ajrud," in *The Anchor Bible Dictionary*, vol. IV, ed. D. N. Freedman (New York: Doubleday, 1992) 103–9.

SUGGESTED READINGS

Chapter One: The Pentateuch and History

GENERAL INTRODUCTORY BOOKS ON THE PENTATEUCH:

Blenkinsopp, Joseph. *The Pentateuch: An Introduction to the First Five Books of the Bible*. New York: Doubleday, 1992.

Friedman, Richard. *Commentary on the Torah: With a New English Translation*. San Francisco: HarperCollins, 2001.

Van Seters, John. *The Pentateuch: A Social-Science Commentary*. Sheffield: Sheffield Academic Press, 1999.

Whybray, R. Norman. *Introduction to the Pentateuch*. Grand Rapids: Eerdmans, 1995.

REFERENCE TOOLS FOR THE STUDY OF THE BIBLE:

The Anchor Bible Dictionary. Edited by D. N. Freedman. New York: Doubleday, 1992.

Ancient Near Eastern Texts Relating to the Old Testament. 3rd ed. Edited by James Pritchard. Princeton: Princeton University Press, 1969.

The Ancient Near East in Pictures Relating to the Old Testament. 2nd ed., with supplement. Edited by James Pritchard. Princeton: Princeton University Press, 1969.

A Dictionary of Biblical Interpretation. Edited by R. J. Coggins and J. L. Houlden. Philadelphia: Trinity Press International, 1990.

Dictionary of Deities and Demons in the Bible. Edited by Karel van der Toorn, et al. Grand Rapids: Eerdmans, 1999.

Eerdmans Dictionary of the Bible. Edited by D. N. Freedman. Grand Rapids: Eerdmans, 2000.

Harper's Bible Dictionary. Edited by P. Achtemeier. San Francisco: Harper & Row, 1985.

The New Encyclopedia of Archaeological Excavations in the Holy Land.
Edited by Ephraim Stern. Jerusalem: Israel Exploration Society
and Carta, 1993.
The New Jerome Biblical Commentary. Edited by R. Brown, et al.
Englewood Cliffs, N.J.: Prentice-Hall, 1989.
Oxford Bible Atlas. 2nd ed. Edited by Herbert May. New York: Oxford
University Press, 1974.
The Oxford Companion to the Bible. Edited by B. Metzger and M.
Coogan. New York: Oxford University Press, 1993.

HISTORICAL AND RELIGIOUS BACKGROUND:
Ahlström, Gösta. *The History of Ancient Palestine.* Minneapolis:
Fortress Press, 1993.
Albertz, Rainer. *A History of Israelite Religion in the Old Testament
Period.* 2 vols. Louisville: Westminster/John Knox Press, 1994.
Ben-Tor, Ammon, ed. *The Archaeology of Ancient Israel.* New Haven:
Yale University Press, 1992.
Berquist, Jon. *Judaism in Persia's Shadow: A Social and Historical
Approach.* Minneapolis: Fortress Press, 1995.
Bright, John. *A History of Israel.* 3rd ed. Philadelphia: Westminster
Press, 1981.
Coogan, Michael, ed. *The Oxford History of the Biblical World.* New
York: Oxford University Press, 1998.
de Vaux, Roland. *Ancient Israel: Its Life and Institutions.* London: Dar-
ton, Longman & Todd, 1973.
Halpern, Baruch. *The First Historians: The Hebrew Bible and History.*
University Park, Pa.: Pennsylvania State University Press, 1996.
Hayes, John, and J. M. Miller, eds. *Israelite and Judaean History.*
Philadelphia: Trinity Press International, 1977.
Lemche, Niels Peters. *Ancient Israel: A New History of Israelite Soci-
ety.* Sheffield: JSOT Press, 1988.
———. *The Israelites in History and Tradition.* Louisville: Westminster/
John Knox Press, 1998.
Mazar, Amihai. *Archaeology of the Land of the Bible, 10,000–586 BCE.*
New York: Doubleday, 1990.
McNutt, Paula. *Reconstructing the Society of Ancient Israel.* Louisville:
Westminster/John Knox Press, 1999.
Niditch, Susan. *Ancient Israelite Religion.* New York: Oxford University
Press, 1997.

Chapter Two: How the Pentateuch Was Written

Campbell, Anthony, and Mark O'Brien. *Sources of the Pentateuch: Texts, Introductions, Annotations*. Fortress Press, 1993.
Friedman, Richard. *Who Wrote the Bible?* Englewood Cliffs, N.J.: Prentice-Hall, 1978.
Noth, Martin. *A History of Pentateuchal Traditions*. Englewood Cliffs, N.J.: Prentice-Hall, 1972.
Rendtorff, Rolf. *The Old Testament: An Introduction*. Philadelphia: Fortress Press, 1986.
Van Seters, John. *Prologue to History: The Yahwist as Historian in Genesis*. Louisville: Westminster/John Knox Press, 1992.
Wellhausen, Julius. *Prolegomena to the History of Ancient Israel*. Atlanta: Scholars Press, 1994.
Whybray, R. Norman. *The Making of the Pentateuch: A Methodological Study*. Sheffield: JSOT Press, 1987.

Chapter Three: Genesis 1–11

Brueggemann, Walter. *Genesis*. Atlanta: John Knox Press, 1982.
Speiser, E. A. *Genesis*. New York: Doubleday, 1964.
Van Seters, John. *Prologue to History: The Yahwist as Historian in Genesis*. Louisville: Westminster/John Knox Press, 1992.
von Rad, Gerhard. *Genesis: A Commentary*. Rev. ed. Philadelphia: Westminster Press, 1972.
Westermann, Claus. *Genesis 1–11*. Minneapolis: Augsburg, 1984.

Chapter Four: Genesis 12–50

Axelsson, Lars. *The Lord Rose Up from Seir: Studies in the History and Traditions of the Negev and Southern Judah*. Stockholm: Almquist & Wiksell, 1987.
Brueggemann, Walter. *Genesis*. Atlanta: John Knox Press, 1982.
Speiser, E. A. *Genesis*. New York: Doubleday, 1964.
Van Seters, John. *Prologue to History: The Yahwist as Historian in Genesis*. Louisville: Westminster/John Knox Press, 1992.

———. *Abraham in History and Tradition*. New Haven: Yale University Press, 1975.

von Rad, Gerhard. *Genesis: A Commentary*. Rev. ed. Philadelphia: Westminster Press, 1972.

Westermann, Claus. *Genesis 12–36*. Minneapolis: Augsburg, 1985.

———. *Genesis 37–50*. Minneapolis: Augsburg, 1986.

Chapter Five: Exodus 1:1–13:16

Childs, Brevard. *The Book of Exodus: A Critical, Theological Commentary*. Philadelphia: Westminster Press, 1974.

Fretheim, Terence. *Exodus*. Louisville: Westminster/John Knox Press, 1991.

Hoffmeier, James. *Israel in Egypt: The Evidence for the Authenticity of the Exodus Tradition*. New York: Oxford University Press, 1996.

Nicholson, E. W. *Exodus and Sinai in History and Tradition*. Richmond: John Knox Press, 1973.

Propp, William. *Exodus 1–18*. New York: Doubleday, 1999.

Redford, Donald. *Egypt, Canaan, and Israel in Ancient Times*. Princeton: Princeton University Press, 1992.

Van Seters, John. *The Life of Moses: The Yahwist as Historian in Exodus–Numbers*. Louisville: Westminster/John Knox Press, 1994.

Chapter Six: Exodus 13:17–40:38

Blenkinsopp, Joseph. *Wisdom and Law in the Old Testament: The Ordering of Life in Israel and Early Judaism*. New York: Oxford University Press, 1995.

Childs, Brevard. *The Book of Exodus: A Critical, Theological Commentary*. Philadelphia: Westminster Press, 1974.

Fretheim, Terence. *Exodus*. Louisville: Westminster/John Knox Press, 1991.

McCarthy, Dennis. *Treaty and Covenant*. 2nd ed. Rome: Pontifical Biblical Institute, 1978.

Nicholson, E. W. *Exodus and Sinai in History and Tradition*. Richmond: John Knox Press, 1973.

Niditch, Susan. *Ancient Israelite Religion*. New York: Oxford University Press, 1997.

Van Seters, John. *The Life of Moses: The Yahwist as Historian in Exodus–Numbers*. Louisville: Westminster/John Knox Press, 1994.

Chapter Seven: Leviticus

Cody, Aelred. *A History of Old Testament Priesthood*. Rome: Pontifical Biblical Institute, 1969.

Douglas, Mary. *Purity and Danger: An Analysis of the Concepts of Pollution and Taboo*. London: Routledge & Kegan Paul, 1966.

Gerstenberger, Erhard. *Leviticus: A Commentary*. Louisville: Westminster/John Knox Press, 1996.

Haran, Menahem. *Temples and Temple Service in Ancient Israel: An Inquiry into Biblical Cult Phenomena and the Historical Setting of the Priestly School*. Winona Lake, Ind.: Eisenbrauns, 1985.

Hartley, John. *Leviticus*. Dallas: Word Books, 1992.

Milgrom, Jacob. *Leviticus 1–16: A New Translation with Introduction and Commentary*. New York: Doubleday, 1991.

———. *Leviticus 17–22: A New Translation with Introduction and Commentary*. New York: Doubleday, 2000.

———. *Leviticus 23–27: A New Translation with Introduction and Commentary*. New York: Doubleday, 2000.

Chapter Eight: Numbers

Axelsson, Lars. *The Lord Rose Up from Seir: Studies in the History and Traditions of the Negev and Southern Judah*. Stockholm: Almquist & Wiksell, 1987.

Budd, Philip. *Numbers*. Waco, Tex: Word Books, 1984.

Levine, Baruch. *Numbers 1–20: A New Translation with Introduction and Commentary*. New York: Doubleday, 1993.

———. *Numbers 21–36: A New Translation with Introduction and Commentary*. New York: Doubleday, 2000.

Chapter Nine: Deuteronomy

Miller, Patrick. *Deuteronomy*. Louisville: John Knox Press, 1990.

Nicholson, E. W. *Deuteronomy and Tradition: Literary and Historical Problems in the Book of Deuteronomy*. Philadelphia: Fortress Press, 1967.

von Rad, Gerhard. *Deuteronomy: A Commentary*. Philadelphia: Westminster Press, 1966.

Weinfeld, Moshe. *Deuteronomy 1–11: A New Translation with Introduction and Commentary*. New York: Doubleday, 1991.

———. *Deuteronomy and the Deuteronomic School*. Winona Lake, Ind.: Eisenbrauns, 1992.

INDEX